CU00325948

Advance Praise

'It is a thought-provoking book where you learn about operational excellence not only from the author's experience but also from stories and events beyond the business world....'

Bhargav Dasgupta,
MD and CEO,
ICICI Lombard General Insurance Co. Ltd

'It is a s superb collection of examples and lessons learned, which will avail the reader with a wealth of opportunities to focus on the right topics to improve operations and, more importantly, avoid making the mistakes others have already done.'

Anatolijus Fouracre,
CEO, Swiss Post Solutions, Vietnam;
Member of the Executive Board, Swiss Post Solutions

'In his book on *Little BIG Things in Operational Excellence*, Debashis Sarkar provides a comprehensive view of sustainable operational excellence. His numerous practical examples from various domains will provide an actionable road map to create operational excellence in one's own organization. I am looking forward to reading this book with great anticipation.'

Dr Manu K. Vora,
Chairman and President, Business Excellence, Inc., USA;
Fulbright Specialist, US Department of State, USA

'I have known Deb for 10 years. He is an outstanding individual and a man of high integrity and ethics. He leads from the front and is a very inspiring leader—notably humble. His knowledge is profound and intense. There is tremendous learning from him. He explains the most difficult and complex content in a very simple way so that everyone can understand. He is always up to date. I would recommend and encourage everyone to read this book. We will be the beneficiaries.'

Vishwanathan Gopalan,
Director—Finance, Global Delivery Centre,
BNY Mellon

'*Little BIG Things in Operational Excellence* is a delightful read, evidence based and full of insights. Debashis has this amazing ability to unearth nuggets from compelling stories. Clearly, these can come handy as we navigate the challenges of operational excellence.'

Sashidharan Menon,
Group Head of Compliance and
Corporate Governance, Bank of Sharjah, UAE

'Operational excellence is pivotal to achieving competitive advantage. The compelling stories and experiences shared by Debashis make the book one of the finest in the field of operational excellence. The 'little big things' can do wonders; I enjoyed reading every bit of it.'

Gautam Mahipal,
Managing Director, APAC Regional
Controller at State Street

'Debashis's book is a must-read for operational excellence practitioners who want to bring people, processes, operations strategies and technologies together to deliver value in a changing world.'

Alice Crochet,
Editor, Process Excellence Network, UK

'I have known Debashis for his work in operational excellence over more than a decade. He has this innate ability to offer simple guidance but produce big impact transformationally. The book brings simplicity to the field of operational excellence. I wish the readers of the book a wonderful useful voyage into how to make business perform better.'

Ravi Krishnamurthy,
President, SBILIFE

LITTLE

BIG

THINGS IN

OPERATIONAL
EXCELLENCE

DEBASHIS SARKAR

LITTLE
BIG
THINGS IN
OPERATIONAL
EXCELLENCE

Los Angeles | London | New Delhi
Singapore | Washington DC | Melbourne

First published in 2021 by

SAGE Publications India Pvt. Ltd
B1/I-1 Mohan Cooperative Industrial Area
Mathura Road, New Delhi 110 044, India
www.sagepub.in

SAGE Publications Inc
2455 Teller Road
Thousand Oaks, California 91320, USA

SAGE Publications Ltd
1 Oliver's Yard, 55 City Road
London EC1Y 1SP, United Kingdom

SAGE Publications Asia-Pacific Pte Ltd
18 Cross Street #10-10/11/12
China Square Central
Singapore 048423

Published by Vivek Mehra for SAGE Publications India Pvt. Ltd. Typeset in 10.5/13.5 Adobe Caslon Pro by Fidus Design Pvt. Ltd, Chandigarh.

Library of Congress Control Number: 2021943005

ISBN: 978-93-5479-006-5 (PB)

SAGE Team: Neha Pal, Megha Dabral, Ankit Verma and Dally Verghese

*Dedicated
to
Ma and Baba
and
Mr K. V. Kamath
(First President, New Development Bank)*

Thank you for choosing a SAGE product!
If you have any comment, observation or feedback,
I would like to personally hear from you.

Please write to me at **contactceo@sagepub.in**

Vivek Mehra, Managing Director and CEO, SAGE India.

Contents

Preface

The idea of this book took birth almost by serendipity. I was between two client sites and was on a flight between Pune and Mumbai. Sitting on the first row of the now-defunct Jet Airways flight, I was trying to reflect on my experience over the years as an operational excellence (OPEX) practitioner. A kaleidoscope of images passed as I tried to remember the various contexts wherein, I had the opportunity to make an impact.

While I may have touched lives and helped businesses to climb the curve of performance, I too had benefited from each of the interactions, experiences and engagement.

As I continued my reflection, one thing became increasingly clear that the most challenging trysts with business improvements were not the technical aspects of the problems but the softer dimensions of deployment. They often don't get discussed yet play a big role. They are what I call the 'little big things' that make a business better. They often appear insignificant yet play a big role in making businesses customer-centric and operationally excellent. The solutions to these problems were not taught in a classroom. I gathered them from the following:

- My personal experience
- Events in the business world
- Events beyond the business world
- Behavioural science

Clearly, there is a lot that we can learn from other domains which can be adapted to make businesses profitable and better. The *Little BIG Things in Operational Excellence* is a book that has an assorted set of those learnings.

The book is a definite guide to smoothen rough edges in OPEX. It will ventilate your existing approach by providing a fresh perspective on how to navigate challenges that come in the way of making your business perform better. The book has a universal appeal. From senior executives to middle managers to someone working in the frontline, everyone will find it useful.

The book is organized in such a way that you can begin reading from any chapter and go forward or backwards. The focus of the book is such that every minute you spend with it, you'll get a new idea that is sharp and actionable. The terms 'operational excellence', 'operational transformation', 'business improvement' and 'making business better' have been used synonymously. While OPEX stands for operational excellence, OPEX pro is a short form of OPEX professional. It refers to any change agent who is involved in making businesses operationally excellent. The pronoun 'he' has been used as a gender-neutral pronoun. Many of the insights in this book are backed by the work of eminent scholars and researchers. If you want to explore a topic further, the references are at the end of each chapter. Every lesson has been written in a jargon-free manner for people to understand the topics easily. The focus is to provide insights into how to use it to deliver results. There are case studies and real-life examples for you to assimilate the chapters easily.

One principle that I tried to follow in this book is Pfeffer's law. Proposed by Stanford Professor Jeffrey Pfeffer, the law says, 'Instead of being interested in what is new, we ought to be interested in what is true'. Successful OPEX executions depend on small things done remarkably well, and the book tries to provide those foundational insights.

Embedding OPEX is both science and art because the 'little big things' make a big difference.

Hope you find the book useful.

I look forward to hearing from you. I can be reached at DebashisSarkar4@yahoo.com and debashis.sarkar@proliferator.net Happy reading!

Debashis Sarkar
August 2021

Acknowledgements

This book would not have been possible without the contribution of the client organizations for being laboratories where I tried my ideas on OPEX. I would thank the CEOs and C-suite members for giving me an opportunity to solve some of their toughest problems which forced me to unlearn what I knew. I would also like to thank the senior executives, whose questions on workplace dilemmas brought new perspectives. It also goes out to the business leaders from all over the world (from Detroit, Winterthur, Stockholm, Brussels, Ann Arbor, Shanghai, Singapore, Dubai, Toronto, etc), who were kind enough to open the doors of their company and share their trials and tribulations.

I would also like to acknowledge my colleagues for supporting me in efforts to make businesses perform better, thought leaders whose work is listed in detail at the end of each chapter and my late mom, who was always supportive of my auctorial pursuit.

Also, I am thankful to my daughter, Trisha, and wife, Sudeshna, for bearing with my selfish pursuit of putting pen to paper, which could otherwise have been time spent with them. I would also like to acknowledge Neha Pal, Commissioning Editor at SAGE, for being a great project manager. I also want to thank Ankit Verma, Production Editor at SAGE, for being a great support during the entire editorial process.

Chapter 1

Many Hues of Operational Excellence

The concept of excellence is not new. Ancient Greeks had a philosophical term, *'arete'*, which meant virtue or excellence. To be a person of *arete* was to exemplify the greatest ideals of humanity as the Greek people understood them.[1] For someone to be called as having the quality of *arete*, one had to truly excel. The word meant fully achieving one's potential or purpose. The idea of excellence was very contextual. For a soldier displaying prowess in battle was being *arete*. A dog guarding its owner's home meticulously and herding his sheep with care was being *arete*. The person of *arete* had the highest level of effectiveness.

Greek philosopher Aristotle's perspective on excellence was as follows:

> Excellence is an art won by training and habituation. We do not act rightly because we have virtue or excellence, but we rather

have those because we have acted rightly. We are what we repeatedly do. Excellence, then, is not an act but a habit.

—**Aristotle**

In the business world too, excellence is not achieved by fluke. It's an outcome of millions of large and small acts, performed by tens of thousands of employees every day. CEOs want their businesses to be profitable and efficient while consistently meeting the changing needs of the customers.

CEOs who aspire to make their businesses operationally excellent accomplish it through a well-thought-out strategy and pursuing it as a part of their business philosophy and culture.

But what is operational excellence (OPEX)?

Over the years, experts, scholars and practitioners have defined OPEX in myriad ways. Each one of them has added their perspective to it. There are also various OPEX models which aim to propel companies to new levels of performance. What's common to all of them is that they aim to unleash efficiencies and performance improvement, which impacts the firm's profitability and positively impact customers. OPEX is no more a matter of choice for businesses. It has become an imperative for survival amid rising complexity, changing customer needs, burgeoning risks, increased competition and a world which is digitally connected like never before.

Let's get a sneak peek into how OPEX has been defined. Refer to the collage (Figure 1.1).

Let's also look at a few OPEX models.

CHEVRON MODEL

American multinational energy corporation, Chevron, has an in-house Operational Excellence Management System (OEMS), which is used to embed OPEX culture and improve our health, environment and safety performance. The model was updated in 2018 to emphasize more linkages between risk, assurance and safeguards and a stream-lined approach to manage risk (Figure 1.2).

'It isn't necessarily a destination; rather, it is an ongoing journey that organizations continuously travel. It focuses on minimizing and managing downside risks while maximizing an operation's performance and shareholder value.'
—Brian Rains[2]

'Operational excellence is defined as the process of executing a business strategy more consistently and more reliably than the competition, resulting in increased revenue, lower operational risk and lower operating costs.'
—Jonathan Trout[3]

'Operational excellence improvement goes well beyond cutting costs. It's about achieving greater flexibility, agility, and higher levels of responsiveness to increase competitive advantage and fuel growth.'
—TBM Consulting[4]

'Operations Excellence is a set of approaches, practices, and tools that target maximizing efficiency in operations without losing focus on time, quality, cost, and employees. Many elements of it are common across various organizations (e.g. lean, digitization, etc.), some can be though unique and reflect company-specific culture.'
—Burnie Group[5]

'We define operational excellence as a continuous improvement journey that essentially never concludes, but positions an organization to endlessly progress forward in the areas most critical for achieving and sustaining market leadership.'
—LNS Research[6]

'Operational excellence is a mindset, not a methodology. It is the relentless pursuit of finding ways to improve performance and profitability. It is finding money and performance boosts in areas that organizations don't normally look.'
—Andrew Miller[7]

'Operational excellence (OpEx) is the goal of improved business performance. It usually means using lean manufacturing techniques, made popular by Toyota with its Toyota Production System (TPS). For many organizations, OpEx is the set of TPS "tools" that help eliminate waste—"Muda" in Japanese terminology—and lower production time and costs.'
—Dr Joseph A. DeFeo[8]

'Operational excellence can be defined as executing a business strategy more effectively and with a higher level of consistency than your competition. For this to be achieved, every employee must have the capacity to see the flow of value to the customer and fix this as and when interruptions arise.'
—Ideagen Software[9]

Figure 1.1. OPEX Defined Collage

Source: Chevron. Operational excellence management system. n.d., https://www.chevron.com/about/operational-excellence/oems (accessed 23 February 2021).

Figure 1.2. Chevron's OEMS

THE SHINGO MODEL™

The Shingo Model from Shingo Institute and Jon M. Huntsman School of Business is another holistic model to steer an organization towards OPEX (Figure 1.3).

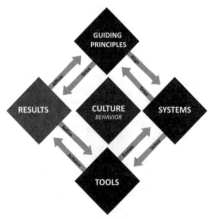

Source: Shingo Institute and Jon M. Huntsman School of Business. The Shingo Model. n.d., https://shingo.org/shingo-model/ (accessed 23 February 2021).

Figure 1.3. Components of Shingo Model

 LITTLE BIG THINGS IN OPERATIONAL EXCELLENCE

The other model which is very popular is Toyota Production System, which has been applied by corporations the world over. This is not just a technical model but also a philosophy, where quality is built into the manufacturing process and productivity is improved by making 'what is needed, when it is needed, and in the amount needed'.

VALUE DISCIPLINE AND COMPETITIVENESS

One of the powerful ways to understand OPEX is to look at it through the value disciplines model proposed and solidified by Michael Treacy and Fred Wiersema in their book *The Discipline of Market Leaders* (Figure 1.4).[10]

According to the authors, for a business to be competitive, they need to do well in all the following value disciplines:

- Product leadership
- OPEX
- Customer intimacy

Source: Treacy M and Wiersema F. *The discipline of market leaders.* Boston, MA: Addison-Wesley, 1995.

Figure 1.4. Value Disciplines

However, if they wish to differentiate in the marketplace, they need to excel in one of the areas. Let's understand what they mean.

- **Product leadership:** This entails offering leading-edge products and services to customers, which consistently exceed customer expectations and make rivals goods obsolete. Companies which follow the strategy of product leadership are at the forefront of innovation and raise the bar of the market and industry at large.

  Examples of such companies include Apple and Nike. Apple is considered among the top global innovators. Its products have not only created new markets but also changed the habits of consumers. Nike is another company known for innovation which it achieves by a supporting culture and by continually adapting to existing and emerging technologies.

- **Operational excellence:** This is about having a deep focus on embedding efficiency in the company. This is achieved by optimizing processes, reducing overhead costs, eliminating steps, etc. Here, the focus is on delivering reliable products or services to customers at competitive prices and minimal inconvenience. Examples of such companies include Walmart and Toyota. Walmart's operational efficiency strategies allow them to offer products at lower prices than any other competitor. Toyota delivers cars that are known for quality and reliability and benchmarked as best in class by competitors. Not surprisingly, its OPEX is emulated by companies the world over.

- **Customer intimacy:** This entails pursuing a strategy of customer intimacy continually tailor and shaping products and services that continually meet customer needs. These companies enmesh detailed customer insights with operational flexibility so that they can respond to almost any needs of customers. These companies create huge customer loyalty. Examples of such companies include Nordstrom and The Ritz-Carlton. Both these companies are known for their legendary customer experience. They adopt a host of strategies and tactics to make it happen. Let me give you one example from each of the companies. At Nordstrom, employees are given unusual latitude to take their calls on how to solve customer problems. At The Ritz-Carlton, employees adhere to 'Gold Standards', which comprise Motto, the Credo, Three Steps of Service, Service Values, the 6th Diamond and the Employee Promise.

The understanding of the concept of value disciplines is very important, as the way I look at OPEX includes all of the above.

HOW DO WE DEFINE OPEX?

As we have seen above, OPEX gets defined in various ways. Some of them are very narrow, while others are broad and vague. There are some which have been developed based on the unique needs of a specific company or an industry, while others have a fairly universal appeal which can be applied to companies across industries and sectors.

So how do we define OPEX?

It is about creating a sustained shareholder value by focusing on what the customers want, consistently delivering to their expectations, driving internal efficiencies and remaining competitive in the marketplace.

It is achieved by creating an operating model which aligns people, process, technology and other organizational assets with strategic objectives and aspirations of the firm.

A typical OPEX effort includes working on elements such as customer focus, leadership, business strategy, employee involvement, organization structure, product portfolio, culture and climate, accountability and ownership, financial and operational management, innovation, value chain, competitive insights, community relationships, rewards and recognition, digital transformation and risk management. What should also be remembered is that it is just not about designing new processes and business systems but also educating the employees on new ways of working and then getting continuously better at it.

There are myriad benefits of OPEX which include profitable growth, improved operating margins, optimization of the bottom line, lower operating cost, better productivity, best-in-class performance, flawless customer experience, engaged employees, reduced complexity, enhanced organizational efficiency and consistent quality.

Embedding OPEX requires a structured and disciplined approach which is owned and led by line managers. The focus is not just on bottom-line improvements but also on establishing a core which can sustain the gains.

The post-COVID-19 world is very different. Businesses need to gear up for the new normal, where the pace of change is like never before. Consumer behaviours are changing, and one sees a preference for digital commerce and solutions. Incumbents are increasingly facing stiff competition from start-ups. There is accelerated adoption of digital technology by businesses. It is increasingly becoming their backbone, and there is a need for changing the way how businesses are run and managed. An OPEX engine will not only help to build a change-ready culture but also aid in building an enterprise which is future-ready.

There are four important dimensions which are an integral part of OPEX journey. These are as follows:

- **Operational discipline:** This is about consistently complying and executing defined processes by every member of the organization every time day after day. Operational discipline embeds predictability while infusing efficiency and quality in the operations. This includes adoption of myriad technology solutions that increase process speed, reduces costs, builds quality, enhances consumer experience, increases resilience, optimizes decision outcome and solidifies compliance.

- **Continuous improvement:** This entails continually improving business processes, practices and products to meet the current and future needs of the customers (both internal and external). Improvements can be incremental or breakthrough based on the requirement. This includes adoption of myriad technology solutions that increase process speed, reduces costs, builds quality, enhances consumer experience, increases resilience, optimizes decision outcome and solidifies compliance.

- **Culture:** This is about changing the ways of working of the organization so that employees can demonstrate the right set of behaviours which enable the journey of OPEX.

- **Leadership:** The top management of the company needs to clearly define what is OPEX for the firm, how success will be measured and how people are going to be rewarded. They are also the role models for the right behaviours, act as coaches and make OPEX their personal priority. They enable people by providing resources, skilling them, removing barriers to implementation and installing the right context and governance structure which makes the journey to become operationally excellent frictionless.

REFERENCES

1. Mythology Source. Arete: The spirit of excellence. 2020, https://mythologysource.com/arete-greek-goddess/ (accessed 10 February 2021).

2. Rains B. The path to operational excellence through operational discipline. *IndustryWeek*, 20 May 2014.

3. Trout J. Operational excellence: An overview. *Reliable Plant*, n.d., https://www.reliableplant.com/operational-excellence-31886 (accessed 10 February 2021).

4. TBM. Operational excellence. n.d., https://www.tbmcg.com/solutions/operational-excellence/ (accessed 10 February 2021).

5. The Burnie Group. What is operations excellence? n.d., https://burniegroup.com/capabilities/operations-excellence/#:~:text=Operations%20Excellence%20is%20a%20set,quality%2C%20cost%2C%20and%20employees (accessed 10 February 2021).

6. LNS Research. Operational excellence: A data-backed guide for manufacturers. 2014, https://blog.lnsresearch.com/blog/bid/195529/Operational-Excellence-A-Data-Backed-Guide-for-Manufacturers (accessed 10 February 2021).

7. Miller A. *Redefining operational excellence: New strategies for maximizing performance and profits across the organization.* Special ed. New York, NY: AMACOM, 2014.

8. DeFeo JA. What does operational excellence look like? Juran, 5 August 2020, https://www.juran.com/blog/introduction-to-operational excellence-opex/ (accessed 10 February 2021).

9. Ideagen. What is operational excellence and how can it be achieved? 3 December 2020, https://www.ideagen.com/thought-leadership/blog/ what-is-operational-excellence-and-how-can-it-be-achieved (accessed 20 February 2021).

10. Treacy M and Wiersema F. *The discipline of market leaders*. Boston, MA: Addison-Wesley, 1995.

Chapter 2

7 Ps of Operational Excellence

While embarking on an OPEX effort, it's important to make sure that all the 7 Ps are in place. The 7 Ps are the building blocks of an OPEX transformation (Figure 2.1). Missing any of the Ps can make the OPEX effort go astray.

PURPOSE

Before embarking on the OPEX effort, it's imperative to ascertain the larger purpose of the effort. How would it impact the strategic objectives of the enterprise? If the larger purpose is not clear, I would recommend not to begin the work. An OPEX effort without a larger purpose is like a ship without a rudder. It can lead to frustration.

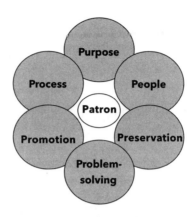

Figure 2.1. The 7 Ps of OPEX

PATRON

Every OPEX effort needs to have a customer. The customer could be outside the enterprise or within the enterprise. Before beginning the transformation, did you ascertain the customer requirements well? What are his needs which he is explicitly stating and what are his wants or what is his deeper purpose from the project, which he may not be stating? When the requirements of customers are fuzzy or not clear, it results in confusion.

PEOPLE

Under people, we need to answer the following set of questions:

1. Have the leaders who will sponsor the effort been taken on board?

2. Are we involving the right set of people in the project?

3. Towards achieving the improved state, is there a need for learning and unlearning that the teams need to go through? What sort of capability development or enhancement needs to happen?

4. Are there any structural changes required as a part of the transformation?

5. What do we have to do to change the mindsets and behaviours?

When people are not involved in the transformation, it results in resistance, which could either be active or passive in nature.

PROCESS

Processes are the heart of the OPEX. If you are not modifying or improving a process, you are not doing an OPEX work. All work is a process, and OPEX is working around them. Processes are strategic assets of an enterprise and help to achieve enterprise outcomes. When core processes are improved, it has a positive impact on strategic outcomes. When there is no process involved in an OPEX outcome, it results in a false start.

PROMOTION

Any transformation effort needs marketing and communication. This is required to communicate to those directly or indirectly impacted on why we are doing what we are doing. Also, it is required for the required excitement and buzz for any transformation. A good communication plan helps all those directly or indirectly impacted by the transformation to be informed on what is happening and the progress being made. Transformations can have dull moments, and a good communication plan can help to address this problem. When there is no promotion, the outcome of the OPEX effort is local or siloed, that is, confined to a pocket.

PROBLEM-SOLVING

Any OPEX effort is essentially a problem-solving effort. Hence, there is a need for clarity on the problem-solving approach which would be followed. The problem-solving approaches could be Six Sigma, Lean, Theory of Constraints, 8D, 7S, PDCA, A3 Problem-solving, Agile, various in-house problem-solving approaches of companies, etc. Without a structure the outcome is uncertain. The right approach is critical for the success of OPEX effort. It not only provides a blueprint stating what should be the sequence of steps but also helps in project management.

PRESERVATION

Once the OPEX transformation is done and the benefits are achieved, how would you go about sustaining the gains? The following are the questions that you need to answer:

- Would there be a need for putting together a new process documentation?
- What sort of metrics would be tracked?
- What would be the management review process? Who would be doing the reviews and at what frequency?
- Would there be a need for audits to ascertain if processes/ procedures are being followed as they had been implemented?
- Do we need a control plan?

When this P is missing in any OPEX transformation, the impact is temporary and does not last for long.

The impact of missing Ps is summarized in Figure 2.2.

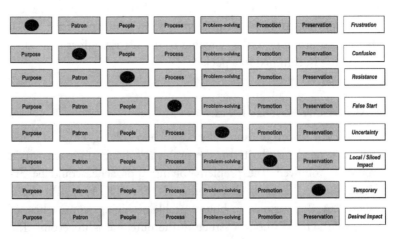

Figure 2.2. Impact of Missing Ps in OPEX

LITTLE BIG THINGS IN OPERATIONAL EXCELLENCE

Chapter 3

Energizing an Operational
Excellence Transformation

While embarking on an OPEX transformation in our focus on getting the results, we should never forget the power of narrative in getting the desired results. We tend to focus on various technical elements such as process, technology, structure and capabilities. One thing that we don't put sufficiently is the power of stories in getting the employees on board. Without an engaging story around why we are embarking on the effort, it becomes difficult to bring about sustainable change. A successful outcome is one in which employees are actively involved in the OPEX effort. It is achieved when teams are emotionally connected to the effort. This is where the power of stories comes to play. A good story stimulates the senses of employees, and they get connected emotionally and intellectually to the OPEX effort.

Before rolling out any transformation effort, I always spend a day with the top management to carve out the story which will be shared with the company. The objective of the narrative is to tell the employees why the initiative is being taken and the rationale. The right story can not only grab attention but also influence people to join the transformation journey. It can create buzz and energize the enterprise. These stories should not just be told by the top management but also activate their team members to further tell the story to people around them and even to the customers. An OPEX transformation needs people who are loyal to the improvements underway in the firm and should be loud about it.

Leaders should be consistent with the story which is shared around the OPEX. It should not leave the employees confused.

Some people ask me that won't repeating the same story look phoney. When stories are similar, it shows that the leaders are aligned with the larger purpose. Most importantly, when it is repeated, it creates a solid awareness of the purpose of the OPEX roll-out. Remember that no one gets engaged by data. What engages them are stories.

However, stories that we see in movies and books have suspense. People are willing to get confused and ready to wait till the end. In business world, this will not work. If you don't begin with the end, the employees would tune out.

Some business leaders do tell a story around the need for change in the organization, but it's largely around the company. It is typically one of the following:

- Company performance is below par and needs to adopt OPEX for survival.
- Company is doing well but wants to be more competitive in the marketplace.
- Company is doing very well but wants to be the best in the marketplace.
- Company is doing well and wants to build a culture of continuous improvement.

While the above are indeed logical reasons, they all meander around the company. This only does not have sufficient meat for employees to come on board. They would like to know the impact on them and those around.

While embarking on an OPEX journey, here is a structure which I follow, which I learnt and adopted from Scott Keller and Colin Price's book *Beyond Performance*.[1] It has worked both for me and my clients. Given that it encapsulates benefits beyond that to company, it connects much better.

So what are the components of a story?

1. **Where are we now?** Provide an overview on the company and how we have been performing over the last few quarters/years. Focus on highlighting the key achievements or the key misses—the former when the company has been performing well, while the latter when the performance has been subpar.

2. **Where do we want to go?** Elaborate the larger vision and how we see our company in next few years. The image of the vision has to be very engaging. Try and make this description very visceral so that people can feel excited about it. Talk about unique elements of the future which will make the employees want to get associated with it. For example, a client of mine in packaging space talked about creating the most customer-centric and competitive company not just in the category it operated in but also among all packaging players.

3. **How would OPEX help in our journey?** Here, the talk should be about how OPEX will enable the achievement of the larger vision.

4. **What is the benefit that this effort would provide to the following?**

   a. **Industry/market/ecosystem at large:** Talk about how the transformation would impact the industry and market at large.

   b. **Society:** Give an idea about how the improvement efforts will impact the society at large. In case there are none, you can skip this point. But I would recommend you to look for connection with the society.

c. **Customers:** Provide details on how customers will receive it and how it will impact their experience with the product or service.

d. **Employees:** Share how the transformation would impact the employees and their workplace. Talk about the improved company, how it creates competitiveness and the resulting sense of belonging for the firm.

e. **Individual:** What is it in for an individual? How will it impact his life, career, opportunities, compensation, engagement, etc.?

With my clients, I typically hold a day's workshop with the top management. In this, I work with the CEO and his leadership team to create their stories and make them share with each other. They critique each other and finally, by the end of the workshop, there is one story which is created which shall be shared by them.

A few things which need to be remembered are as follows. Stories should stir up emotions. The emotion which you elicit should help you to connect with the end goal. But make sure it does not create a sense of fear. I am not a supporter of burning platform principles as it often makes people flee from the change that you want to embark on. Don't make the story humorous, as it can communicate non-seriousness about the issue.

A good story not only provides a coherent narrative but also acts as a glue and connects people across functions for OPEX. It removes uncertainty and provides comfort to the employees, as they know that they are in the right organization. A good story engages our right brain and triggers our imagination, which further stirs our emotion. This makes us participants in the narrative of OPEX.

Whatever story you create, tell it often and on all possible occasions. Use various modes of communication such as video and town hall.

Storytelling should also be used to share success stories, what's worked and what's not worked. Sometimes it makes sense to hire a person in the OPEX team as a chief storyteller. His focus would be to interpret and translate the OPEX strategy for the employees. He also goes around the enterprise to look for stories which can be shared with others. I also recommend OPEX professionals undergo a training session on storytelling so that it can be a handy tool.

REFERENCE

1. Keller S and Price C. *Beyond performance: How great organizations build ultimate competitive advantage.* Hoboken, NJ: John Wiley & Sons; Times Group Books, 2016.

Chapter 4

When a Rejected Take-off Is Imminent

Having seen an opportunity in OPEX transformation, I have seen companies not being able to take off. This is not because they don't want to do it but because of a lack of strong leadership, clarity haze and bureaucratic processes which stop them from beginning the work. Last year, a CEO of a leading home finance company approached me to guide them on a journey of OPEX. The CEO introduced me to the COO, who he said would take things forward. The COO kept on saying how relevant it was at that phase of the finance company's journey. He said that he would like me to meet his key team members in the next meeting before the journey kicked off. The second meeting was barely for 15 minutes, and he concluded it by saying that he should now be able to take it forward. Then I got a call from him two weeks later, telling me that he would like to meet again. I visited his office and he again emphasized the need for OPEX in the company but wanted to wait for a new hire who had to join in a month's time. He then requested a fourth meeting, wherein he introduced me to the new person but told me that he would like the initiative to go through the internal buy-in process. Five months passed and nothing moved. Then I again got a request from him to once again share the benefits of the OPEX effort. I shared with him the impact on key financial ratios and company profitability. He profusely thanked me for the details and said that he should get back to me in two weeks' time on deployment detail. Nothing happened for the next three months. Then after two and a half months, I got a WhatsApp message from him, requesting a Skype call. I obliged, clearly knowing that nothing would move. In the call, he told me that he had called me to inform me that the OPEX roll-out was going through internal committees. The logic he presented was that them being a finance company, any hiring of a consultant needed to go through the internal processes, hence the delay. It's going to be two years now, and I have not heard from him. What I also got to know from other sources was that they have yet to begin their OPEX roll-out. I also wonder how serious the CEO was about OPEX.

These things are quite common in companies. You need to know when the OPEX effort will never really take off. Here are some of the cues which would signal that it would not take off.

WHEN THERE IS NO HURRY TO MAKE DECISIONS

When decision-making is slow, and there is no sense of urgency to take the decision, and every step of the decision-making goes through endless scrutiny, you can be sure that the OPEX journey which is being envisaged is more of an intent than execution.

WHEN THE DECISION-MAKING HAPPENS THROUGH CONSENSUS

When the culture of the enterprise is to take decisions only after everyone has been taken on board, this approach to 'management by consensus' is a passe. This may have worked 20 years back, but today when things are changing so fast around us, every decision cannot happen through consensus. Quite often it's about taking a decision and making it happen. Clearly, that is the case with OPEX. If this is the approach, making change happen will not be possible. Instead, the CEO or COO, whoever is responsible, has to take a decision and make things happen.

WHEN THERE IS LACK OF UNIFIED DIRECTION

When the CEO has not articulated a vision because of which leaders don't really know where the company is going or the CEO has articulated a vision, but it has not been brought by the leaders below, such lack of unified direction galvanizes the troops because of which the organization operates like a fragmented entity. Each of the leaders below act as mini-generals, which makes all of them wanting to go their way. The result is that the CEO has ceded power to these independent-minded leaders who want to tread in various directions. In such a case, a journey of OPEX is not likely to succeed.

WHEN LEADERS DROWN THEIR HEADS LIKE AN OSTRICH

This often happens when the company has been doing well, and they believe that they don't need to improve further. The general view of CEO and top management ignore the various voices which include the voice of customers, voice of competition, voice of context and voice of partners. While they do pay lip service when it comes to these voices and say that they will look into it, in reality they just shrug it aside, knowing that the volumes would come as it is, so why bother. Any suggestion of improvement is looked at as an interference to their so-called well-oiled machine which has been delivering the desired company performance. While they don't say it themselves, in their mind they believe in the fact that becoming competitive is not for them as they are successful.

WHEN THE COMPANY HAS 'WE DON'T NEED IT HERE' SYNDROME

When a conversation around improvements is brought up for discussion, the general response is 'we don't need it here'. This is resonated by the members of the C-suite too. Leaders believe that what they do is unique and their work does not require any improvement. The other thing that happens here is that leaders don't talk about competitors who are doing better or some company that does something better somewhere. Their belief that they are paragons for what they do puts them in a state of denial.

WHEN THERE IS BUREAUCRATIC DECISION-MAKING STRUCTURE

There are companies wherein such initiatives go through committees which have representation of leaders from various functions. Each member has a veto power, which can stop an effort. Any decision on any change effort or major activities that the company takes up has to go through it. Members in the committee look at things from their own silos because of which they don't want change efforts to go through because it can expose them or may not put them in the right light. Or there could be turf wars which may push one member to veto the effort. The tyranny of the committee sometimes just kills an intent to begin an OPEX journey.

WHEN LEADERS LOOK FOR APPROVAL

Outside consultants are brought in for OPEX. This is not to catalyse improvements but to validate the status quo. The consultants come in and finally share a report that the company does not need to spend time and resources on OPEX.

WHEN THERE IS PROTECTION FROM GOVERNMENT

There are times when the company is protected by the government. This could be due to regulations because of which the company has never really had to bother about competition. There may have been a monopoly because of this. It could also be that performance does not matter as the government is there to bail you out. Don't we remember some of the public sector companies in India in the 1980s? Clearly, this sets in complacency in the company, and talks about OPEX would be futile.

The journey of OPEX will only succeed when the CEO puts his might behind it. He does not wait for long-drawn consensus building. He at the most bounces off with his key deputies and just tells his teams to get going. After all, OPEX is a change effort, and many people would not like to be a part of it, as it would require them to change the way they get things down.

Chapter 5

Power of Early Wins

OPEX effort in an enterprise is typically a multi-year effort, wherein large projects take time to reap benefits. This is where the power of early wins comes to play. I have seen business leaders only focusing on big ticket projects and not paying attention to the wins that are possible in the first few months of the journey. Any company embarking on an OPEX journey should design in early wins to keep the momentum going.

What are early wins?

These are successes that one sees in the first few months of OPEX rollout. They can be projects, actions, rituals, behaviour or symbolic act.

PROJECTS

Projects are typically an improvement effort. These are low-hanging fruits which deliver benefits within a short period of time. The project outcomes should typically result in operational and financial improvement. These could be a mix of projects which get done in 30–60 days.

Example: As a part of OPEX roll-out, a company decided to install end-to-end metrics for the key processes. Within 30 days, there was a dashboard ready for everyone to see the progress. This gave a big fillip to the workplace, as the employees could, for the first time, see how the top processes were performing. This triggered many improvements, which were initiated by the employees.

ACTIONS

Actions are execution of decisions and action plans that have been agreed upon and have been pending for long. Rituals are habits that influence and inspire people.

Example: A CEO decides to take an action on the pending infrastructure issue which was not being owned by anyone due to political reasons.

RITUALS

Rituals are habits that influence and inspire people. These are actions, emotions and gestures which are repeated to communicate a certain message. This is done to institutionalize a certain way of thinking in the enterprise. The objective is that people repeat it so that it slowly becomes a habit or changes the way they look at things.

Example: As a part of OPEX roll-out, one company came up with a two-minute anthem, where teams would stand and speak to reinforce that they were a part of the journey.

BEHAVIOURS

Behaviours are changes that employees see in the way they conduct themselves. Non-verbal actions can be a powerful way to communicate about the upcoming change.

Example: As a part of OPEX roll-out, a CEO a top management of a shared services took a call that meetings would start and end on time. They followed it religiously.

SYMBOLIC ACT

A symbolic act could be a one-time action taken to demonstrate that things are not going to be the same again. It denotes that business as usual is something of the past and change is underway.

Example: A CEO who had OPEX on his mind, the first few days of his joining, visited the manufacturing plant. There he was appalled to see the condition of toilets. This was something overlooked by the previous CEOs and the entire C-suite. Within seven days of joining the company, he took a call that all washrooms of the company should have a bare minimum standard. And this he made happen within 40 days.

What do early wins do?

Early wins act as a catalyst for sustaining the momentum which was there on the launch of the OPEX transformation. They help in gaining the confidence of the employees who often wonder if this is another of the management's buzz words that is being thrown at them. It also helps in reducing resistance, especially from those who don't want to come on board because they are still not sure what this is all about. There are others who are hesitant to lead or be a part of any OPEX initiatives because of fear of failure. The early wins convince them that they can also win. Employees are generally not keen to participate in a transformation effort if the likelihood of success is not seen. The early wins bring that assurance to them that they are going to be part of something that is going to meaningful and also successful.

Carefully choosing what's on the list of early wins is very critical. This is because getting them wrong can dissuade people from coming on board. Don't take up things that you are not sure would be successful. Any decision that you take should be visible to the employees. It could be need of a metrics moving or change of behaviour or closing a long-pending action.

Communicating the gains from the early wins is key to mobilize the company. But it's important to not overdo this. Share successes with people and call out names of those who made it happen. However, employees should know that they have just scratched the surface, and the journey has just begun. Any exaggeration could give a false sense of progress. Small recognitions are fine, but avoid big celebrations. Yes, you should also not be quiet about your early wins. Trivializing their success could be a missed opportunity; hence, it should be narrated well. It is recommended that you use influencers to spread the word around, as informal sources of communication can be very powerful.

Remember that early wins play a big role in an OPEX roll-out. It is imperative to design them into the transformation effort.

Chapter 6

How to Lose Friends and Alienate Staff

Every textbook you read on carrying out an OPEX transformation talks about the importance of getting 'top-down' support. Management must be fully on board, understand the basic tools and techniques, and help to ensure buy-in at lower levels in the organization.

In reality, however, we often deal with less than ideal circumstances.

One particular piece of work springs to my mind.

Our task was to catalyse a Lean transformation event in the process shop of a services organization. The objective was to look at opportunities for enhancing productivity and streamlining process efficiencies. The sponsor of the intervention was Ms Vandana John, a leader who claimed to be passionate about improvements; during my pre-engagement discussion with her, I realized that she understood some of the basic Six Sigma tools. She was quite proud of how she was a part of a few quality projects in her previous company that had delivered huge financial returns.

She assured me that she would provide all the necessary support to make sure that impediments were removed during the execution.

The words were what I wanted to hear, but I finished the meeting with a mixed view. Was she a real 'performance-improvement convert' or a 'glib talker'?

The Lean breakthrough event started on the scheduled date, and Vandana was there to set the context and communicated to all how important the project was and what it meant for her business. For the uninitiated, a Lean breakthrough or a kaizen event is one when a set of people come together and work day and night on a problem with an objective to deliver a spectacular result within a short period of time.

I was quite happy with the way the event got launched. The team began work as per the predefined schedule, going through the typical due diligence of comprising value stream walk, detailed process dissection, takt time calculation, etc.

But then things started to go awry at the end of the second day when Vandana made a sudden unannounced visit to the war room.

At first, she seemed pleased with the maps, coloured post-its, easel chart papers, etc., adorning the walls all over. However, her eye went to the value stream map and the detailed process dissection comprising value-add/non-value-add analysis, and that's when it all started to go wrong.

Vandana didn't understand why 'electronic inventory' showed in the value stream map and was keen to challenge us on it. She argued that 'service requests' were not inventory, as they were not tangible. She went on to imply that this was not usual practice as her previous employer had not included 'electronic inventory' in the value stream map.

Patiently, we explained the concept of inventory in Lean thinking and seemed to win her round to our thinking, but not without a fight.

Next, she shifted her focus to data accuracy. She kept on questioning the source of data and who had provided them. We finally had to call the person in her team who had provided the data to reassure her that they were correct.

Her next focus was on the detailed process dissection comprising 'VA–NVA' analysis and the identified eight wastes.

In total, the interrogation went on for four hours.

The team was able to successfully address all her concerns, but the problem was that they shouldn't't have had to.

This is a very good example of unconstructive micromanagement. Certainly, as the process-improvement sponsor, she had every right to challenge us on our work, but the problem is that she clearly didn't have as much Six Sigma experience as she thought she did. She wasn't challenging us on the work we were doing as much as questioning the very basic tenets of Lean and Six Sigma.

Her intervention distracted our project team from focusing on the task at hand and left everyone feeling frustrated.

But then it got worse.

She was back at the end of the fourth day. This time she wanted to understand the 'opportunities' that had been identified for improvement and was told that our intervention had freed up around 21 people.

She wasn't happy.

She called the process owner and gave him an earful, rebuking him for how inefficient he had been in holding so many unproductive team members and warning him that his year-end performance rating would be impacted.

This was the worst thing that could happen.

On hearing this, I realized that I couldn't be a bystander any longer. I led her out of the room and talked her through the leadership behaviours required for building an improvement culture.

Vandana's behaviour in this instance was exactly what you shouldn't do to create an environment conducive to performance improvement. The rebuke to the process owner, and threats to undermine his year-end performance rating, would only lead to staff hiding problems and inefficiencies. Instead, she should encourage teams to report problems and process deficiencies.

So what do we learn from all this?

I don't want to disparage Vandana John's character, as I believe that she thought she was acting in the best interest of the business. I think what this example highlights, though, is how important it is that business leaders are properly equipped with the right tools and necessary understanding of Six Sigma and Lean to be effective managers.

I think that there are four main ways in which the pitfalls that I've described could be avoided:

- **Before embarking on Lean transformation, make sure that business leaders have undergone a session on Lean fundamentals:** I should have ensured that Vandana had undergone a proper training session. So many of the problems we encountered with her during the transformation would have been covered during the leadership alignment session and would have helped us avoid them in the first place.

- **A Lean performance improvement coach should spend time to coach leaders:** Even the best athletes in the world rely on coaches to improve their performance and understanding of the game; why should it be any different in business? I think that a coach can help business leaders understand the best way for them to contribute to process improvement.

- **Let leaders experience a Lean performance improvement before they sponsor a project:** I think we learn best by doing and I think that in an ideal world, all project sponsors would have participated in a Lean improvement before taking charge of their own.

- **Encourage teams to report problems and reward them for taking the initiative to solve them:** This is probably the single most important takeaway from all this! If we wish to foster a culture of continuous improvement, then we must ensure that people are not put on the defensive. We want to foster an open environment that rewards staff for flagging up problems and then having the gumption to solve them.

As for the project, the Lean event got over as scheduled on the seventh day, and all the counter-measures had been implemented as planned. The results spoke for themselves. And Vandana? Her closing remarks were: 'Good job, but we have just scratched the surface.'

While the above pertains to a Lean improvement the lessons hold true for any OPEX transformation.

Chapter 7

><·<■□——□·>·<

10 Laws of Process Work

Processes are the linchpin to organizational performance. While companies are typically structured vertically across functions, it's the workflow that moves horizontally and touches the customers. It's the processes that deliver value to customers and help in achieving objectives of the enterprise. Process improvement and OPEX go hand in hand. Rather without looking at the process, OPEX is not possible. When processes are the heart of this effort, it is imperative to understand the laws that govern processes. As someone who catalyses OPEX, you should know them. They tell you the essential elements which drive process improvement. It elaborates when you should take them and what needs to be done to manage them.

ALL WORK IS A PROCESS

All work that happens in an enterprise irrespective of the functions are processes. Look at them carefully and you will find that they have inputs which converted to outputs after some value addition. These help to serve the needs of various stakeholders such as external customers, internal customers, shareholders and community.

PROCESSES HAVE A LARGER PURPOSE

Every process has a larger purpose. They are defined by the needs of the stakeholders. The output that a process produces impacts the larger purpose. This essentially defines a larger reason as to why a process exists. Keeping the purpose on the radar is a must while designing, managing or improving a process.

PROCESS COMPETENCY TAKES TIME TO DEVELOP

Competence is the ability to demonstrate skills required to do a job. The competency around management and improvement of processes takes time and grows organically. There are no shortcuts here. There are three types of broad competencies that you need here. You need skills in process design, process management and process improvement. You can't master them by just attending a workshop. You have to back a classroom training with hands-on experience, coaching and project execution. This takes time, and there is no magic wand to reduce the duration of this process.

CORE PROCESSES ARE STRATEGIC ASSETS

Core processes are the strategic assets of an enterprise. These are those processes which have a direct impact on strategic objectives such as revenue, customers and employee engagement. Ensuring the health of the core processes is critical for enterprise success. What is key in an OPEX journey is to have identified the core processes and keep your eyes on the health of these processes. The health of these processes will determine the quality of outcome from your core processes.

HEROES DON'T BUILD A CONTINUOUS IMPROVEMENT CULTURE

While improving processes, companies often swoop in OPEX experts who catalyse improvements and then fly out. This is a short-sighted approach. It promotes individualism and not collaboration. A continuous improvement engine sticks when it is owned and led by the teams running the process. Getting experts who come in and then vanish for making changes does bring about some change, but they don't create a mechanism for the change to happen on an ongoing basis. The right approach is to have OPEX experts amid the process teams. They work with those who are a part of the process and help to make change happen.

LOCAL IMPROVEMENTS DON'T MOVE THE NEEDLE OF ORGANIZATIONAL PERFORMANCE

Improvements carried out locally may bring about change in components of a process but do not have an impact on overall process performance. Real benefit is seen when an end-to-end process is taken up for improvement. This is the reason why companies don't see the dial moving on overall company performance despite executing a large number of local improvement efforts. Hence, the choice and scope of the process is an important factor in getting meaningful benefit from process improvement work.

ANALYSE BUT DON'T GET PARALYSED

While working on process improvement, we know that analysis is important. But don't analyse so much that it delays the process and does not lead to any incremental benefits. What matters in a real business setting is the speed of execution. It's better to go for a less than perfect solution than looking for a perfect solution which takes an inordinate amount of time. The complexity of problems and business need should decide the level of analysis. While approach matters, don't do things on the pretext of rigour that add little value.

SHUN PROCESSES IN TRANSITION

Processes which are undergoing a change or are ill-defined should never be taken up for improvement. If changes are being made, wait for it to be fully implemented. Only after it's fully implemented and stabilized should we take it for improvement. In case of ill-defined processes, the start point, end point, inputs, resources and even output may not be clear. Hence, they are also not candidates for improvement. A well-defined process is a prerequisite for process improvement.

UNDERSTAND THE INTERACTION AND INTERDEPENDENCIES OF PROCESSES

Processes in an enterprise are interlinked with each other. They not only interact among themselves but are also interdependent on each other. When you improve one process in an enterprise, it could have an impact on other processes. Hence, it's always important to assess the impact of one process being changed on others which have not been taken up. Here, an interaction diagram and a macro map of how processes are interdependent on each other can be of help.

JUST NOT PROCESSES

A process improvement often requires a new way of working to sustain the benefits. This may require changing the underlying mindsets of those involved in the process. This is not an easy process and takes time. Sometimes project/transformation teams work on the process changes but don't focus on behaviours. As a result, whatever change that has been carried out vanishes after sometime, as people continue to operate in the old way and don't adopt the new way to get things done. If those involved don't change the underlying mindsets and behaviours, and continue doing things the way they have done, the change would not sustain.

Keeping the above laws in front is a must while catalysing an OPEX endeavour.

Chapter 8

Make Better Decisions by Questioning

Assumptions are beliefs which we consider to be true without data or proof. They are invisible, taken-for-granted beliefs which have not been examined. We consider them true and think they would happen without concrete evidence. They develop from our knowledge, heresies or learnings from events and experiences. The problem is that the assumptions are often based on half-baked information, obsolete data and past experience. We make assumptions when we don't fully understand the situation and feel the need to make sense of what is happening.

Assumptions shape our judgements and influence how we make decisions. They help us to draw a conclusion about what's happening and what others are thinking about us. When assumptions are wrong, even the smartest people can go wrong.

What we humans don't do quite often is questioning these assumptions. When we ask instead of assuming things, it brings better clarity to what we are doing.

Confronting assumptions is key in the journey of OPEX. When you don't do that, it can lead to making wrong conclusions, barking up the wrong tree, creating obstacles, causing misunderstandings and not doing what is required.

Here is a set of assumptions that we need to question in a journey of OPEX.

YOU UNDERSTAND WHAT THE CUSTOMER WANTS

Many of the projects that you take up will have a direct bearing on customers. It's important to understand the customers and their persona well. We should know their needs, wants, what they say and also what they don't say. Understanding customers entails how they act, think and feel as they come in contact with the customers. Many improvements go wrong because of the wrong assumptions that leaders ha/e about customers which they try to push through. If your perceptions about customers are based on assumptions, it's time to pause and question them.

YOU KNOW YOUR COMPETITORS

Knowing who is your competition is critical in OPEX. Often, competitors could be whom you know and you don't know. There could be current competitors whom you know and about whom you don't know. There could be an underdog whom you are taking lightly. There could also be future competitors which you may not be considering. Ascertain the market disruptions which are happening in the environment and how these are impacting the competitive landscape. Before jumping to a conclusion, do some work on assessing the competitive landscape of today and tomorrow.

THOSE AROUND HAVE CONTRIBUTED AND BOUGHT INTO THE SOLUTIONS

While working on OPEX projects, there would be many times when you have to brainstorm solutions and agree on a way forward. This is where you have to make sure that everyone in the team has contributed and bought into the solutions that have been agreed upon for future. It's important to make sure that there is sufficient debate and all the concerns have been surfaced. This is possible when the team members trust each other, have an open mind, engage in unfiltered passionate debate, come up with a clear plan of action and then commit to what needs to be done going forward. What's important is that when they leave the room, they are all aligned and will go all out to work on the actions that have been agreed upon.

THIS IS HOW IT IS DONE IN THIS INDUSTRY

Sometimes it may be required to challenge the preconceived notions that we may have about an industry. List all the assumptions that have been navigating the industry. Are there rules that need to be revisited? For example, Southwest Airlines challenged the assumption that there needs to be fixed seating.

MESSAGES BEING COMMUNICATED ARE EFFECTIVE

When an OPEX programme gets rolled out, a lot of messages on myriad issues will fly around. This could be from the vision of the OPEX programme, why we are embarking on it, the critical success factors, progress reports and so on. Various approaches could be used to do this, such as email, town halls, videos, Google Hangouts and telephones. This is where it is important to understand not only what is being communicated but also their effectiveness. Make sure that the intent of the message is clear and what you want them to take away with them. So never assume that just sending out a message will get absorbed by the participants. One approach that is adopted by a few leaders is telling employees to repeat the message that they have heard. Also, make sure that the overarching message is communicated in all possible opportunities.

LEADERS HAVE BOUGHT INTO OPEX

While rolling out OPEX, don't assume that leaders have bought into it. Despite commitment from the CEO and C-suite, there could be leaders at middle management and other levels who are not convinced about it. Hence, the change catalysts are required to constantly ascertain if the leaders are on board. For this, they have to be trained on it. This can be done by engaging them and observing the type of questions that they are asking and the level of involvement during the preparatory phase of the project and even during roll-out. In case there are gaps, make efforts to take them on board.

SUCCESS STORIES OF THE PAST CAN BE REPLICATED

There is this belief held by business leaders that solutions to problems of past and success stories can be applied to similar problems in the future. This assumption may not be true. The pace at which things around us are changing is unthinkable. With advances in technology and morphing customer expectations, the solutions of yesterday may not be relevant. For example, if we look at process improvement in 2007, we adopted methods of Lean, Six Sigma, etc. In 2020, when we spoke about process improvements, we adopted solutions using Lean, Six Sigma, intelligent automation, RPA, etc.

WE ARE DOING WELL AS FAR AS CUSTOMER SERVICE IS CONCERNED

Business leaders sometimes have this belief that they are doing well as far as customers are concerned, and nothing much needs to be done. Even if this is true, this assumption has to be questioned. Irrespective of the way the customer is getting served today, a company needs to continually find better ways to serve the customers. This could be through innovative products or services. Rather, a company serious about customers should have a deep obsession for it.

OPEX IS FOR PRACTITIONERS

OPEX isn't just for practitioners. Practitioners have to work with the other leaders and employees across the organization to catalyse the required improvement. For OPEX to be successful in a firm, it has to be everyone's business. The experts and practitioners have to handhold and work with them to make the larger vision of OPEX a reality. An OPEX programme which is just run by experts is bound to fail. A living OPEX programme is one in which the improvements are run by the line managers, and experts come in to handhold when required.

REFRAME THE PROBLEM

The way you frame the problem decides the approach which will be taken up for transformation. Hence, start by questioning the question.[1] For example, a company always worked on enhancing customer engagement by framing the questions as 'How does the company reduce customer complaints?' Or 'How does the company improve quality defects and reduce lead times?' Embarking on this approach will result in two very different sets of solutions. By posing the two questions it was being assumed that customer engagement will be improved by either reducing complaints or improving quality and lead time. However, when a new CEO came on board, he urged the teams to change the question and ask: 'How does the company provide a memorable experience?' Framing the question changed the focus of the team, and different and much more holistic solutions were found.

Remember, when you don't question the assumptions, you are somehow encouraging the status quo and using the full potential of the transformation.

REFERENCE

1. Fast Company. Three ways to reframe a problem to find an innovative solution. 8 September 2015, https://www.fastcompany.com/3050265/three-ways-to-reframe-a-problem-to-find-innovative-solution (accessed 3 February 2021).

Chapter 9

The Bed Sheet Scandal

In 2016, a leading Indian manufacturer of home textiles was hit by a scandal. The company has been known around the world for its towels, bath robes, bath rugs/mats, area rugs, carpets and bed sheets. The company had captured market share in the USA by partnering with its customers on solutions, and not just commodity textile products. This manufacturer had supplied premium quality bed sheets to retailers such as Target and Walmart—except that said sheets were actually made of low-grade cotton blends, not the Egyptian kind as promised.[1] Investigators from Target probed the fibres of the bed sheets under a microscope and then tracked the global supply chain touching Minnesota, Cairo and Mumbai.[2]

The company not only acknowledged the issues, but the correction was led by the chairman himself. The top management took it upon itself to communicate with all stakeholders on what actions were taken to ensure such an incident does not repeat. The company roped in management and media consultants on how to address the issue. The chairman's wife who is also a part of the top management travelled around the USA to meet every client and asked them if they needed to indemnify them from any potential liability to ensure that their interest is not jeopardized.[3] A slew of measures were put in place around beefing up processes and technology. New products were also introduced. The outcomes of the efforts were positive, and the company was out of the woods within a year's time.

The objective of this chapter is to not delve into the root causes that led to this specific scandal. However, it brings to fore the necessity for businesses to introspect and see if there are issues which could lead to this type of reputation-damaging problem. This becomes imperative when efforts are underway to make businesses operationally excellent. Towards this, there is a need to find answers to the following questions.

ARE STRATEGIC OBJECTIVES CREATING BEHAVIOURAL DISSONANCE?

Strategic objectives help an organization to steer their course. They provide clarity on the prize ahead for organizational teams. They unite the organization in a common purpose, challenge individuals and aid in planning for success. But these objectives when not carved well— especially when their impact is not thought through—can drive undesirable behaviours. Let me give you two examples.

- **Perils of contradictory objectives:** Have a look at your strategic objectives and see if they are contradictory in nature. The first goal should be to avoid such contradictory goals. But when it is not possible to avoid, take care to see how they are being communicated to employees. The focus should be on ascertaining if the contradictory goals could trigger behaviours which could negatively impact the larger interest of the organization. Here's an example: One of the reasons for the Volkswagen emissions scandal was that the CEO had set three contradictory goals— demonstrate energy efficiency, price competitiveness and environmental safety.[4] The company had to pass the tough emission standards while making sure that the prices did not go up or impact fuel efficiency. The result was that engineers came up with software that made cars emit less toxic fumes during test conditions.

- **Sharp targets which have to be achieved at all cost:** Has the CEO set sharp targets without really thinking through the consequences? The famous example of this is the Ford Pinto scandal of the 1970s. At the time, Ford president Lee Iacocca wanted his team to build a car weighing less than 2,000 pounds and costing not more than US$2,000 within 25 months. Given the pressure, the product was sent to the market with design faults. The engineers were aware of the defect which could be hazardous to human life yet decided to send it to the market as the cost–benefit analysis found that it was cheaper to pay customers than correct the problem. It was a commercial success until *Mother Jones* magazine exposed how this car could cause a fire at the rear end and lead to human deaths.[5]

Businesses in both the manufacturing and service sectors have to be careful about not falling into a similar trap. Given the pressure to remain competitive, sometimes companies set targets to meet requirements of customers. For example, let's say there is a demand from an international retailer to deliver a certain product at a certain price. While there is no harm in the target per se, organizations need to ensure that a proper structure is followed to design a new product and no shortcuts are taken.

HOW OFTEN ARE THE CORPORATE VALUES REINFORCED?

Most progressive manufacturing companies have values which they mention in their website, company brochures and even on their premises—these values take pride of place along with their vision and mission. There are two issues here. The questions to ask are: When were the values decided? And are they sufficient for allowing the organization to wade through current challenges? For example, if the company competes in a market where customers expect an ecologically friendly product, then does it have 'going green' as a corporate value?

The other issue is making sure that the values remain central to everything that the organization does. Are they being lived by the leaders and the employees on a daily basis and do they guide all decisions and actions taken by them? This is easier said than done. The values cannot just be communicated once and forgotten. Their overarching importance has to be repeatedly communicated by leaders across various forums. It has to be ensured that systems, policies and practices align with these values. Remember that values, if not reinforced, decay over a period of time and hence need to be regularly brought to life.

IS THERE A CULTURE OF SILENCE IN YOUR COMPANY?

By culture of silence I mean instances when things are not right, yet people don't speak up. There could be many reasons why employees do this. One reason could be because employees don't find it safe to raise a flag if things are not as they should be. This could be because the organization does not have a culture of openness and trust.

Employees find it too risky to bring out issues which could put them under the spotlight. They don't want to get rebuked or challenged for something they are not responsible for. There could also be a fear of losing their job. What pervades in the organization is a 'this is not my responsibility' mindset. Why bother about something that does not pertain to my area of work? It could also be because when employees reported a problem, the bosses said things like 'Don't come with problems but with solutions.' Don't we remember the recalls of small cars made by General Motors (GM) in 2014 due to a faulty ignition, which shut off the engine during driving and prevented the airbags from inflating? Although the employees of GM knew about the problem for many years, the company decided to recall the cars only when GM was sued by a family for a death caused by the fault.[6]

This is why it's imperative for business organizations to build a culture of trust and openness and drive an environment of accountability. If things are amiss, employees should not shy away from holding people accountable irrespective of their hierarchy or organizational standing.

ARE 'NOT ACCEPTABLE' PRACTICES BECOMING 'ACCEPTABLE'?

Are practices which are normally not acceptable in your company becoming acceptable? This is something leaders need to be always careful of. This is called normalization of deviance. This is a term coined by sociologist Diane Vaughan, which refers to the practice where 'deviance' from the norm or standards slowly gets institutionalized in the company. This happens when teams find it difficult to adhere to standards due to factors such as time pressure, resource constraint and limited budget. As a result, they accept the current subpar standard as a benchmark. There may be a belief that the slip in standards is temporary, but often it becomes permanent. Your normal behaviour becomes what you have got accustomed to and not what the original standard was. The psychology behind this is that we humans have a natural tendency to take shortcuts and deviate from established standards. If nothing bad happens, we don't mind repeating such behaviour and before we know it, it's a new norm.

This is something that the CEO and top management should have zero tolerance for. They should come down heavily on actions and behaviours which may not lead to the best outcomes for the organization. Remember that when there is a quality drop in the marketplace, it does not suddenly happen. It happens because someone someday compromised some standard somewhere which later became a norm. Hence, business leaders need to not only watch out but also identify potential deviances which may occur in the organization and take proactive steps to arrest them.

REFERENCES

1. Chauhan B. Welspun record undermined by bed sheets controversy. BloombergQuint, 25 August 2016, https://www.bloombergquint.com/business/welspun-indias-30-year-track-record-undermined-by-bed-sheets-controversy (accessed 2 February 2021).

2. Bloomberg. Scandal could be the unmaking of India's bedsheet industry. *IndustryWeek*, 14 Nov 2016, https://www.industryweek.com/supply-chain/article/21988667/scandal-could-be-the-unmaking-of-indias-bedsheet-industry (accessed 2 February 2021).

3. Datta A. Welspun India: Out of the woods. *Forbes*, 11 May 2017,https://www.forbesindia.com/article/8th-anniversary-special/welspun-india-out-of-the-woods/46931/1 (accessed 2 February 2021).

4. Halfond J. Speaking ethics to power: Lessons from Volkswagen. HuffPost, 12 July 2017, https://www.huffpost.com/entry/speaking-ethics-to-power-_b_10880852 (accessed 2 February 2021).

5. Wojdyla B. The top automotive engineering failures: The Ford Pinto fuel tanks. *Popular Mechanics*, 20 May 2011, https://www.popularmechanics.com/cars/a6700/top-automotive-engineering-failures-ford-pinto-fuel-tanks/ (accessed 2 February 2021).

6. Wikipedia. General Motors ignition switch recalls. n.d., https://en.wikipedia.org/wiki/General_Motors_ignition_switch_recalls (accessed 2 February 2021).

Chapter 10

Taking the OPEX Flight

Before embarking on an OPEX journey, don't forget to understand the context. By context, I mean the setting within which an organization operates and also the environment within the company. This is required for making sure that the transformation efforts are pivoted in the right direction. I have seen people jumping to working on a project or a change effort without really pausing and trying to make sense of the big picture.

Context is about trying to understand a situation from multiple perspectives. Every project is unique in a way. The scope, people, processes, stakeholders, competitive forces, industry in which it operates, technology changes, etc., will affect the way you design and deliver the OPEX transformation. I have developed an approach called APPLE, where each letter stands for the areas that we need to look at to ascertain the context.

A = ASPIRATIONS

What is the vision of the enterprise? What are its goals? What is the strategic plan for the enterprise? What are the key metrics which they are targeting in the next 12–18 months? What are the chronic pains? What do the CEO and top management expect from OPEX?

P = PRODUCT

What are the products and services of the enterprise? What are their USPs? How do we stack up in the market? How do we distribute our products? What sort of channels do we use? How do customers experience value in what we deliver?

P = PEOPLE

Walk around the company and get sense of the people who are there. Who are the key stakeholders, which are the power centres? How engaged are the employees and who are the voices that matter? Understand the culture of the company, how things get done there, how their performance is measured and how they are recognized. Get an idea on the political undertones of the company and what could make or break a project. If possible, meet all the leaders who matter and capture what they say and what they don't.

L = LANGUAGE

This is about ascertaining the verbal and written language which you hear about the company. What sort of language do people use when they talk about the company? What sort of adjectives do they use? What messages do you hear about the company? What are the views of the shareholders? What do analysts say about them? What is the general perception among customers? What does the company stand for in the market it operates? What murmurs does one hear in the company's corners? What sort of language do you read about the company in the media?

E = ENVIRONMENT

Understand the environment well. Who are competitors? What are technological disruptions which are impacting the industry? Where do you see the industry and market-moving at large? Who are your competitors? Are there players who may be your competitors but you are not aware of?

Remember that an OPEX endeavour depends a lot on the context. Even if you have done all the right things and used the right approaches and tools, it may go awry because we have not understood the context. The following are some of the approaches which I follow to understand the context.

- **Interviews:** Meeting and having conversations with relevant stakeholders can provide a lot of insights into the context. The meetings could be with key leaders in the company or even with key customers, shareholders, partners, etc. It is very critical to go to these meetings with prepared questions.

- **Observation:** Observation is a powerful tool to know a context. What's required here is to look at things with an open mind as they are happening. This is about capturing what you see in the company, what sort of conversations you hear, the energy which you feel and the way things get done.

- **Research reports:** Going through annual reports, analyst reports and views in media can provide a lot of data about the company. I suggest that you browse through the things which matter and not really getting lost in trivial details.

- **Focus group:** Focus groups are used to gather views of groups of people on the company and the market it operates in. This can be done with customers, suppliers, industry experts and so on.

You can use the approaches based on the need. However, please don't skip the process.

Chapter 11

Alan Kurdi, Fukushima and Emotional Connection

The year 2015 was filled with stories and insights on passion, persistence, perseverance, human spirit, leadership and more. It's not that other years did not have such stories, but one incidence of 2015 stands out. This was the image of little Alan Kurdi.

This was probably the most saddening picture not just of 2015 but also last few years. I am sure that everyone who saw it must have been heartbroken and realized how dangerous the world is today. The picture of the three-year-old Syrian boy, who drowned with his brother and mother when their boat capsized in the Mediterranean Sea, became a symbol of the extent of the refugee crisis.[1] While the world was aware of the problem, this picture made a visceral impact. All of us have been seeing the extent of damage in Syria on TV, but seeing a cute little boy being swept aside to the Turkish shore connected to all our senses and awakened us.

Not surprisingly, many world leaders reacted sharply to this event. Leaders such as French President François Hollande, British PM David Cameron and Irish PM Enda Kenny voiced that a lot more needs to be done for these refugees. The image brought focus and a sense of urgency to this problem. And countries in Europe, the US and Canada took a series of measures to help to settle these migrants.

So how does it connect to OPEX?

If you are trying to change or improve something in your organization and wondering where to start, look for events which communicate a sense of urgency to all your employees. See how the need for change can be connected with the senses of all, so that they come on board and willingly participate in the effort.

Look at the image of lifeless Alan Kurdi—it is very different from what we had earlier seen of the Syrian war. It juxtaposes two contrasting moods. On one side, there is the desolate figure of the prone child on the beach and on the other there is this bright background of lovely blue serene Mediterranean waters. The contrast of mood accentuates the pain in the image and stimulates our five senses. Anyone seeing the picture can almost feel the tragedy and would like to do something about it.

Another example is the images of the Fukushima nuclear disaster of 2011 and how the event triggered a debate on usage of nuclear power and created a sense of urgency among nations to reduce their dependence on it.[2] The images of Fukushima triggered actions such as Germany deciding to phase out of nuclear power by 2022, France deciding to reduce its share of nuclear power from 75 per cent to 50 per cent by 2025 and Italy deciding a target of 25 per cent of electric generation from nuclear power by 2030.[3]

What's important to remember in OPEX is that individuals have to 'see' and 'feel' the message for them to act. When a message triggers an emotion, the likelihood of taking actions is greater.

Clearly, when seeking employees to be a part of a change effort, it's important to have visceral connection which can be achieved by stories, images and voices.

STORIES VERSUS DATA AND STATISTICS

To understand this further, let's look at the research done by Deborah Small, George Loewenstein and Paul Slovic, who wanted to see how people respond to charitable contribution for an abstract cause versus a charitable contribution to a single person.[4] The participants were divided into two groups. Both of them received an envelope with a letter inside.

In one, the people received a letter with the following details:

Food shortages in Malawi are affecting more than three million children. In Zambia, severe rainfall deficits have resulted in a 42 per cent drop in maize production from 2000. As a result, an estimated three million Zambians face hunger. Four million Angolans—one-third of the population—have been forced to flee their homes. More than 11 million people in Ethiopia need immediate food assistance.[4]

In the other, the people were provided a letter giving information about a single girl:

Any money that you donate will go to Rokia, a seven-year-old girl who lives in Mali in Africa. Rokia is desperately poor and faces a threat of severe hunger, even starvation. Her life will be changed for the better as a result of your financial gift. With your support, and the support of other caring sponsors, Save the Children will work with Rokia's family and other members of the community to help feed and educate her, and provide her with basic medical care.[4]

What was found was that people who read the first letter donated on average $1.14, while those who read about Rokia donated on average $2.38.

Clearly, the story of Rokia had stirred people's emotions, and they donated more. The reason why people did not contribute to option one was that they felt that their small donation will have little impact. This is what is called 'drop in the bucket effect'.

The researchers carried out a third study. Here, they put both the letters in an envelope and gave them to the participants. The impact was that the average donation came down to $1.43. Although there was a story about an individual called Rokia and statistics about the country, the people became less charitable. The researchers concluded that when people think analytically, they are less charitable. Cleary, sympathy and aid-giving are often irrational.

As a part of OPEX, when nudging people to change, what plays a big role is a powerful story, and the corresponding emotions that are evoked. Often logic may not work, but a powerful story which emotionally connects with people can do wonders.

CEOs, business leaders and change agents keen on driving change should use impactful stories and images to drive engagement on a change effort. For example, an organization facing major customer issues may decide to embark on a quality improvement programme. To get employees on board, it could use real videos of irate customers which are played across the length and breadth of the firm.

When a food manufacturer was concerned with sliding volumes, the reason expressed was the poor condition of packing of the jam bottles. The packs were dirty, and labels had dog-ears or were torn. These bottles had gone through a couple of rounds. The factory manager had spoken about it with the shop-floor staff, and somehow it did not connect. He even shared the data that also had little effect. The CEO had an idea. He placed the defective packs with customer feedback on display on the factory floor. The customer stories were read, narrated and discussed during shift meetings and daily huddles. The staff could see for themselves the quality of products that had left the plant. They seemed to feel a bit embarrassed seeing that. The exercise had not only stirred their emotions but also reinforced the need for change. What data and statistics could not do was done by a set of stories and images.

BRAIN PROCESSES NEGATIVE AND POSITIVE INFORMATION DIFFERENTLY

The human mind registers negative information more than positive information. We all tend to remember the negative experiences of our lives more than positive. We may forget the positive experiences of childhood but may not forget how someone had misbehaved with us.

This happens because our brain processes negative and positive information differently. While pondering on negative emotions, we process them more thoroughly than positive information or emotions. As Baumeister et al. mentioned in a paper in 2001, 'Research over and over again shows this is a basic and wide-ranging principle of psychology.'[5] 'Bad emotions, bad parents and bad feedback have more impact than good ones. Bad impressions and bad stereotypes are quicker to form and more resistant to disconfirmation than good ones.'

Professor Clifford Nass mentioned in an article in *The New York Times* that we tend to see people who say negative things as smarter than those who are positive.[6] Thus, we are more likely to give greater weight to critical reviews.

The reason for this is evolutionary. As Baumeister mentioned in the article, being more attuned to bad things would have been more likely to survive threats and, consequently, would have increased the probability of passing along their genes. Survival requires urgent attention to possible bad outcomes but less urgent with regard to good ones.

While driving change, when we hear a story or see an image which pertains to a negative experience which the organization has had with a customer or any other stakeholder, it will register and more likely be remembered by the employees. This can be a big propellant in changing things and making things better. So negative images do create a sense of urgency among people to change things.

UNDERSTANDING EMOTIONAL MOTIVATORS

To drive emotional connection with staff in an OPEX effort, we can also leverage the power of emotional motivators of the employees and position the roll-out accordingly. Emotional motivators are inner motivations of individuals which help them fulfil deep, often unconscious desires.

Scott Magids, Alan Zorfas and Daniel Leemon of Motista, a consumer intelligence firm, has assembled a list of more than 300 emotional motivators which help brands to connect with customers.[7] Although they are meant for external customers, they can be used to position an OPEX transformation. The list of emotional motivators includes the desire to 'stand out from the crowd', 'enjoy a sense of well-being', 'protect the environment', 'feeling secure', 'succeed in life' and 'feel a sense of belonging', to name just a few.

What needs to be done is to find out the emotional motivators of the team who are going to be a part of OPEX. This can be ascertained by having conversations with employees and getting a sense of what really excites them, and then positioning the transformation in a way that the teams feel connected.

When a shared service centre was undergoing a finance OPEX transformation, the CEO ascertained that one of the subconscious needs of the staff was to be looked as working for an organization which 'stands out in the market'. This was because the perception among the employees had been that they were just doing a grunt work which had been offshore to them. Hence, he decided to position the transformation as an effort to create the best shared services in the country. He told the employees in a town hall that irrespective of the role that one played in the centre, going forward they were contributing towards this lofty vision. This seems to have resonated with the staff, as it had addressed the internal motivator of 'standing out in the crowd'. When a data entry operator was asked what he did, his answer was that he was on a journey to build the best finance shared service centre in the nation. The shared service centre was able to achieve its goals from the OPEX transformation two months ahead of the agreed time frames.

Emotional motivators work very well when you want to give a positive spin to your change efforts. What this means is that your improvements are triggered by a negative incident but to take the company to a new level of performance.

LET EMPLOYEES AIR THEIR FEELINGS

As we go about establishing emotional connect with employees, we should make sure that there are opportunities for them to air their views and feelings. This is required to make sure that they feel heard. Remember that if you don't provide a forum, they will share their views in private. The views can be both positive and negative, but what is required is to make sure that they are addressed immediately. Even if they are not addressed, we should tell them why it's not being down. Your communication on the benefits of OPEX will fall flat if people are not able to air their concerns. Letting employees air their concerns also provides an opportunity to modify the way the improvements are being rolled out. As Colin Powell had once mentioned, 'The day soldiers stop bringing you their problems is the day you have stopped leading them. They have either lost confidence that you can help them or concluded that you do not care. Either case is a failure of leadership.'[8] Clearly, listening to the employees is a basic prerequisite to achieving an emotional connect with OPEX.

REFERENCES

1.   Gunter J. Alan Kurdi: Why one picture cut through. *BBC*, 4 September, https://www.bbc.com/news/world-europe-34150419 (accessed 2 February 2021).

2.   *The Telegraph*. Japan's Chernobyl: Abandoned town in the Fukushima nuclear exclusion zone. 11 March 2013, https://www.telegraph. co.uk/news/picturegalleries/worldnews/9923033/Japans-Chernobyl-abandoned-town-in-the-Fukushima-nuclear-exclusion-zone.html (accessed 2 February 2021).

3.   World Nuclear Industry Status Report. *The world nuclear industry status report 2012*, https://www.worldnuclearreport.org/The-World-Nuclear-Industry-Status.html (accessed 2 February 2021).

4.   Small DA and Slovic P. Sympathy and callousness: The impact of deliberative thought on donations to identifiable and statistical victims *Organ Behav Hum Decis Process* 2007; 102(2): 143–153.

5. Baumeister RF, Bratslavsky E, Finkenauer C, et al. Bad is stronger than good. *Rev Gen Psych* 2001, 5(4): 323–370. doi:10,1037/1089-2680.5.4.323

6. Tugent A. Praise is fleeting, but brickbats we recall. *The New York Times,* 23 March 2012, https://www.nytimes.com/2012/03/24/your-money/why-people-remember-negative-events-more-than-positive-ones.html (accessed 2 February 2021

7. Magids S, Zorfas A and Leemon D. The new science of customer emotions. *Harv Bus Rev* 2015; November: 66–74.

8. Seijts G, Farrell GO and Farrell GO. Engage the heart: Appealing to the emotions facilitates change. *Ivey Bus J* 2003; January–February.

Chapter 12

It's Not WHAT but HOW You Say

Information is a key element in any OPEX endeavour. Without the right set of information, an OPEX effort can get lost and desired benefits may be a mirage. Information comprises myriad things such as metrics, customer's feedback, employee voice, procedures, policies and statutory documents. What's critical is to not only have the right set of information but also use them properly so that they deliver the desired benefit. Hence it's important to discuss the concept of framing and how it can be used in OPEX.

Framing refers to the way information is structured and presented to an audience so that it influences how people process information, actions they take and choices they make.[1] The words which are used, reference points which are mentioned and what we emphasize influence people's actions. When we consciously share a certain frame, it consciously or unconsciously drives our decisions. The other thing to be kept in mind is that when we negate a frame, we strengthen a frame.[2] So if you tell your team, 'Don't think about job security,' you will see that they are forced to think about it.

POWER OF METAPHORS

In an OPEX effort, this tactic can be used to bring a new meaning to the effort. Changing the metaphor in communication can be used to change perception, influence people's beliefs, drive actions and even solve problems.

An interesting research study was done by Paul H. Thibodeau and Lera Boroditsk.[3] The participants were given brief passages about crime in a hypothetical city by the name Addison. They were divided into two groups. For one group, the passage was altered and the crime was referred to as 'beast preying' on the city of Addison, while for the other group the crime was referred to as 'virus infecting' the city.

The participants were asked how they would recommend solving Addison's crime problem. What the researchers found was that the participants exposed to the 'beast' metaphor thought that the crime should be dealt with by law enforcement such as calling the national guard, instituting harsher penalties and building more jails, while those who were exposed to the 'virus' metaphor thought that it needed reformative strategies such as getting into root causes, improving education and providing healthcare.

A metaphor had made so much of a difference in the approach. What was interesting to note was that when asked what influenced the decision, they did not point to the metaphor; instead, they pointed to the statistics and other information presented to them.

A similar approach was taken by a financial services company which had been facing a downward trend in its mortgage business. The sales conversion figures were very low, and the company was struggling to get new customers. The sales had been impacted by a new home loan company which had been eating into its market. The new chief sales officer who came on board decided to reframe the problem differently. Instead of appertaining to someone who was trying to catch up, he pitched the problem as that of a conqueror. Instead of telling them to increase sales, he told them that he was declaring a war on competition. The metaphor of war had changed the game. Suddenly, the team started looking at the problem differently. They thought of themselves as the aggressor who was setting the rules of the marketplace and not playing catch-up. He painted the picture of competition as enemies who had to be dealt with not with kid gloves but iron fists. Within 18 months, the company became a market leader. This is the power of metaphor.

SHARING GOOD AND BAD

The same message framed differently has a different impact on the recipient of that information. When a message has both the 'good' and 'bad', it's looked at very differently versus the one which is either 'good' or 'bad'.

Researchers Derek D. Rucker, Richard E. Petty and Pablo Briñol carried out a study to examine the qualitative differences that message framing has on consumer judgement.[4] Their experiments were focused on ascertaining how message framing (one-sided versus two-sided) impacted messages' persuasiveness. One-sided messages were those which just spoke about positives, while two-sided messages focused on both positives and negatives. Participants were provided with a set of products which were framed as either one-sided or two-sided. Then they were asked to share (a) product certainty or how they liked the product and (b) attitude certainty or how certain they felt their attitude towards the product was correct which led to the purchase.

What the researchers found was that message framing did not have any impact on product certainty. However, attitude certainty was higher in two-sided frames compared with a one-sided frame. When consumers are provided with both positive and negative information about a product, their concern on whether negative information has been considered can be kept aside; hence, they are more certain about their attitude. What the study also threw up was that when negatives are presented as few or inconsequential, consumers tend to believe that there are negative attributes which are not known or have not been shared. When negative attributes are not mentioned, they have lesser attitude certainty, which means that they are less sure to buy the product. Clearly, the chances of consumers purchasing a product with two-sided messages are much higher, as they have got a holistic picture of the product. As the authors mentioned in Kellogg Insight, 'Attitudes held with firm certainty exert a stronger influence on behavior, are more likely to persist over time, and are more resistant to attempts to change them.' What they also mentioned was that

> It's important for marketers to understand not only what consumers think about a product, but also how certain those consumers are in their judgments. Gaining loyal customers may not simply mean fostering positive attitudes toward a brand or product, but also creating attitudes held with high certainty.[4]

So what are the takeaways for OPEX professionals?

Customer Feedback

When seeking customer feedback on e-commerce sites or online channels, specifically ask for both positive and negative observations. This can help customers make better judgement calls.

Product Attributes

While sharing product attributes to customers, be explicit about what it can do and what it can't. This will give great confidence to customers, and they will know what they are buying. Industries such as banking and insurance where mis-selling[1] is rampant can benefit from this approach. It can help in building their credibility before the customers.

---

[1] Mis-selling is the practice where a product is misrepresented to complete a sale. For example, a customer who has no dependents is sold a life insurance product.

Expectation Management

While sharing or even selling details about a specific improvement methodology (such as Lean, TPM, Six Sigma and TOC) to the senior management, be explicit about what it can deliver and want it can't. If you don't do this, the top management can have faulty expectations. When a company implemented Six Sigma, the CEO thought that it can solve all types of business problems.

Technology Solutions

Before adopting any IT solution, ask the technology company to be explicit about both the positives and negatives. If you hear the negatives, your antennas should go up that probably something is being hidden.

HIGHLIGHTING POSITIVES OR NEGATIVES

Another approach to framing information is by highlighting the positive or negative aspect of a decision which changes their attractiveness. To understand this better, let's look at an example.

You are at a supermarket looking for a sanitizer. You find two brands of sanitizers on the shelf. Let's call them Brands A and B. The label on the sanitizer bottle from Brand A says, 'Kills 95% viruses and bacteria', while the label on the bottle from Brand B says, '5% bacteria and viruses survive'. Which one will you buy? In all likelihood, your option will be Brand A.

The same information had been presented differently, and this had an impact on your purchase decision. The effectiveness of the product was the same, but the decision taken by you was different. Brand A focused on the positive trait (kills viruses and bacteria), while Brand B focused on the negative trait (viruses and bacteria that were not killed).

This can be explained by the 'prospect theory' proposed by Daniel Kahneman and Amos Tversky.[5] According to that, people put more effort into preventing a loss than winning a gain. They consider loss to be more significant, hence go out to avoid it even if there is an equivalent gain. They use relative assessment of losses and gains and value losses more than gain

What needs to be kept in mind is that dressing information as a loss instead of gain or neutral, the loss will be avoided. This is even when both the information are mathematically identical.

So how can this be used for OPEX?

Compliance

When seeking compliance, which could be behaviour change, IT system adoption, penetration of an initiate, etc., share information and data on the number of people who have complied with it and not the other way round. This is to send a signal to the many people who are already on board. For example:

- Eighty per cent employees are using the new human resource system.

- Sixty-five per cent of the employees have taken up small improvement projects.

- Six out of ten people have completed the RPA certification.

Meetings

When holding review meetings, always begin by talking about what has been accomplished and not what has not been achieved. Talk about the actions which have been closed, number of projects which have moved further or anything else. This will make the participants more open and not make them defensive. So when we discuss about what's not been done later, it will be much easier.

Value Proposition

While elaborating value proposition for customers, use the frame based on the type of product. For example, use negative framing when the focus is to illustrate risk (e.g., insurance products). Use positive framing when you want to sell a product or service, though in certain instances you may want to share both positives and negatives about a product about which we have discussed earlier.

Non-compliance

If punishments are to be used for non-compliance, share data which make it explicit for all to realize how horrible it would be if they did not do what they were supposed to do.

REFERENCES

1. Fairhurst G and Sarr R. *The art of framing*. San Francisco, CA: Jossey-Bass, 1996.

2. Rathje S. The power of framing: It's not what you say, it's how you say it. *The Guardian*, 20 July 2017, https://www.theguardian.com/science/head-quarters/2017/jul/20/the-power-of-framing-its-not-what-you-say-its-how-you-say-it (accessed 2 February 2021).

3. Thibodeau PH and Boroditsky L. Metaphors we think with: The role of metaphor in reasoning. *PLoS ONE* 2011; 6(2): e16782. https://doi.org/10.1371/journal.pone.0016782

4. Rucker DD, Petty RE and Brinol P. What's in a message frame? Kellogg Insight, 1 May 2009.

5. Tversky A and Kahneman D. The framing of decisions and the psychology of choice. *Behavioral Decision Making* 1985; 25–41. doi:10.1007/978-1-4613-2391-4_2

Chapter 13

Story of an Unsung Pioneer

This is a story of an unsung pioneer whose contribution has made our life safer. He is credited with uncovering the role of hygiene in the prevention of diseases' outbreak.

We are talking about Ignaz Semmelweis.[1]

He was a Hungarian physician, who worked at the maternity department of a hospital in Vienna, where he joined in 1844. The hospital had two maternity wards. In one of them, the pregnant women were treated by doctors and medical students. In the other ward, the women were treated by midwives. Both the wards were for the under-privileged.

Although each of the wards offered similar facilities for patients, what Ignaz Semmelweis found was that the mortality rate of the ward attended by the doctors was much higher than the one attended by midwives. What was believed was that the deaths were caused by corrosive air, overcrowding and an unhealthy diet.

He tested a number of hypotheses to ascertain what caused the deaths. He looked at myriad causes such as women's position during childbirth, the embarrassment of being examined by male doctor and priests attending the patients dying of the fever scared them to death. Finally, he discovered that the cause was the cadavers. On investigation, he discovered that the ward which was managed by doctors not only delivered babies but also handled cadavers. What he also found was that both these activities were performed without appropriately washing their hands in between.

In 1847, Dr Semmelweis instituted a policy which forced doctors to wash their hands with chlorine solution before examining any woman in the two maternity wards.

The outcome was that the mortality rates came down drastically. Ignas had pioneered handwashing and discovered the wonders of basic hygienic practice as a way to stop the spread of infection. He meticulously kept all the data but was quite hesitant to publish or deliver public lectures.

He tried to sell this idea of 'handwashing' to other doctors. But they rejected it. Semmelweis was outraged by the indifference. He finally wrote a book, *The Etiology, Concept and Prophylaxis of Childbed Fever.*[2] But what was disturbing was that part of the book was vicious criticism of all those who doubted him. He even went around insulting those with differing viewpoints. He called the prominently European obstetricians as murderers.[3] After struggling to get his idea adopted, he had a severe mental breakdown and had to be admitted to an asylum. He died at the age of 47.

In the recent pandemic, 'handwashing' had been one of the most potent weapons against the coronavirus. Thanks to Semmelweis for the pioneering work. It was almost 20 years after his death that his idea of handwashing was accepted.

The story has a couple of takeaways for OPEX.

KNOW ABOUT SEMMELWEIS REFLEX

We humans have a tendency to reject new ideas, information and knowledge which contradict and challenge the existing thinking and beliefs. This happens no matter how compelling the evidence for the new idea or the information is.

This is known as Semmelweis reflex.

We all come across instances where new ideas are rejected.

This is not driven by personality or one's knowledge but by how deep one's belief is about something.

A food company was on a journey towards building an operationally excellent organization. A middle-level manager came with an idea on how the distribution and logistics could be redesigned, which would not only make it more efficient but also provide a better experience to the customers as well as those involved in the process. The CEO who had been running the business for the last 40 years outrightly rejected the idea, saying that the idea would not work as he knew what worked and what did not in a business like theirs.

Confidence and belief in yourself are good, but that does not mean one should close oneself to new ideas.

Not surprisingly, start-ups which disrupt the industry are founded by those outside the industry.

NEVER DISPARAGE THE CHANGE AGENTS

The second takeaway is that while driving a change, don't make the change agents your enemies. Semmelweis identified the doctors as a problem and even called them unclean and murderers. Doctors hated this idea of them being called unclean when they examined the patients.

Their work gave them social status, which was being tarnished by someone then. They resisted. When we drive a change, it's important to make the change agents the hero not the villain.

For example, when Deb Cooper wanted to drive a process trans-formation in the human resources function, he met with resistance from those working in the department. Instead of listening to them out, he started accusing them and branding them as 'change resistant'. The outcome was that the initiative never took off till Deb was associated with it.

MANAGE THE CONCERNS OF THOSE IN POWER

Those in power are more likely to dismiss others' opinions. Semmelweis's boss was Professor Johann Klein, who had been teaching his students that the mortality of the patients was due to noxious atmosphere which hung over the city. He dismissed Semmelweis's view that the deaths were due to germs. Klein did not want to appear like a fool in front of his students, as someone was telling him to change what he had been teaching so far. So next time you go with a new idea to your boss, don't be surprised if he instantly dismisses it. This may happen because it may need changing their position which they have taken so far. This can also happen as there could be many responsibilities on the executive. A new idea may need a change and may upset smooth functioning. For such people to accept ideas, you have to also tell them ways in which they can unwind their position. And also share with them tactics on how issues around operational disturbance can be addressed.

DON'T ALLOW THINGS TO BACKFIRE

When people are made to see evidence which disapproves their existing beliefs, they reject the evidence and strengthen their support for the original stance. This is called the backfire effect and seems to have also happened in case of Semmelweis. To argue against the unwelcomed data, they end up arguing more to support their existing beliefs. Another thing which one needs to be mindful of is that showing people that they are wrong can sometimes be ineffective. This happens because people feel threatened, and this causes them to generate negative emotions. This especially happens when beliefs which you want to change are a part of their self-concept and internal part of their identity.

With such people, data may not work. Try and present information in a way that does not threaten their identity. Share in a way that is digestible to them.

GENEROUSLY SHARE THE DATA

Semmelweis was very hesitant to share or even publish the data which he had meticulously collected. When driving OPEX, let the key information on as-is state, progress metrics, financial data, etc., be shared generously. Those impacted by the change should know what's happening. This is needed to not only keep them posted but also take the doubting Thomases on board. I am not saying that you share confidential information. But all other relevant information should be shared, displayed and communicated for all to know. Let there be a person who takes ownership of this activity.

DON'T LET KNOWLEDGE BECOME A CURSE

While selling ideas, if they get rejected by the audience, don't give up. Ascertain what could be the possible reasons for it. One of the common reasons is the 'curse of knowledge'. This happens when better-informed people find it difficult to put themselves in the position of audience and understand their background and how it impacts their understanding. Semmelweis assumed that everyone would understand what he was talking about. After all, it was a new concept for them, and they would have found it difficult to appreciate his ideas on 'handwashing'. Instead of coming to a common ground, he started accusing the doctors.

Those involved in OPEX need to know that their knowledge about tools, improvement methodologies, etc., may not be easily understood by others in the company, as they may not have been exposed to them. So when talking to them, use the language and terminology which they will understand.

For example, if you are talking to a CEO and trying to sell your OPEX journey, avoid technical terms, methodologies and solutions (such as Lean, Six Sigma, Theory of Constraints, Design of Experiments, 8D and so on) which he may not understand. Instead, speak the language of money and other things which he will understand. If you try to show off your knowledge by using technical terms, you may lose the CEO's attention.

When communicating, learn what the audience values. A guest of the Ritz-Carlton and one of Holiday Inn Express value different things, yet they both want a hotel.

BEHAVIOUR CHANGE DOES NOT HAPPEN WITH COERCION

Semmelweis tried to change behaviour by coercing people to wash their hands. Instead, he should have been patient and inspired them. Behaviour change is an integral part of OPEX. You can't push people to adopt new behaviours. Instead, there may be a need to do myriad things which gradually change behaviour over a period of time. This could be inspiring them, explaining them reasons, changing the social context and so on.

REFERENCES

1. ScienceAlert. Who is Ignaz Semmelweis? n.d., https://www.sciencealert.com/ignaz-semmelweis (accessed 3 February 2021).

2. Semmelweis IP. *The etiology, concept, and prophylaxis of childbed fever.* Translated by CK Codell. Madison, WI: University of Wisconsin Press, 1983.

3. Flynn M. The man who discovered that unwashed hands could kill—and was ridiculed for it. *The Washington Post*, 23 March 2020.

Chapter 14

Using Neuroscience to Manage Change

A key element of OPEX is change. Understanding how the brain works can help to manage change better. There is a framework which was developed by David Rock in 2008, which can come very handy here. It's called the SCARF model and has five domains which influence how we behave in a social situation.[1] Based on neuroscience, the model describes the specific interpersonal threats and rewards which have the most power to affect us. By embedding this framework in thinking and leadership behaviour, we can use principles of neuroscience to drive change.

When a person senses something unexpected, the limbic system of the brain is activated and there is a 'minimize danger, maximize reward' response. Neurons are activated and hormones are released to ascertain whether it is a situation for reward or potential danger. If it's the latter, there is a threat response which is also called 'fight or flight' response to avoid the response. Have we not felt this when there were life-threatening situations?

A similar response is triggered even in social situations. This is why how we interact with team members and stakeholders can have such a deep effect on all organizational initiatives. The model helps to anticipate and interpret emotional response in others in response to change. It can also help employees to decipher the reason for your responses to organizational strategies and what you can do about it. Probably the biggest benefit is that it helps you to decide on the strategies for employee engagement.

The five universal principles of human social experience of the SCARF model are detailed in Figure 14.1. Each of the five social domains mentioned in the model activate the same type of reward and threat in the brain that we rely on for physical survival.

A person's behaviour would be based on whether he feels threatened or rewarded in each of the domains of the SCARF model. How they experience each of the domains would influence their ability to manage and react to change.

Let's understand the impact of each of the domains in OPEX.

STATUS

Due to the change which happens during an OPEX transformation, if an individual feels his status getting threated in any way, such as

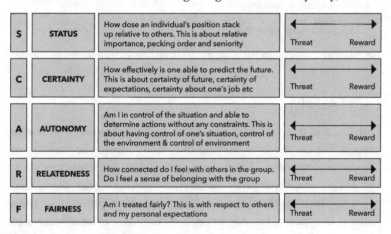

Figure 14.1. SCARF Model

feeling left out, feeling less important, change of pecking order, reduction in position in company hierarchy and feeling belittled in a conversation, it can evoke myriad reactions.

He could be belligerent. He could defend a position which may not make sense. This happens as decrease in status creates anxiety that results in the release of hormone cortisol by the adrenal glands as part of fight-or flight response. This is physically manifested by heightened levels of breathing and heart rate. However, if we feel rewarded there is a rush of dopamine in our brain that elevates our mood. Hence, while driving change through OPEX extra care has to be taken to sense and respond if the status of employees are diminished.

Things that you need to keep in mind are as follows:

- Avoid getting into situations wherein employees look bad
- Acknowledge good work and achievements
- Acknowledge people's skills and contribution
- Empower people so that they give feedback on their own performance
- Engage with stakeholders to understand their concerns our status issues
- Seek other's opinion
- Include more people in management meetings wherever possible
- Let employees go through professional development programmes

CERTAINTY

Our brain craves certainty. We want to predict what is going to happen. We do this by retrieving information from the memory of our past experiences. When we're acting with sufficient certainty, our brain senses patterns, successfully predicts next steps, and operates much more efficiently. Anything which prevents us from doing it is a threat. In such cases, the brain uses extra resources to process the information. This involves the more energy-intensive prefrontal cortex, to process moment-to-moment experience. This not only drains our energy but also takes our attention from the task at hand. For example, as a part of a productivity project, if you get a sense that your role may not exist, your attention will go away from the project and you will start worrying about your survival. As a result, you will not contribute what you are supposed to in the project. The antidote to such situations is leaders communicating upfront that there would be no job loss and everyone would be accommodated suitably in the company in other roles.

Things that you need to keep in mind are as follows:

- Overcommunicate
- Give people more information about the change which you are pursuing
- Reduce ambiguity around the change which is underway
- Break complex projects into smaller projects
- Share clear expectations
- Clearly tell stakeholders what to expect and what not to expect from a transformation
- Regularly share company and OPEX performance
- Open book management

AUTONOMY

Increasing a sense of autonomy is always rewarding, and employees feel a sense of control. The lesser the autonomy a person experiences, the situation is a threat for the individual. When people have a sense of autonomy, the workplace is stress-free. Being a part of the team reduces autonomy; hence, it's critical here to provide clear guidelines within which employees operate, which gives them a sense of control. The best performance is achieved when teams are given autonomy.

Things that you need to keep in mind are as follows:

- Give people choice or even perception of choice
- Don't micromanage your subordinates

- Policies should not get into minute details that employees feel claustrophobic
- Allow people to organize their work
- Involve them in decision-making
- Reach out for improvement ideas
- Address issues around work–life balance

RELATEDNESS

Human beings have this affinity to be a part of a tribe. Relatedness is about being a part of a group which is familiar. They want to be a part of a group wherein they feel safe, secure and bereft of judgement. How we interact with others impacts how we behave and the type of decisions we make. People feel comfortable to interact with those who they are comfortable with, trust and feel connected with. When we connect with others, it increases our hormone called oxytocin, which has been found to increase our collaborative behaviour. When we discuss something common, shake hands or swap names, oxytocin is released, which makes us feel comfortable with each other. Relatedness is simply about who is in and who is out of a social group. As a result, this has the potential to create organizational silos. When the size of a company increases, one has to find innovative ways to stay connected with people, and this is something that OPEX professionals should remember. The more socially connected you are, the easier it would be for you to catalyse initiatives of OPEX. So how does one manage this in amidst organizational diversity. What needs to be kept in mind here that differences are more effectively addressed after a sense of relatedness has been established.

Things that you need to keep in mind are as follows:

- Create an environment wherein employees feel psychologically safe to speak and share their views
- Reach out to people
- Make social connections

- Share your personal stories which will help them to connect
- Mentor and coach during change
- Make personal connection with people
- Give time to your employees to connect with each other
- Before putting together a diverse team, make deliberate effort to ensure less infractions

FAIRNESS

This is about having the perception of fair exchange between people. In a workplace where employees have a fair exchange, they find it rewarding. People who perceive a person as unfair do not feel empathy for them. And also when the unfair person is punished, they feel rewarded. Similarly, if a person has a low status and thinks that it's fair, he is fine with it. The cognitive need for fairness is so much that human beings are ready to fight for the cause they strongly believe in. In an organization, you cannot afford to create a perception of unfairness. This can attenuate trust and impact collaboration.

Things that you need to keep in mind are as follows:

- Be transparent with employees
- Explain reasons for specific decisions
- Give everyone an equal opportunity to contribute and win in change efforts
- Ensure consistency in policy around rewards, performance evaluation and benefits
- Let employees decide how work is allocated
- Openly communicate business issues
- Share the impediments to OPEX projects
- Never play favourites

The SCARF model is a brilliant framework which guides you on how to communicate and engage those around in an OPEX transformation.

Every decision you make in this collaborative journey either supports or undermines the perceived levels of status, certainty, autonomy, relatedness and fairness in your organization. The model acts as an aid to reduce the pain caused by change. It can help to spot negative emotions (such as fear, shame, anger, anxiety) and unbecoming behaviours (such as defensiveness, denial, attack and withdrawl) triggered in you and others, that come in the way of transformation delivery. Using the SCARF model helps to prevent, prepare, sense and respond to such occurrences during the various phases of an OPEX exploration. The focus in every phase has to be to increase sense of reward and eliminate perceived threats of those involved and impacted by the transformation.

REFERENCE

1. Rock D. SCARF: A brain-based model for collaborating with and influencing others. *NeuroLeadership J* 2008, http://www.scarf360.com/files/SCARF-NeuroleadershipArticle.pdf (accessed 3 February 2021).

Chapter 15

Pressing the Idea Button

Have you observed one thing about toothbrushes?

We all want it, we all need it, yet no self-respecting person wants to use anyone else's toothbrushes.

We find a similar phenomenon in the business world. And this is with respect to ideas.

We all want ideas, we all need them, but there are groups or organizations who do not want to use anyone else's ideas.

This is called not-invented-here (NIH) syndrome. Scholar Dan Ariely calls it the toothbrush theory.[1]

So what is NIH syndrome?

It is a tendency of a group or an organization to resist and reject ideas, solutions and knowledge which emerge from outside.

The impact of NIH syndrome is that companies reinvent the solutions, even though they exist somewhere else. It causes organizational blindness to potential growth opportunity.

In NIH syndrome, the lack of receptivity to ideas emanates just not from outside the organization but also within the organization. In the latter case, there could be NIH syndrome between two teams in a company or between two individuals in the same department.

It's said that Apple had this culture in the 1990s when employees rejected outside ideas, and it was called 'reality distortion field'.[2]

WHAT ARE THE SYMPTOMS OF NIH SYNDROME

In a company infected with NIH syndrome, one gets to see many instances where there is rash reinventing of wheels. New Ideas are rejected and the pace of innovation slows down, which impacts organizational performance. There is a biased evaluation of knowledge from outside. Knowledge from outside does not percolate within the organization or trickles in with a lot of difficulty. What is also seen is that the teams tend to believe that they possess a monopoly of knowledge of the domain in which they operate.

The voices that are heard in the company include 'This will not work here,' 'We know what works for our customers,' 'We have tried this before' and 'We can do it ourselves.'

WHY DOES THIS HAPPEN?

There can be myriad reasons for it to happen. Let me share the main causes.

Idea Usefulness

People tend to overvalue the usefulness of one's ideas. For example, Edison, who had developed direct current and felt that it was the best method to transmit electricity to masses, discredited alternating current developed by Tesla, only to be proven wrong later.[3]

Market Position

The company can be a dominant player in the market, for example, Kodak's refusal to address the rise of digital technology over film, which led to the fall of the company.[4]

It's Not Ours

The company has a philosophy that if something is not invented by them, it has nothing to do with them. Sony's digital music failed as they were not made compatible with MP3s, as it had not been developed by them. This resulted in iPod becoming the successor of Walkman.[5]

Identity Issues

The groups feel threatened of losing their identity, distinctiveness and self-esteem; hence, they don't allow outside ideas. This is strongest when the outside entity from which the idea is being sourced has similar expertise and operates in the same domain or product market. The people who are within the in-house team feel threatened and worry that their position and importance can get jeopardized.

Overconfidence

A person who is in a position of influence is overconfident and prejudiced. He is closed to new ideas from outside as he believes that he has all the solutions. We saw this evidence during the recent pandemic when a few global leaders ignored scientist, researchers and economists and took steps of reopening which caused many lives.

Past Accomplishments

The team has high confidence in its expertise and what it has achieved so far. It is also very proud of its achievements and could be even known in the marketplace for it. This decreases the readiness to accept knowledge from the outside. Their know-it-all mindset stops them from seeking external insights.

Relationships

It's also observed that when team members have worked in a team for long and have a stable relationship among themselves, it builds understanding among them and also enhances working relationships. It also helps to build each other's capabilities and of the technologies that they are entrusted with. However, as found by researchers Katz and Allen, team membership reduces communication with outside groups and external parties.[6] They also tend to isolate themselves from sources providing critical evaluation and do not align with the group ideas.

Performance Measurement

The reason why NIH syndrome happens can be the way the performance of the team members gets measured. Their incentives may be based on recognizing their brackets of expertise. There could also be a culture that celebrates the accomplishments of experts.

Processes

NIH syndrome also happens because of unfriendly processes which inhibit communication and interaction with external parties. It can also be because people are not aware of how to gather insights from outside and there are no processes for the same.

Organization Hierarchy

NIH syndrome happens when the knowledge has to cross organizational hierarchies. For example, a senior leader may reject an idea which has come from a junior person. In the book *Men, Machines and Modern Times*, author E. Morison[7] talks about US Navy, where a junior offer pioneered an innovation which enhanced the accuracy of guns used from ships. A senior naval officer rejected it for many decades till President Theodore Roosevelt intervened.

Domain Expertise

NIH syndrome can also occur within a team when two members in a team operating at the same location have different backgrounds.

An accountant may reject ideas from an engineer. For example, as I. Lakatos mentioned in his 1978 book, Leibniz and Huygens had rejected Newton's concept of universal gravity due to their distinct scientific philosophies, even calling the concept occult.[8]

Certainty

People want to maintain the status quo; hence, they reject ideas from outside. Humans seek security. When external knowledge enmeshes with their existing work, it creates uncertainty, which makes people feel uncertain. Rejection is a way to ensure the existing certainty.

Prefrontal Cortex

The scientific explanation of NIH syndrome is that absorbing new ideas and knowledge taxes our prefrontal cortex in the brain.[9] This is where we do our thinking. By avoiding external ideas, we preserve our energy which may be required to focus on the new knowledge. After all, we have a tendency to preserve our mental resources. We also don't want to experience the discomfort and eerie feeling as results of the extra work that the brain needs to do to process the new set of information.

Emotional Investment

New ideas are also resisted because of significant emotional and financial investment in internal initiatives. People don't want to look foolish and weak in front of others, as they have been a votary of way of doing things which may be questioned and even undone by the outside ideas. Also, it could lead to losing control of what they have been part of. After all, no one likes ideas getting killed which they may have created.

HOW TO OVERCOME NIH SYNDROME?

So how do organizations address NIH syndrome? The following are the suggestions which can be adopted based on the context and where they are applied.

Create Opportunities

Don't push people to adopt ideas from outside. Instead, create opportunities for them to look at ideas from outside and decide for themselves where they can apply those in their workplace. This is to ensure the issue around ownership. No team is keen to undo the practices it has created. By following this approach, it will also address issues around pride which can result in them rejecting the ideas.

Evangelize

Evangelize within the company to learn from outside the organization. Tell employees that it's okay to pick up ideas from everywhere including competitors, another industry, another sector or an area no way connected with what the company does. Exhort them to adopt Pablo Picasso's famous quote: 'Bad artists copy, great artists steal.' Narrate stories of leaders like Steve Jobs and how they picked ideas from others and created their own products. As US politician Nancy Pelosi mentioned in 2016 Mid-Atlantic Democratic Platform Forum, iPhone had been made up of components such as GPS, voice recognition, alloys and compression algorithms for wireless data, which came from federal investments in research.[10] As she mentioned, 'They say Steve Jobs did a good idea designing it and putting it together. Federal research invented it.'

Open Innovation

Encourage and institutionalize open innovation where ideas from outside are used to achieve strategic goals. In 2000, when P&G appointed A. G. Lafley as the new CEO, he realized that its method of 'invented-here' approach to innovation was not capable of meeting the top-line growth. He mandated that 50 per cent of new products should be developed outside the company. The company also launched Connect+Develop, a systematic, company-wide open innovation programme charged with bringing outside-in innovation. By 2005 , P&G had achieved its goal of 50 per cent of its innovation fuelled by outside partnership.[11] Today, Connect+Develop looks for innovative solutions for all areas of business from products to process to packaging.

Network

Create a knowledge network outside the organization comprising experts, thinking partners, organizations, collaborators, social media, etc., who can be a source for inputs. Be part of trade shows and conferences to understand what's happening outside both in your industry and outside the industry. Install a mechanism for regular competition reviews and scan the larger environment to know what's happening outside the company.

Hackathons

Hold hackathons where diverse talent from outside are invited to solve problems of an organization.

Recognition

Recognize and incentivize employees for building on ideas which have emerged outside the organization. People should be incentivized on how much outside knowledge they have used to solve organizational problems. The key performance indicators (KPIs) are going to be driven by the context and should capture ideas leveraged both from within and outside the organization.

Partnerships

Forge partnerships with entities outside the organizations. For example, GE Digital had been trying to do lots of things by itself in the technology space. It practised a mantra of NIH. The company invested large sums to build a Silicon Valley presence for its software, hired engineers, built its own infrastructure and so on. Things changed when John Flannery served as the CEO from August 2017 until October 2018 joined the company. In 2018 Minds + Machines conference in San Francisco, he announced that going forward GE would work more closely with its partners.[12] Just a few months later, one heard that GE's partnership with Microsoft would bring together operational technology and information technology 'to eliminate hurdles industrial companies face in advancing digital transformation projects'. This was reported in a media blog from Microsoft.

Critique

Be open to get your ideas critiqued by those outside the organization. Regularly invite experts and thought leaders to come and look at what you are doing. In the first month of new joiners, let them come with a list of areas which need improvement.

Competitions

Companies can hold a competition to seek outside ideas and collaboration to solve organizational problems. For example, in 2009, Netflix launched an open competition called Netflix Prize.[13] The competition sought to get the best algorithm to predict user ratings for films. It aimed to substantially improve the accuracy of predictions about how much someone is going to enjoy a movie based on their movie preference. The BellKor's Pragmatic Chaos team was the winner. It received the grand prize of US$1,000,000.

Outside Perspective

Within the existing teams, include team members with external knowledge and outside perspective. This should be a regular process within organizations and should be done for all departments. Doing this can help to arrest NIH syndrome. This was validated by H. Mehrwald in a 1999 study involving 50 R&D managers and 89 scientists in over 50 of Germany's companies.[14]

REFERENCES

1.   Ariely D. *The upside of irrationality: The unexpected benefits of defying logic at work and at home.* London: HarperCollins, 2011.

2. Kenehan S. How an undetected problem might be hurting your learning product. n.d., https://learnosity.com/not-invented-here-syndrome-explained/ (accessed 3 February 2021).

3. Borowski S. The brilliant and tortured world of Nikola Tesla. 29 May 2012, https://www.aaas.org/brilliant-and-tortured-world-nikola-tesla (accessed 3 February 2021).

4. Amann M and Granström G. *Mitigating not-invented-here & not-sold-here problems.* Industrial and Management Engineering, Master's-level Thesis, Luleå University of Technology, Sweden, 2019, http://www.diva-portal.org/smash/get/diva2:1322767/FULLTEXT01.pdf (accessed 3 February 2021).

5. Surowiecki J. All together now. 3 April 2005, https://www.newyorker.com/magazine/2005/04/11/all-together-now-3 (accessed 3 February 2021).

6. Katz R and Allen TJ. Investigating the not-invented-here (NIH) syndrome: A look at the performance, tenure and communication patterns of 50 R&D project groups. *R&D Man* 1982; 12: 7–19.

7. Morison E. *Men, machines and modern times.* Cambridge, MA: MIT Press, 1966.

8. Lakatos I. Falsification and the methodology of scientific research programmes. In: Lakatos I (ed.) *The methodology of scientific research programmes.* Cambridge, UK: Cambridge University Press, 1978, 8–101.

9. May MR. Overcoming the Not-invented-here mindset. 8 May 2018, https://www.disruptorleague.com/blog/2018/05/08/overcoming-the-not-invented-here-nih-mindset/ (accessed 3 February 2021).

10. DNA. Apple founder Steve Jobs did not invent the iPhone, then who did? 13 June 2016, https://www.dnaindia.com/technology/report-apple-founder-steve-jobs-did-not-invent-the-iphone-then-who-did-2222018 (accessed 3 February 2021).

11. P&G. Partnering with the world to create greater value. n.d., https://www.pg.com/en_US/downloads/innovation/C_D_factsheet.pdf (accessed 3 February 2021).

12. Mintchell G. GE Digital ends not invented here syndrome. 19 July 2018, https://themanufacturingconnection.com/2018/07/ge-digital-ends-not-invented-here-syndrome/ (accessed 3 February 2021).

13. Netflix. Netflix Prize. n.d., https://www.netflixprize.com (accessed 3 February 2021).

14. Mehrwald H. *Das 'not invented here'-syndrom in Forschung und Entwicklung.* Wiesbaden: Deutscher Universitaetsverlag, 1999.

Chapter 16

When Good Is the Enemy of Better

Let me begin this chapter with a few examples.

1. When a credit card company saw a downward trend with sales conversion, the new chief sales officer who had come on board thought that to be a familiar field. He had worked on similar problems in the past. Without further ado, he went ahead and implemented the solutions which had worked in the past. The outcome was that the conversion figures did show an upward trend but not as much as he wanted.

2. A QSR business had a problem of sagging customer experience. The new head of customer experience decided to adopt Lean Six Sigma for this purpose. He looked at the process in detail and ascertained what caused friction. He then went ahead eliminating them. He had successfully used

this approach in the past and thought that it would give results. The result was that the errors in the process did come down, but there was marginal improvement in customer satisfaction levels. What the person seems to have missed is to look at the entire customer journey before zooming into processes. What he also did not look at was how one can embed a customer-first mindset.

3. The CEO of a conglomerate hired a business leader to take a retail business of electronic to a new level of performance. This person had a name in the market for having successfully led two retail companies in two different companies. Both these companies had seen an increase in not only revenue but also customer engagement levels. The broad strategy which he had taken in both those retailers was making them lean and efficient and then providing a good experience. The media had given him a name as the 'Lean Machine', about which he was very proud of. On joining this company, he did not waste time in understanding the uniqueness of this business. He instead started adopting the solutions which had worked in his last two success stories. With a focus to drive efficiency, he closed down stores and even laid off employees. He felt that the company was over-staffed and had a very high store density. He launched a channel migration strategy to take customers to the online channel. In his hurry to get down to execution, he seems to have missed the positioning of the retail business. This was positioned as The Ritz-Carlton of retailing which encouraged customers to come and experience their products. The focus of his transformation should have been on enhancing consumer experience and look at creative approaches to increase the revenue. By the time he realized that his strategies had been wrong, 18 months had passed. The profitable business went in the red. The CEO who was supposed to be an expert of retail transformation had messed up. He had to go finally.

The above cases are examples of our pre-existing knowledge impeding our ability to reach an optimal solution.

These are the examples of what psychologist Abraham Luchins had called the Einstellung effect.[1]

Einstellung is a German word, which literally means 'setting', 'mindset' or 'attitude'.[2]

WHAT IS EINSTELLUNG EFFECT?

This is a cognitive trap where a person has a tendency to solve a problem by adopting familiar solutions or methodology which have been experienced in the past.

He does this even though there are better methods to solve the problem.

His previous experience tends to blind him from addressing the problem in a new or better way. This can result in less optimal solutions.

What happens here is that the first ideas that come to his mind are based on familiar dimensions of the problem. He sticks to it, even though it may not be the best solution.

We have seen this behaviour among experts. When they make mistakes, it's because they assume that the situation is similar, so past solutions will work. I know of an OPEX expert who believes that Six Sigma is the panacea for all types of problems without really realizing that the type of the problem decides the methodology which has to be adopted. Whenever a problem comes before him, without much thought, he will use the DMAIC (define–measure–analyse–improve–control) and the tools within. Has he been successful in solving all problems? He has not. But he has always discounted the issue telling that it's a problem of poor adoption of tools and not the approach.

Clearly, our past knowledge stops us from looking at alternatives.

Why does this happen?

BRAIN WANTS TO TAKE SHORTCUTS

Our brain looks for ways to simplify the way we process information. It uses shortcuts and saves mental energy for harder tasks. Hence, it takes shortcuts and refers to past solutions to solve a problem. The familiar thoughts inhibit our ability to generate novel solutions.

Our brain sabotages our ability to come up with novel ideas. Hence, you have to look for ways to break the pattern.

If problem 'A' has been solved in a specific way in the past, when problem 'B' occurs which is similar to problem 'A', our brain tells us to take the same approach adopted earlier.

Clearly, our past knowledge stops us from looking at alternatives.

This is what happens to experts who steadfastly stand by what they know and have done in the past. Their rigidity blinds them from interesting possibilities.

What happens here is that we tend to use similar thought patterns and past experiences to solve a problem if when it may not be relevant. We are stuck with ideas from the past which prevents us to step back and look at alternatives.

FUNCTIONAL FIXEDNESS

This is a cognitive bias that makes people to see objects in a particular way as a results they become trapped in a conservative view. A person believes that an object has a certain purpose and should function in the same way in all situations. They have preconceived notions on objects and how they should be used for solving problems. For example, hammers have been used to punch nails on the wall, but they can also be used as paperweights. Or a pencil is used for writing, but it can also be used as a bookmark. Due to rigidity in thinking, the problem-solver does not look at using the object in a new way.

So how does it connect with OPEX? Functional fixedness causes a person to look at all problems in one specific way. He believes that the approach which he knows and has practised in the past can be used to solve them. He does not look at alternate approaches, which constraints his being able to adopt solutions which will deliver optimum results. For example, I discussed earlier about the Six Sigma expert who claimed that Six Sigma could be used to solve all types of problems.

When functional fixedness is prevalent in a company, it can prevent them to develop breakthrough products and solve problems which address pressing issues. Employees soak in familiarity and don't venture into doing things which are uncomfortable. The more successes that they have had with their approach to problem-solving in the past, the harder it becomes for them to imagine a different method.

Researchers Munoz, Olson and James have established that functional fixedness impairs our ability to think of novel solutions to a problem.[3] Functional fixedness makes it difficult when we want to be creative in our problem-solving approach and embed outside-in thinking.

PepsiCo addressed functional fixedness in an innovative way. It wanted to find a way to reduce sodium in potato chips without reducing the salty flavour. It looked for options across food and snack industry but could not find a solution. So it changed the brief so that it could cast a wider net. The brief was that it was seeking 'formulation and delivery of nano-particle halide salt'. Responses came in from myriad industries such as pharma, fuels and engineering services. The winning proposal was from the orthopaedics department of a global research firm.[4] Although this was not a final solution, PepsiCo got a valuable partner to take the problem further and find a solution.

Functional fixedness strengthens with time. The more a person has solved a problem in a certain way, the harder it is to look for alternative approaches.

EXECUTION ON STEROIDS

Bias for action is always welcome in business. But trying to close initiatives, projects and transformations as the CEO believes in that is what I call 'execution on steroids'. What this means is drastically cutting down the timelines of projects by management on the pretext of driving the sense of urgency, embedding a high-performance culture and driving action bias. This typically emerges from a CEO who is larger than life and no other leader including the top management speaks the truth before him.

As a result, when teams share timelines of initiatives with the CEO or top management, they cut it down by 50–75 per cent, resulting in teams perennially hurrying to close projects. Sometimes it's just not about unrealistic timelines but also unrealistic targets set by the top management. Hence, teams don't do adequate due diligence on the right approach which should be used for projects. They adopt the approach which they have successfully used in the past even if that may not be the best thing to do. As a result, the results are suboptimal on many occasions. The CEO and top management are in a state of denial. They proclaim that even if the teams are achieving 50 per cent of the outcome, they are happy. They say that it creates a sense of urgency and builds a high-performance culture in the company. They don't realize that they are pushing their company to a sea of mediocrity where innovations and novel solutions don't flourish. Also, many of the problems may erupt again, as the solutions have been less than optimal.

HOW TO ARREST THIS PHENOMENON

First thing first, people should know about this cognitive trap. Beyond this, the following approaches can be adopted to arrest the Einstellung effect.

Jumping to Solutions

When you are entrusted with solving a problem, don't jump into brainstorming solutions. Instead, pause and reflect. Understand the context. Deep dive into the issue. And then decide what needs to be done. Get your approach critiqued by others in the company. Talk to companies not just in your industry but beyond on how they have solved such problems. Have a chat with experts from different domains. Even though you may have solved similar problems in the past, find out what's different in the current problem. Every problem has a customer. Understand what his explicitly stated problem is and what is implicit. Understand if the problem statement reflects the issue or needs to be received to represent the reality.

Searching the Horizon

Regularly carry out searches to find out how problems are being solved across industries, disciplines and functions. Ascertain how different ways are being used to solve problems. This will not only open up your mind but also provide the potential and power of other approaches. Distantly related domains can provide novel solutions which we may not realize till we go through the process. A small team can be entrusted with this responsibility. They hold regular sessions to share what new they have discovered in their searches.

Seeking Outside Voice

Set up a team with a mandate that they have to find solutions from outside their organization. This team ascertains how problems have been solved outside their industry wall and collaborate with them to solve organizational problems. This can set the foundation for addressing the Einstellung effect in the company. When other employees see how innovative approaches are being used to solve problems, there is always the rub-on effect.

Stare Vacantly

Gaze mindlessly into the open space while not looking at anything nor thinking of anything either. You stare at the clouds, look into the garden and stare at the leaves without thinking. There is a word in Japanese called *boketto*.[5] It literally means to gaze vacantly into a distance without thinking anything. This is an opportunity for the mind to take rest. There may be a status symbol in being busy and demonstrating actions every time. Practising *boketto* is healthy. It reduces our heart rate and clears our mind. It also increases our creativity to problem-solving.[6]

Problem-solving When Drained

Avoid solving a problem when you are tired. Research work of Daniel Frings has shown that fatigue has positive impact of Einstellung effect.[7] When people are tired and fatigued, they experience greater Einstellung effect. However, when working in a group, the impact is much lesser. When working in teams, members are motivated to perform well and they compare solutions with one another. Hence, despite the fatigue, the teams display less inflexible thinking.

Breaks

Take regular breaks. During that time, do something else or just let your brain take rest. Go for a walk, take a swim, run on a treadmill, go around on your bike, go through a book of art, etc. When you are taking a break, your thinking is unconsciously re-energized. New ideas start getting germinated in your brain. This is called a period of 'incubation' by psychologists. So when you will be back on the problem, new ideas will emerge. The other thing to do is to sleep over the problem, after which you may be taking a shower, walking through your garden, cooking a meal, doodling aimlessly or just working out in the gym, and suddenly a solution to the problem may pop up. It's almost like a eureka moment.

Diverse Background

Let a team comprising people from different backgrounds work on the problem. It's important to have a mix of experts and non-experts. This will reduce the likelihood of falling prey to a cognitive trap. We shall delve more into diversity in Chapter 37.

Adopt a Beginner's Mindset

A beginner's mindset is an inclination to periodically question and reassess deeply held theories, archetypes and conventions to devise new and fundamentally innovative solutions—either because reality has changed or because the current approach is based on flawed thinking, faulty premises or a different consumer or technological landscape.[8] In a beginner's mindset, we look at things free from the experiences of the past. This mindset is observed when we try something for the first time. When a beginner's mindset is adopted, it opens up different possibilities. To cultivate a beginner's mindset, ask the following questions before solving any problem:

- What if the existing approach will not work despite the best evidence?
- What if the solutions that worked in the past are no longer valid?
- How will my approach change if there are no constraints?
- What will be my approach if I were not an expert?
- What will I hear when people poke holes in my approach?
- What will I do if I am the founder of the company? (I can't let my business fail)
- Where/which business does exactly opposite of my approach?
- Under which situation will my approach not work/has not worked?

REFERENCES

1. Luchins AS. Mechanization in problem-solving: The effect of Einstellung. *Psychol Monogr* 1942; 54(6): i–95. doi:10.1037/h0093502

2. Luchins AS and Luchins EH. *Rigidity of behavior: A variational approach to the effect of Einstellung.* Eugene, OR: University of Oregon, 1959. OCLC 14598941

3. Munoz-Rubke F, Olson D, Will R and James KH. Functional fixedness in tool use: Learning modality, limitations and individual differences. *Acta Psychol (Amst)* 2018; 190: 11–26.

4. Zynga A. The cognitive bias keeping us from innovating. (7 August 2014), https://hbr.org/2013/06/the-cognitive-bias-keeping-us-from (accessed 3 February 2021).

5. Palmer, T. Boketto: Discover the importance of not doing. *medium. com*, 2 November 2019, https://medium.com/the-ascent/boketto-ce7a95217ff4 (accessed 4 May 2021).

6. The Decision Lab. Do you fall prey to the Einstellung effect in problem-solving? n.d., https://thedecisionlab.com/biases/functional-fixedness/ (accessed 3 February 2021).

7. Frings D. The effects of group monitoring on fatigue-related Einstellung during mathematical problem-solving. *J Exp Psychol Appl* 2011; 17 (4): 371–381.

8. Finzi B, Lipton M and Firth V. A beginner's mindset: Leading organizations in new directions. 4 February 2019, https://www2.deloitte.com/content/dam/insights/us/articles/4814_A-beginners-mindset/4814%20A%20Beginner%27s%20mindset.pdf (accessed 7 March 2021).

Chapter 17

It's Not about Cost Cutting

Whether you like it or not when CEOs and CFOs talk about OPEX, they have cost reduction in mind. Their focus is on how one gets maximum cost advantage which can not only improve competitiveness but also help in achieving profits.

As competition intensifies, margins tighten and stakeholders demand higher performance, many C-suite members equating OPEX to cost reduction is a new normal. This is seen more in the post-COVID-19 world. Sadly, they often don't include customer-centricity or product innovation within the world of OPEX. This is a reality which should be accepted. For many of them, every rupee spent on OPEX effort should result in improvement in operational efficiency which should positively impact the financials.

Hence, it becomes extremely important for the OPEX team to understand the strategies which can be adopted to get the costs down.

What's important to remember is that there is a difference between cost reduction and cost efficiency. The former is about unilaterally cutting costs across the board, which could lead to competitive disadvantage, while cost efficiency is about gathering long-term competitive advantage by following a structured approach to achieve gains. Although the latter takes time to yield benefits, it helps to push the company towards high performance. The problem with cost reduction programmes is that they are like a crash diet. They do reduce overheads, but the costs slowly come back to haunt the enterprise.

Typical cost reduction efforts are reducing the headcount, across-the-board budget cuts, cutting on travel expenses, slashing costs on employee training, removing employee benefits, making senior executives travel in economy class, etc., while cost efficiency efforts typically entail working with the 7 Ps about which we have discussed. Cost reduction efforts are 'just do it' efforts. Someone takes a decision around an action which will reduce costs and then people work to make it happen, while cost efficiency efforts are much more elaborate and require whole host of actions around structured problem-solving, strategic choices, aligning cost structures, building capabilities, rejigging organization construct, etc., which need to be adopted to arrive at actions which would need to be implemented; hence, they take time for execution. They are about making a deliberate choice on where to cut costs ruthlessly, where to cut costs thoughtfully and where to invest for profitable growth. Cost efficiency programmes are implemented as transformation projects. These entail implementing a couple of cost levers to achieve the desired outcome.

In cost efficiency efforts, the resources are aligned to a larger business strategy and deployed towards initiatives which are strategically important and enable a business to differentiate in the marketplace. It requires a need to change the way in which the company operates to sustain the gains and create a lasting value.

Cost reductions are sometimes driven as an austerity programme pushed from the top. The top management mandates that a certain cost item needs to be cut, and it is done across the board. When such programs are not thought through, they impede growth and reduce profits. For example, forcing suppliers to reduce prices can impact raw material quality or cutting down on employee benefits can have detrimental effect on employee morale.

So the focus of OPEX efforts is not cost reduction but cost efficiency. The focus is to protect 'good costs' while jettisoning 'bad costs'.

So what are good and bad costs?[1]

- **Good costs:** Good costs are those expenses which are focused on value-added activities of business. They typically help in business growth, build organizational capabilities and enhance organizational health.

- **Bad costs:** Bad costs are those expenses which may appear necessary yet don't directly contribute to business value. They divert resources from the future growth of the company and building critical capabilities.

Figure 17.1 summarizes the difference between cost cutting and cost efficiency.

A cost efficiency drive under an OPEX programme enables growth while getting rid of bad costs. The focus is on making sure that the strategically important initiatives and capabilities which differentiate the company in the marketplace are adequately funded. All other expenses go through a strict scrutiny. The focus is on getting rid of unnecessary, bad costs by changing the way the company operates, optimizing business elements and redefining how work gets done. This has to be a well-thought-out process and OPEX professionals need to know the levers which they can pull.

WHEN TO TRIGGER A COST EFFICIENCY PROGRAMME

The following are instances when a company may need to embark on a cost efficiency programme:

- When costs burgeon at a faster rate than the revenue
- When there is a need to be competitive in the marketplace

	Cost Cutting	**Cost Efficiency**
Philosophy	Get costs down at all cost by fixing a benchmark.	Build an engine of sustainable cost advantage while achieving profitable growth.
Approach	It is achieved through across-the-board mandate. They focus only on cost cutting.	It's structured and achieved through transformations. They focus on both business efficiency and effectiveness.
Focus	It is focused on pruning costs of selected cost. They often lose sight of protecting differentiating capabilities that matter.	It is focused on investing on differentiating capabilities while eliminating and pruning all other unnecessary costs.
How it is felt	It is often dramatic.	It is usually gradual.
Deployment	Top-down with little focus on taking employee inputs and involving in its design.	Driven like a change programme where all stakeholders are involved and taken on board.
Cost treatment	No special treatment to costs.	Deep dive of cost structures to understand the 'good costs' and the 'bad costs'.
Tools	No specific tool, just 'cut costs'.	Use the various cost levers in the quiver.
Impact after some time	The costs often creep back after some time.	The programme delivers sustainable benefits.
Organization health	Has little impact on the operating model of the company.	Strengthens the organization's core by fundamentally changing the way it operates.
Ways of working	Little focus on changing the ways of working of the company.	Focus on instilling right behaviours that support the effort.
Where it ends	It ends once the target is achieved.	This is an ongoing process in the organization and supported by a continuous improvement engine.

Figure 17.1. Difference between Cost Cutting and Cost Efficiency

- When new competitors are challenging the way business gets done

- When there are concerns with the financial stability of the company

- When some shareholder pushes the company to revisit its cost structure

- When a business needs to transform to meet the changing needs of the customers

- When there is a need to invest in differentiating capabilities and funds are scarce

- When there is a black swan event like COVID-19 about which the company was not prepared

- When shareholders seek greater value creation

- When the financials of the company are stressed and there is a need to conserve cash

- When there is an ongoing regime in the company to eliminate and reduce unnecessary costs

- When the competitive landscape has changed and new entrants are challenging the existing business models

LEVERS OF COST EFFICIENCY

The following are the levers which are available at our disposal. They can be chosen based on the context and unique organizational challenges of the company.

Portfolio Optimization

This is about reducing the number of products, categories and channels, which results in unnecessary complexity and drive-up cost. Typically, such complexity does not create or add value. The focus here is on shifting to profitable products, stock keeping units (SKUs) or channels. What also is done here is to treat high-volume and low-volume products differently and differentiate service levels based on profitability. The way portfolio complexity manifests is that each dollar of revenue comes at a higher cost as it's more expensive to do things without scale. Also, there is a lot of effort that gets into coordination between various teams and departments. An example of portfolio optimization is when a bank reduces the various types of credit cards in it's portfolio. For any business, too large a product or service portfolio or too much of customization, lead to inefficiency and increase costs. Portfolio optimization should be a regular and continuous process in the company.

Zero-based Budgeting

This is a method of budgeting wherein all expenses are justified based on strategic priority and business necessity at the beginning of each new period. The process of zero-based budgeting starts from a 'zero base', and every function within an organization is analysed for its needs and costs. Things are not included just because they were in last year's budget. This is done irrespective of whether each budget is higher or lower than the previous period. Although OPEX should know about this cost lever, this is typically driven by the finance team, and open teams don't play an active role.

Organizational Construct

An organizational construct is the key element of the operating model of the company. It is how the organizational units are structured, how people work together and how that ensures that critical work gets done. The design of the organization directly supports the differentiating capabilities of the firm. Here, the boxes and layers in an organogram are looked into and ascertained if there are opportunities for optimization. The type of things that one would look at here are the consolidation of layers, having the right span of control and shunning 1–1 or 1–2 reporting wherever possible. When organizational layers are reduced, it not only helps in cost efficiency but also simplifies decision-making, improves flexibility and enhances responsiveness. The organizational redesign should always begin with the CEO and his top three layers. Once it's done, it can be replicated by others. Spans and layers are very effective in reduced overheads costs. Spans refer to the number of people that a manager can effectively control. It is the number of direct reports for each position. Layers are the different levels in the organogram. They are the number of hierarchical levels from the CEO to the frontline.

One effective approach for reducing spans and layers is to look at the concept of 'managerial archetypes'. The span of control should be different and based on the type of role. Scott Keller and Mary Meaney in their book *Leading Organizations: Ten Timeless Truths* suggest this approach of 'managerial archetypes' for optimizing spans.[2] They observe that a key driver is how standardized is the work. If a work is completely standardized and minimum intervention is required, the span of control can be higher, while if there are activities where there is no standard work, the span of control is lower. The right span of control also depends on the complexity of the role, degree of judgement required and amount of interaction with others within and outside the company.

Centralization

This is about centralizing activities which may be happening across geographies and regions to a low-wage country where talent is available easily. This is about creating shared service centres for managing processes of finance, human resources, information technology, supply chain, sales, marketing, etc. This not only delivers economies of scale but also results in consistent and efficient delivery.

Outsourcing

This is the practice of farming out activities of organizations to a third party. Typically, non-differentiated processes are handed over to external service providers. It is done to focus on core aspects of the business while spinning off the less critical operations. This is what is typically seen in large companies. In the case of smaller companies, they use outsourcing for growth. They may not have in-house capabilities in critical areas such as R&D, death analytics and product design.

In all cases, the service provider delivers value by leveraging their process competencies, process standardization, cutting-edge capabilities, economies of scale, specialized expertise and labour–cost arbitrage.

Geo Optimization

Geo optimization or geography optimization is a strategy where the focus is on assessing how effectively the various locations wherein the company has a footprint are delivering on a larger strategy. The outcome is typically to have an optimal footprint after looking at customer demand and service-level expectations. The types of things that are looked for are the footprint of production factories, service points, R&D centres, retail branches, support offices, distribution centres, offices and so on. While working on this, one needs to keep in mind the attended risk and the service requirements.

Procurement

This is about looking at the procurement function holistically and making improvements. This begins with getting visibility into what item has been ordered and by which location or plant, how much quantity has been ordered, what price has been paid and who is the supplier. Then the effort looks at opportunities to reduce the cost through myriad approaches such as price negotiation, re-specification, value partnership, integrated operations planning, cost partnership, co-sourcing, demand management, volume bundling and target pricing.[3]

Process Optimization

This is about making end-to-end processes more efficient and effective. This is achieved by using methodologies such as Lean, Six Sigma and Theory of Constraints. These projects typically cut across functions and departments. It also includes manufacturing excellence efforts, supply chain improvement, sales and distribution excellence, etc. The focus is on determining the processes which create that value and simplifying or eliminating others.

Technology and Automation

This is about using information technology for streamlining operations and cutting costs. These also help in reducing the need for manpower, energy cost and errors, enhancing data capture, eliminating manual work, etc. The type of solutions adopted here are intelligent automation, moving IT infrastructure to the cloud, apps, self-service system, blockchain, tools, etc. One of the key focus areas here is to automate manual processes in the entire organization. Automation hopes to reduce cost, improve quality, accelerate production lead times, ensure quicker delivery, provide consumer convenience, etc.

Complexity Reduction

This is about removing unnecessary complexity in the enterprise. They not only choke profits but also add to the cost. The focus here is on reducing value-destroying complexity, which weans away from the customer and pushes the company into confusion. This begins with identifying areas in the value chain wherein there is undesired complexity and then carrying out simplification for value.

Mindsets and Capabilities

To make cost focus a part of the organizational fabric, it should be a part of the company mindset.

The company needs to implement a set of beliefs, mindsets and behavioural changes to help employees and leaders to be cost-focused and compound value. It also includes creating change agents who have knowledge and skills on methodologies which can facilitate cost optimization.

Any cost reduction effort which an OPEX professional takes up should be to make it more competitive and take the company to a path of greater prosperity. Any cost initiative stirs a lot of emotion in the employees, and the OPEX professional with other leaders should be able to convey the rationale and allay any concerns.

THE ROAD MAP

To embed cost efficiency, it's imperative to follow a structured process. What needs to be kept in mind is that a cross-functional team needs to work on it which has diverse capabilities of finance, change, functional knowledge and OPEX tools. The following is an approach that can be followed:

1. Understand the company's vision.

2. Understand what its strategic objectives are.

3. Go through the company's strategy.

4. Understand the company's position in the market vis-à-vis competition.

5. Dive deeply into the company's financials.

6. Ensure top management alignment.

7. Set a target of financial savings with an explicit time frame. These are set by the top management and focus on things such as share price, EBIT margins and cost as a percentage of income.

8. Identify capabilities[1] which will enable the company to differentiate and outperform.

9. Analyse all activities and look at all expenses.

10. Dive deeply into all cost structures. Get into the root causes.

11. List the activities which do not support priority capabilities that enable company to differentiate and outperform. These are the non-differentiating expenses. Segregate the expenses which the company can do without and the ones which are required for legal and regulatory compliance.

12. Inventory the activities which build competitive advantage or enable building capability for business differentiation.

13. Adequately resource activities which enable to build capability for business differentiation.

---

[1] 'Capability is a combination of processes, tools, knowledge, skills and organization. Differentiating capabilities are those that enables a company to outperform.'[1]

14. Scale back or eliminate expenses which focus on non-priority capabilities.

15. Select the cost levers to free up funds which can either go to the bottom line or can be reinvested.

16. Let a senior leader own each cost transformation project with a cross-functional team working with him.

17. Install a governance structure.

18. Execute cost transformation.

19. Embed new ways and working culture to leverage critical behaviours.

20. Create awareness among employees on 'good cost' and 'bad cost'.

21. Communicate with all the stakeholders.

22. Incentivize employees so that they take ownership of cost efficiency.

(The sequence of the deployment of the above points can be changed based on context.)

When a cost efficiency programme is run systematically, it not only impacts the bottom line but also releases cash which can be gainfully invested for building critical capabilities for business differentiation. Never cut costs which impair the differentiating capability of an enterprise.

REFERENCES

1. Couto V, Plansky J and Caglar D. *Fit for growth: A guide to strategic cost cutting, restructuring and renewal.* Wiley, 2017.

2. Keller S and Price C. *Beyond performance: How great organizations build ultimate competitive advantage.* John Wiley & Sons and Times Group Books, 2016.

3. Schuh C, Raudabaugh JL, Kromoser R, et al. *The purchasing chessboard: 64 methods to reduce costs and increase value with suppliers.* 3rd ed. Springer, 2017 .

Chapter 18

Collaboration Wins Games

Have you ever wondered why technology companies offer free food to their employees and why they are pampered with cuisines from different geographies? Companies like Google and Apple started this practice a long time ago, and today many companies are following suit. This was done not because the employees can't buy food for themselves. When employees have meals together, it provides an opportunity for employees to communicate together more often. It's also an opportunity to build trust with others and remove potential barriers. And the free food provides an opportunity for employees to start acting neutrally. Most importantly, these provide an opportunity for serendipitous interaction and collaboration.

The late Steve Jobs was a great believer in it. When he commissioned the headquarters of Pixar film studio in East Bay, he made sure that the building had an open structure. The building was designed in such a way that everything converged to an atrium—where the cafe and a single set of loos was situated, forcing employees to engage with one another. Jobs is quoted as having said, 'Creativity comes from spontaneous meetings, from random discussions. You run into someone, you ask what they're doing, you say 'Wow', and soon you're cooking up all sorts of ideas.'[1] Since then it has been a feature of many technology companies.

At Google, a healthy waiting time is kept during free lunch.[2] This is done to foster innovation among employees. When people wait in queue, they chat. Their conversations translate into ideas, and these ideas become projects. Even at Zappos, the late CEO Tony Hsieh was a great believer in such serendipitous encounters among employees. To make this happen, he closed all secondary exits at their corporate office in downtown Las Vegas so that all employees have a single entryway on their way out or into the company.[3] Such collisions have led to many innovations.

Research done at Cubist Pharmaceuticals found that employees who engaged in such conversations during lunch were more productive and energetic. As found by Boston's Sociometric Solutions, eating together enhances collaboration and cooperation. What they believe is that a cohesive network of people comes up with a lingo for communication, and this becomes very effective while speaking to each other.[4] With programmers, for instance, it can take 32 per cent more time to complete without communication. It's just not about having food together. The size of the table also matters for ultimate interactions. Sociometric Solutions tracked the behaviours of employees at an office cafe which had both tables of 4 and tables of 12. What was found was that employees who sat at the larger table were 36 per cent more likely to interact with each other later during the day. This group was also more engaged. When layoffs occured at this company, those who had sat at the larger tables were 30 per cent more resistant.

Shared meals need to be a part of a company's culture. Businesses need to consciously design in these down times when they can talk about things other than their task and a lot can come out from this exercise. Shared meals help to bring down barriers between individuals and connects people with each other. This brings employees on the same page and reduces the ignorance of those around and those who claim that they don't know what's going on in the company. Shared meals work as a social lubricant and facilitate cross-pollination.

ALLEN CURVE

Massachusetts Institute of Technology's Late Professor Thomas Allen in his 1977 book *Managing Flow of Technology* proposed what is now known as the Allen curve.[5] He did a study to determine how the distance between engineers' offices affects the frequency of technical communication between them. His study revealed a negative correlation between the physical distance and the frequency of communication between workstations.

What he found was that people in the workplace were four times as likely to communicate regularly with others located up to 6 feet away as they were with people sitting 60 feet away. Also, the people on different floors barely communicated at all.

It gave rise to the Allen curve (Figure 18.1).

If you thought that the Allen curve may not be relevant in the digital world, Allen revisited this in his 2006 book *The Organization and Architecture of Innovation*, which was co-authored with German

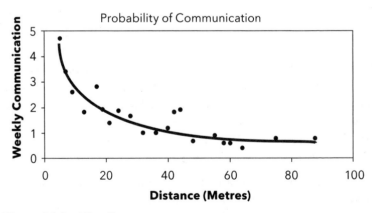

Figure 18.1. Allen Curve
Source: Managing Flow of Technology, Thomas Allen, MIT Press (1984).[5]

architect Gunter Henn.[6] The book explores how office design, physical space, social networks, flows of information and organizational structure must be integrated to drive innovation. As they mentioned in their book,

> Rather than finding that the probability of telephone communication increases with distances, as face to face probability decays, our data shows a decay in the use of all communication media with distance. We do not keep separate sets of people, some of which we communicate in one medium and some by another. The more often we see someone face to face, the more likely it is that we will telephone the person or communicate in some other medium.[6]

Clearly, physical distance between individuals is an essential element in the development of working relationships and the way ideas and information flow. Physical space is integral to innovation.

Those who were co-located connected more frequently over digital media too. If we see people, we are prompted to communicate. The distance from other people also influences the quality of our relationship with them.

A study by Ben Waber, Jennifer Magnolfi and Greg Lindsay also establishes that both face-to-face and digital communication follow the Allen curve. For example, engineers who shared a physical office were 20 per cent more likely to stay in touch digitally than those who worked elsewhere.[7] When they needed to collaborate closely, co-located co-workers emailed four times as frequently as colleagues in different locations, which led to 32 per cent faster project completion time.

It's important to remember that the physical design of the workplace will prompt the right behaviours, which can allow interaction among employees. The Allen curve is still relevant in the digital world.

POWER OF SERENDIPITOUS COLLABORATION

The word 'serendipity' was coined by English author Horace Walpole in 1754. He wrote a story called 'The Three Princes of Serendip', in which the heroes of the story made a number of discoveries by complete chance or happy accident.[8] The word means making discoveries by accident or the phenomenon of finding things not sought for.

Thanks to serendipity that humans have been able to discover Aspirin, Viagra, penicillin, antihistamines, smallpox vaccine, Scotchgard, Teflon, Velcro, nylon, Ivory soap, Post-It notes and so on.

Forward-looking companies create conditions for serendipitous interactions. This cannot be left to chance and has to be engineered to make it happen. Companies will have to create situations so that employees have chance encounters so that it can lead to serendipitous conversations and discoveries. The approach followed is how you slow down people through some bottleneck which makes them come close to each other and have that conversation.

3 PS OF CASUAL INTERACTIONS

For casual interactions to happen, a workplace needs to balance the 3 Ps. This was proposed by Anne-Laure Fayard and John Weeks in a *Harvard Business Review* article.[9] According to them, the most effective spaces bring people together and remove barriers while also providing privacy which people don't fear being overheard or interrupted. The 3 Ps comprise the following.

Proximity

Proximity is much more than how far employees are from one another in a workplace. It depends on traffic patterns which are shaped by social and psychological aspects. The design should be such that it drives traffic to shared spaces such as entrances, restrooms, stairwells, elevators, photocopiers, coffee machines and water cooler. These provide an opportunity for them to interact and cross-pollinate ideas.

Privacy

The workplace should allow people to converse without being an interruption or being overheard. The design is such that others can't see whom a person is talking to and he can see others approaching or within earshot. One solution for this is to have alcoves which lend privacy to public spaces. Alcoves allow people to continue a convention which began in the open to continue in a private space without having to seek a room with a door.

Permission

The management in the company encourages employees to have casual conversations. It conveys about it to employees and nudges them to socialize with others in the company. The top management also participates in having conversation with people in shared spaces. For example, in a design company, the founders, designers, UI/UX experts, etc., are often seen chatting together on the sofa kept in the centre of the office. The CFO is seen having chat with employees in alcoves. All these indicate that the company leadership supports casual conversation and even models behaviours around it.

It has been observed that people do start interactions at a coffee machine or other informal spaces such as a Xerox machine and printers but they come to an end as there is no private space to take the conversation forward. Hence, it's imperative to build in privacy (say by creating alcoves) in the workplace, and there is adequate permission from the leaders to carry on with the casual or serendipitous interactions. The worst thing to happen is a manager's negative comment to employees when they see them having these informal chats.

MAKING SERENDIPITUOUS COLLABORATION HAPPEN

So what are various ways that companies can design in conditions for serendipitous interactions?

- **Proximate design:** The building is designed in such a way that people working there are always approachable and close to each other. For example, when Google's Mountain View 1.1 million square feet campus was set up, the company insisted on a floor plan so that every employee was within two and a half minutes' walk from each other.[10]

- **Bathrooms:** Bathrooms are located centrally. This is what Steve Jobs did when he designed the Pixar headquarters in such a way that the bathrooms were located at a central location. This was done with the objective that employees can run into each other. We will discuss it in detail later.

- **Elevator:** Elevators are so designed that they take people from the ground floor to a cafeteria from where people move to other elevators to go to various floors. The Bloomberg building in New York has a similar construct. Moving past the cafeteria provides an opportunity for serendipitous interactions.[11]

- **Hot desking:** Here, employees take whatever desk is available instead of having an assigned place. It brings unlikely partners to work together. This is another approach which supports a serendipitous workplace.

- **Hallways:** Hallways are designed narrow so that when people walk by, they are forced to take their eyes of the mobile devices and look at people. This is to avoid them bumping into each other. It also provides an opportunity for casual interaction. As mentioned earlier, Pixar's offices in Emeryville, California, were personally conceived by Steve Jobs. Collaboration was a central part of the design. People from all over the campus are drawn to the central atrium, which houses mailboxes, screening rooms, cafes and leisure facilities, where they mingle with people they might not ordinarily see. Originally, the only bathrooms in the building were on the ground floor, which meant that everyone had to walk down the central staircase for a comfort break (although this was later changed, you have to admire the commitment!).[12]

- **Getting rid of coffee points:** Many companies are getting rid of coffee points in every department. Instead, they are creating a centralized coffee area, where everyone comes together for picking coffee. People from different disciplines assemble to refresh and refuel and they strike casual conversations with people whom they may not otherwise meet.

- **Seating in the cafe:** There is bar-style seating for people to have conversations on the fly while having coffee or tea or while they warm their lunch. There are sofas and couches at the centre for having deeper conversations. So they begin the conversation while picking a coffee and sit down on the sofa to have an intimate conversation facing each other. Another approach adopted is that the tables in cafeteria are designed in such a way that they look like those in high-school cafeterias. When these tables are put back to back and people walk in between the chairs, they make people bump into each other. At Google, they call it a 'Google bump'. You bump into someone and then sit down to have a chat.

- **Horizontal layouts:** A cafeteria is designed to have open and horizontal layouts. The design encourages congestion, which fosters encounters. The furniture that is there is lightweight and geometric-shaped. This enables the people to rearrange seating and accommodate groups of various sizes, such as when a friend unexpectedly arrives.

- **Open staircases:** Companies are building open staircases so that it allows employees to be visible and allows serendipitous conversations. This sort of conversation cannot happen in an elevator. The staircases are such that they are visible floor to floor.

- **Food courts:** The food courts and restaurants are built in a way that they are within easy reach of employees. At Google, employees are never more than 150 feet away from food courts, which include coffee shops, restaurants, micro-kitchen, and it provides opportunities for serendipitous interactions.

- **Lunch queues:** Companies design lunch queues in such a way that it encourages 'serendipitous collaboration' among employees, which could later result in better collaboration, breaking barriers or even working on projects.

- **Games room:** Another way to hatch serendipitous inter-actions is creating a games room with pool tables, ping-pong, a pinball machine, etc. These not only keep employees at work for longer but also add to creativity. Employees get in touch with each other with childlike imagination and instincts.

- **Allowing outsiders into the company:** Create a space in the company wherein outsiders can come and work. Achmea, a leading insurance company in the Netherlands, has Lab 55. This is a space within the company where clients, self-employed professionals and start-ups can work from. This was done with the objective that employees of Achmea could work together on multidisciplinary issues.[13] Not only does it provide an opportunity for employees for serendipitous collaboration but also gives different energy to employees.[14] When the employees got back to the office, they came back with a different sort of energy and enthusiasm.

Lab 55 is a platform for Achmea to create a platform where employees and co-workers come together and reinforce each other. This has provided a great opportunity to collaborate with start-ups and local businesses.

REFERENCES

1. Ray T. Steve Jobs said Silicon Valley needs serendipity, but is it even possible in a Zoom world? ZDNet, 24 June 2020, https://www.zdnet.com/article/steve-jobs-said-silicon-valley-needs-serendipity-but-is-it-even-possible-in-a-zoom-world/ (accessed 3 February 2021).

2. Walker T. Perks for employees and how Google changed the way we work (while waiting in line). *Independent,* 20 September 2013, https://www.independent.co.uk/news/world/americas/perks-for-employees-and-how-google-changed-the-way-we-work-while-waiting-in-line-8830243.html (accessed 3 February 2019).

3. Ferraz E. Serendipity without shoes: Promoting collision with remote teams. 15 April 2020, https://www.google.co.in/amp/s/www.entrepreneur.com/amphtml/349289 (accessed 4 February 2022).

4.   Lacina L. The lunch table: The low-tech management tool you're not using. *Entrepreneur,* 11 December 2013, https://www.entrepreneur.com/article/230236 (accessed 3 February 2021).

5.   Allen TJ. *Managing the flow of technology: Technology transfer and the dissemination of technological information within the R&D organization.* Cambridge, MA: MIT Press, 1984.

6.   Allen TJ and Henn G. *The organization and architecture of innovation: Managing the flow of technology.* Oxford: Butterworth-Heinemann, 2006, 152.

7.   Waber B, Magnolfi J and Lindsay G. 'Workspaces that move people. *Harv Bus Rev* 2014; 92(10, October), https://hbr.org/2014/10/workspaces-that-move-people (accessed 19 November 2017).

8.   Wikipedia. The three princes of serendip. n.d., https://en.m.wikipedia.org/wiki/The_Three_Princes_of_Serendip (accessed 5 February 2021).

9.   Fayard A-L and Weeks J. Who moved my cube?' *Harv Bus Rev* 2011; 89(7–8, July–August).

10.   Williams SJ. Promoting collaboration: 4 lessons from Google. 7 February 2014, https://redbooth.com/blog/promoting-collaboration-br4-lessons-from-google (accessed 5 February 2021).

11.   Gilbar S. The importance of serendipity in design thinking. 7 June 2016, https://medium.com/@skygilbar/the-importance-of-serendipity-in-design-thinking-45520e98f13e (accessed 5 February 2021).

12.   Spaceoasis. Serendipitous encounters of the workspace kind. 8 December 2015, https://www.spaceoasis.com/news/2015/12/serendipitous-encounters-of-the-workspace-kind/ (accessed 3 February 2021).

13.   Gen in the Ring. Work with Centraal Beheer Achmea to support their customers with comfortable living. n.d., https://getinthering.co/challenges/work-with-centraal-beheer-achmea-to-support-their-customers-with-comfortable-living/ (accessed 5 February 2021).

14.   Van den Toorn A. Bringing two worlds together in Lab55. 1 June 2015, https://www.linkedin.com/pulse/bringing-two-worlds-together-lab55-andré-van-den-toorn (accessed 5 February 2021).

Chapter 19

Don't Serve Your Customers Deep-fried Lizards

In 2017, it was reported widely in Indian media that a pregnant woman found a fried lizard in her fries in a McDonald's outlet in Kolkata.[1] The news caused much consternation, given that most people believe McDonald's to adhere to international-level hygiene standards. This was clearly a food safety violation which could have caused real harm to consumers.

Now, I have always been a great fan of Ray Kroc (founder of McDonald's) and his example of how to put together a business model which ensures consistent quality across the globe. Indeed, when it comes to standardization and product quality, McDonald's is an often-quoted case in classrooms. Its success, like all such organizations, is founded on robust quality hardware in place, comprising detailed processes, good restaurant infrastructure, certified equipment, good manufacturing guidelines, supplier quality, a food safety management system such as hazard analysis for critical control points (HACCP) and so on.

A company that's serious about food safety can't just have a food safety strategy—it has to have it as a 'corporate value'.

But why then do such food safety hazards happen despite having all the quality hardware?

The answer lies in employee behaviour. If one were to do a detailed root cause analysis of the Kolkata incident, I would think that it would be found that the employees did not do what they were supposed to do.

The objective of this chapter is to not find out what happened at McDonald's but take certain lessons from the incident for food companies/restaurants which invest in quality hardware yet struggle to change employee behaviour. What are some of the things that food companies need to do to make this happen?

LET TOP MANAGEMENT COMMIT TO IT

Without the CEO and top management owning food safety, it can be a mirage for an enterprise. One way to demonstrate top management commitment is to embed food safety as a part of corporate culture which becomes a part of an organization's way of working. My belief is that a company that's serious about food safety can't just have a food safety strategy—it has to have it as a way things get done on the company. The operating model should pivot to support a food safety culture.

When employees of an organization are personally committed to food safety, they will do the right thing even when no one is watching them. The only way to make it happen is a strong organizational culture which has to be designed and led by the top management. They look at culture holistically and address both the explicit and implicit elements. They also work on the elements which influence behaviours. These include, among others, norms, practices, incentives, metrics, procedures, organizational design and standards.

Having installed a new operating model, top management should ensure that it becomes a way of doing business and is practised in all actions by all employees across levels.

For example, at Nestlé, they have something called 'corporate business principles', where product safety features explicitly.[2] These values or principles of business operation resonate in every action of all employees.

ADOPT REAGAN'S 'TRUST BUT VERIFY'

Ronald Reagan, the 40th president of the USA, popularized the phrase 'trust but verify', which he used extensively with respect to the USA's relations with the erstwhile Soviet Union.[3] The concept is very relevant in the context of food safety.

The lesson is to trust the processes and people running them, but to verify their effectiveness.

One prerequisite for embedding food safety is a good management system which prevents the entry of chemical, micro-biological and physical hazards in processes. However, once the systems and processes are built, they need to be verified on an ongoing basis through audits (which need to be performed by someone other than those involved in the process).

For example, at Coca-Cola, there is a global team which does food safety audits on a regular basis, and top leaders take the findings very seriously. Remember that quality assurance processes are fine, but one needs to check their effectiveness through regular audits. So the lesson is to trust the processes and people running them, but to verify their effectiveness.

ALIGN EMPLOYEE BELIEFS WITH THEIR ACTIONS

It's often seen that employees managing a restaurant outlet or those involved in food processing are from the marginal strata of the society, where hygiene does not get the required importance. For them, the stringent practices required for delivering a safe food product is alien.

My first few working years were spent in food companies. One of the things that we often struggled with was to make the food-processing workmen wash their hands with soap after they visited the washrooms. We had put display boards at the entrance of washrooms to communicate this to workmen, yet many came out without washing their hands with soap. On probing, a workman who stayed in a slum nearby told me that he found it wasteful to use the liquid soap every time he went to the washroom—it seemed like a luxury to him, given he came from a background where making ends meet was a challenge.

This is an example of Leon Festinger's theory of cognitive dissonance—when there is a conflict between what a person believes and what he is expected to do, there is a conflict and the person finds ways to avoid it.[4] This he does by not doing what is expected of him. The way to surmount this is clearly just not training employees on food safety practices but also telling them why and how they have to make things happen.

FEAR OF RETRIBUTION UNTIL A CULTURE OF ACCOUNTABILITY SETS IN

The ultimate vision of a food organization should be to create a culture of accountability, wherein employees take ownership and are responsible enough to follow the practices that meet food safety requirements. To make this happen, one strategy would be to clearly state to employees what is expected of them and how success will be measured and rewarded.

If a senior leader walks into the food-processing area without wearing gloves and a cap, even a workman should not shy away from pointing it out.

However, until a culture of accountability sets in, employees should know that if there are food-safety violations due to careless actions, they will be held accountable and penalized. A fear of punitive measures would slowly change behaviour.

Remember that accountability does not just mean the boss holding subordinates accountable but also an employee holding his boss or peers accountable. So if a senior leader walks into the food-processing area without wearing gloves and a cap, even a workman should not shy away from pointing it out and this should not be held against him.

LEARN FROM CRIMINOLOGY

The broken windows theory was first introduced by social scientists James Q. Wilson and George L. Kelling in 1982.[5] Although originally used in criminology, it has been applied in various contexts. The theory says that when a space is left unattended and there are broken windows, after some time a few more windows are broken and even the place is vandalized. It indicates that no one has concern for the place and it is not owned and attended by people. When a space is kept properly, the anti-social activity goes down, as the vandals know that there are people who are keeping an eye on it and they can't mess around.

In a food-processing workplace, if there is an abnormality which an employee has observed, it should be immediately attended to. So if there is a problem in the workplace, it should be addressed immediately even if the problem is small. For example, if a person has seen a rodent in the processing area, he should immediately take action and not let the matter reach the point where a customer finds a deep-fried version of said animal on her plate, as happened in Kolkata!

REFERENCES

1. Gupta S. Pregnant woman served deep fried lizard at McDonald's outlet in Kolkata. NDTV, 3 March 2017, https://www.ndtv.com/india-news/pregnant-woman-served-fried-lizard-at-mcdonalds-outlet-in-kolkata-1665768 (accessed 5 February 2021).

2. Nestlé. *Corporate business principles.* n.d., https://www.nestle.com/sites/default/files/asset-library/documents/library/documents/

corporate_governance/corporate-business-principles-en.pdf (accessed 5 February 2021).

3. Wikipedia. Trust, but verify. n.d., https://en.wikipedia.org/wiki/Trust,_but_verify (accessed 5 February 2021).

4. Wikipedia. Cognitive dissonance. n.d., https://en.wikipedia.org/wiki/Cognitive_dissonance (accessed 5 February 2021).

5. Kelling GL and Wilson JQ. Broken windows. March 1982, https://www.theatlantic.com/magazine/archive/1982/03/broken-windows/304465/ (accessed 5 February 2021).

Chapter 20

Judgement of Paris

It was 24 May 1976 when some of the finest French judges were drawn from oenophiles (connoisseurs of wine) who had assembled at InterContinental Hotel for a blind tasting which pitted some of the finest wines in France against unknown California bottles.[1] This was organized by Steven Spurrier, a British wine merchant who wanted to drum up business for California wine which had landed in his shop. For the French, if it was a great wine it had to emanate from France. For them, it was only in France did you have the perfect climate, perfect earth and perfect grapes which could deliver great wine. Also, in those days, California wines were hardly known to people. What Steven Spurrier found was that the American wines were good. So he took the help of a lady with American heritage Patricia Gallaghar, who suggested that a tasting session be held of California wines in Paris to mark the bicentennial of the American Revolution.

Steven lined up some of the top nine names of French gastronomy which included Odette Kahn, editor of *La Revue du vin de France*; Raymond Oliver of the restaurant Le Grand Véfour; Michel Dovaz of the Wine Institute of France; Aubert de Villaine of the Domaine de la Romanée-Conti; Pierre Tari (French) of Chateau Giscours and so on. They had to taste ten white wines (Chardonnays from California and Burgundy from France) and ten red wines (Cabernet Sauvignons from California and Left Bank Bordeaux blends from France). In the blind tasting the judges were asked to grade each wine on 20 points. When the results came out, it shocked everyone.[2] The American wines were on the top. What also surprised many was that the judges could not distinguish between American and French wine. They mistook American wines for French.

The tasting helped to transform the American wine industry as they believed that they too could make the finest wines. After the tasting, new vineyards bloomed not just in the USA but also in the rest of the world.

It questioned two assumptions: the first one being the superiority of French wine makers and the second the accuracy that judges showed that their expertise did not deliver the desired outcome. Clearly, having expertise does not guarantee superior performance.

TAKEAWAY FOR OPEX

The biggest takeaway for businesses is that having expertise does not necessarily lead to superior performance. It has also been found that having experience does not necessarily lead to performance. Those with more experience were not better than those who had less experience. There is no correlation between IQ and expert performance in fields such as chess, music, sports and medicine. Just practising what a person already knows how to do does not make him an expert. This is done within one's comfort zone. Have we not seen people working in a domain without really improving their performance? The other point to be remembered is that expertise is not a result of natural talent but of hard work. Evidence shows that experts are born and not always made. This is an outcome of what is called 'deliberate practice'. This term was first coined by K. Anders Ericsson.[3] What he found after studying ballet dancers, surgeons, spelling bee champions, violinists, etc., was that nature did not play a role. What differentiated truly exceptional performers from not-so-great ones was this (deliberate practice). There are no shortcuts here and it requires lots of hard work, sacrifice and painful self-assessment

So what is deliberate practice?

Deliberate practice is an approach to improve performance by sustained effort to do something that one is not good at. It is accomplished by continuous feedback and doing things beyond one's comfort zone.[4]

The following are the attributes of deliberate practice:

- A coach or a teacher plays a big role here. The teacher is able to see in you what you probably are not aware of.

- The teacher or coach sets out the goal which has to be achieved by the trainee which he is expected to visualize during practice.

- The teacher or coach describes the steps required to achieve the goal and shares continuous and even painful feedback to the trainee on how he has done that.

- The activity under practice should be done in a learning zone (see Figure 20.1). You must constantly try to get the best out of your ability.

- Task is mentally demanding and requires a sustained effort to accomplish.

- The task requires a lot of concentration and time.

- In certain fields, it requires to be started early.

- Sometimes the coach/teacher under whom you work are themselves exemplary experts.

- It requires breaking skills to sub-skills and training on them separately.

- Deliberate practice is in certain situations conducted in solitude as it needs concentration, and distraction has to be avoided.

Comfort Zone

This is where activities are subconscious and can be done in auto pilot. You are confident and know how to accomplish a task. It's comfortable and safe to stay in this zone. You operate with the skills that you have acquired. There is very little learning and innovation here. A person can even get bored here. You don't need to take risks here. Most of us operate here.

Learning Zone

This lies immediately beyond the comfort zone. This is an uncomfortable zone where you learn by focus, practice and feedback. Here, activities are done consciously, and you expand your knowledge and understanding by looking for new ways for working. Learning and relearning happen, and the person feels challenged. Indeed things are challenging here, but you are motivated and engaged to accomplish your objectives.

Panic Zone

This zone is beyond the Learning zone. It is a difficult zone where we are unable to learn. Here, the focus goes into managing the anxiety, so there is no energy left for learning. Here, you are attempting something far beyond your reach. Your are also under huge stress. Sometimes you may land up here because of a problem, but staying here long can be bad for health.

While in deliberate practice, you need to be careful that you don't go too much out of learning zone into pan zone.

Figure 20.1. The Three Zones

As K. Anders Ericsson et al. defined in a *Harvard Business Review* article,[5] the expertise that one develops should pass the three tests:

1. It must lead to performance that is consistently superior to that of the expert's peers.

2. It must produce concrete results.

3. It must be reputable and measurable in a laboratory.

The following are a few examples of above application in operational excellence:

1. The Japanese concept of 'kaizen' focuses on solving small problems. Teams take up small issues in their workplace and work on them. Over a period of say a year or so, a large number of projects are done. These could be in thousands. These are problems which have a specific objective, have a structure and are done beyond their day-to-day work. It pushes employees out of their comfort zone, and this is done under the guidance of a coach. Over a period of time, not only does it help to raise the performance of the company, but it also builds problem-solving capability of the employees,

2. Teach OPEX experts various improvement methodologies using case studies. Let them stretch their minds to fathom how business problems can be solved. They go through it and come up with solutions that they share with others. Also, expose them on real life success stories so that they also learn from it. Such case based problem-solving should be done regularly so they continually sharpen their skills.

3. Make people learn through simulation also helps in deliberate practice. We have seen astronauts and pilots doing it where they are pushed beyond their comfort zone and they learn from their experience. To build a problem-solving culture in the company let employees learn the tools and then solve business problems. The training should not be declared complete till they have solved a few business problems.

STEPS FOR DELIBERATE PRACTICE

Here are the steps which can be followed with an example.

1. **Set goals:** Let's say an organization is focused on improving productivity of sales force. Identify a set of employees who will

work on solving this problem and sharpen their selling skills. These are the people you believe are ready to go through the efforts and pains of the journey. It's no use spending time on those who are not interested. The people who go through the practice should know why they are getting into it and that they are not going to quit. Set a measurable goal for the team.

2. **Identify a coach:** Identify a coach who can take the selected people through the journey. The coach should not only know how to do it but should also be a good trainer and guide. He should have himself been an exemplary salesperson who has achieved demonstrable results in the past. What's important to keep in mind is that the coaching will happen one on one.

3. **Pick the right approach:** The team should use the right selling strategies and tactics. The coach can help the team if they are not familiar with what they should do. Using ineffective methods of the past may not lead to results. Hence, the coach guides the team to select the right approach. Whatever practice is chosen, it should be among the best.

4. **Focus on the 3 Fs:** As suggested by Anders Ericsson in his book *Peak*, focus on the 3 Fs. They are focus, feedback and fix it.[6] Keep your focus. Remove anything which can be a distraction. Seek feedback from the coach/trainer and fix areas which need correction.

5. **Break goals into milestones:** Break the larger objective into smaller goals. Practise for not more than 4–5 hours a day. As a salesperson, do the new ways of selling for around 3–4 hours. Avoid going beyond that, as it can be exhausting. Whatever time you spend doing it, make sure it's done with full concentration. The person has to look for and create opportunities for deliberate practice. For example, a salesperson may try his selling skills beyond work at home or with friends.

6. **Measure and stay the course:** Whatever you take up, it should be measurable. Be ready to shun short-term pleasures, as the practice will be painful and exhausting. As you practice, build

visualization of what success looks like and then 'self-evaluate' it So the salesperson should know what an ideal sales process work is towards it and constantly self-monitor how they have done against what they think is the best. Hence, measuring progress is very important.

7. **Move past plateaus:** There will be times when you will feel like quitting. Hence, it's important to keep the motivation going. This can be done by surrounding yourself with people who encourage you. Also, keep tracking your progress and seeing the small improvements which you are making. As you do all these, start stretching yourself. For example, if a salesperson closes three accounts a week, he can take it up to five accounts a week by tweaking his strategies.

8. **Take a break:** It's important for you to take rest. Deliberate practice beyond 4–5 hours can be mentally taxing. When you take rest, counteract the intensity of deliberate practice with deep rest. As a salesperson, this can be done in myriad ways such as spending time with one's toddler, reading a book, going for a walk in the woods, etc.

What OPEX professionals need to remember is that just getting certified in a specific domain does not make you an expert. You need to do deliberate practice and stretch yourself in the process. There are no shortcuts; you have to struggle, sacrifice and often carry out painful deliberate practice under a coach.

REFERENCES

1. Godoy M. The judgment of Paris: The blind taste test that decanted the wine world. NPR, 24 May 2016, https://www.npr.org/sections/thesalt/2016/05/24/479163882/the-judgment-of-paris-the-blind-taste-test-that-decanted-the-wine-world (accessed 5 February 2021).

2. Steinmetz K. How America kicked France in the pants and changed the world of wine forever. TIME, 24 May 2016, https://time.com/4342433/judgment-of-paris-time-magazine-anniversary/ (accessed 5 February 2021).

3. Ericsson KA. Superior working memory in experts. In: Ericsson KA, Hoffman RR, Kozbelt A, et al. (eds) *The Cambridge handbook of expertise and expert performance*. 2nd ed. Cambridge: Cambridge University Press, 2018, 696–713. doi: 10.1017/9781316480748.036

4. Farnam Street. What is deliberate practice. n.d., https://fs.blog/2012/07/what-is-deliberate-practice/ (accessed 5 February 2021).

5. Ericsson KA, Prietula MJ and Cokely ET. The making of an expert. *Harv Bus Rev* 2006; 85(7–8, July–August):114–121.

6. Ericsson A and Pool R. *Peak: How all of us can achieve extraordinary things*. Vintage Digital, 2017.

Chapter 21

Power of Past Accomplishments

When Shaun Gomez[1] took up as the head of a global finance shared service centre, he wanted to change things. He was a CFO of a leading bank in Indonesia and had played a key role with the CEO in reversing the sagging fortunes of a struggling bank. Having become a part of C-suite at an early age, he thought he could achieve anything by his drive and focus. However, his new role was very different. Unlike what he had done before, he had to lead a transformation of a shared service centre which was struggling on major metrics. The productivity levels were low, employees were disengaged, internal customers complained about quality issue and most stakeholders felt that they were not getting the benefit of centralizing all processes in a shared service centre. Shaun's work was cut out. He had to transform five shared service centres located in five different locations and make

---

[1] Not the real name.

this happen by leading a team of 15,000 people. Being quite a flashy person, he started with a big bang. He began his journey by laying out a vision of what he had planned to do. However, what he did was criticize the efforts of the past leaders and how it led to the dismal state as it was today. While he had a great vision of what the transformation could do and also had the drive to make it happen, his repeated mentioning of the ills of the past leadership and their actions put many employees off. What Shaun was missing was that indirectly he was also blaming the employees who were all a part of the past design and roll-out. Many of them found Shaun to be arrogant and, as a result, started derailing the efforts. Every transformation effort has people who resist change. But what was different here was that the influencers were getting antagonized. And they slowly started forming a coalition on how not to make things happen. The result was that they did not fully adopt the changes and the benefits were not seen. The productivity levels drastically plummeted and employee engagement was all time low. The CEO had to finally leave the organization within 18 months of coming on board.

A leader driving a transformation should remember never to undermine the efforts of the past. However bad the organizational health, he should always be forward looking. Rather, he should build on the past. There are always accomplishments and traditions that you can build on.

Here are a few things that organizations should do to build from the past.

LOOK FOR BRIGHT SPOTS

Whatever be the state and health of the enterprise, there are always bright spots in the enterprise. These are pockets of excellence which the leaders should talk about. They could also be some award or recognition which the employees are very proud of. Reach out to employees for sharing the critical success factors of the past achievement. Tell them to share the behaviours that made it possible. Give credit for the achievement and make them feel proud of what they have done in the past. Ask them how they can do an encore and repeat a similar performance. The process of identifying bright spots can not only make employees feel good but also identify change leaders who made it possible. Bright spots and past achievements can be great ways to build for the future.

BRING BACK THE LEADER THAT EMPLOYEES ADORE

There could also be individuals in companies who the company may look up to. He could be someone who in the past could have been a significant impact on the company who took the company to a new level of performance. He could also be someone who could have built the organization. He could be a founder or a professional CEO or an inspirational leader who led the company to success.

PAST TURNAROUNDS

There might be instances where a company might have had a bad phase but had come out of it. Share those stories about how the company came out of the mess. Talk about the grit and determination of employees that made it possible. Let employees know that they have seen the worse and can come out of the current challenges too. For example, when Mylan, a global pharmaceutical major, went through a crisis in October 2008 at the height of financial crisis when its stock price sank to $6[1], in the subsequent months, the leaders made it a point to share with the employees how the company flirted with bankruptcy twice and came out of it. The tales of past struggles and how the company came out of them can be a great force to boost confidence among employees.

HERITAGE STANDS FOR STRENGTH

When a company has a long heritage and been there for decades, it shows that it has navigated the rough and tumble of business cycles. These companies have survived generations, and the employees know that it would also wade through the current change. The employees know that the company would never fold up even if there is a downward spiral. They know that the roots and leadership pipeline of the company are deep and can take up any challenges. This is something a change leader should reinforce while embarking on a change transformation. Think about Tata Group's companies. Anyone who joins them knows that the company would never fold up. Even if there are challenges, it would overcome it. Tata Group's companies have also had their challenges, but they have successfully come out of those. Their strong heritage is a big strength in their change transformation.

STORIES FROM PAST REINFORCE THE VALUES

Stories from the past can be a great way to share the values and business principles that a CEO or a business leader wants his teams to follow. They help in reinforcing what the company stands for. The founders of Infosys have already stood for integrity and ethical practices. Their employees are aware of the story during the early days when Narayan Murthy and other founders set up their first office and needed a phone. At that time, it was difficult to get a phone without paying a bribe to the person who installed the phone. Murthy and team always wanted to create an institution which is known for integrity and ethical practices; hence, they refused to pay.[2] Without the phone, the founders had to go to the nearby telephone booth to make business calls. Even though the bribe amount was very little, they decided to take the pain of going there but not bribe the telephone installer. At times this did impact their business. When every sale mattered to the business, he was ready to live with it. When a real story like this is told to employees, they know what exactly it takes to live a value. It also restates what we state.

CHANGE PLANNING

When a leader looks at a company's history if it is documented in some form, it can give an idea of what change effort has worked and what has not. Knowledge and understanding of the past can help in change planning. It can also give you an idea of how the company had addressed a similar problem later. It can also provide ideas on how similar problems were addressed in the past.

While embarking on a journey of operational excellence, never demonize the past. Rather, look for strategies on how you can build on historical facts and traditions to enrol the employees in your journey. The history, tradition and past accomplishment are power tools for change leaders working towards embedding excellence. Ignoring them would mean missing out on an important tool. Great leaders use these for the experience of the past to motivate employees and embrace the future change.

REFERENCES

1. Seaman J and Smith GD. Your company's history as a leadership tool. *Harv Bus Rev* 2012; 90(12, December): 44–52.

2. Nohria N. Global consequences of corruption. 14 January 2015, https://www.livemint.com/Politics/NPByprN1TpN8qJ42r1xa6I/Global-consequences-of-corruption.html (accessed 5 February 2021).

Chapter 22

Complexity Management

Complexity is a reality of many businesses. Given the demands of customers, growth pressures, rapidly changing technology landscape, need to generate new products and revenue streams and demands of the regulator, increased complexity is inevitable. The pace with which complexity is increasing makes it very difficult for companies to respond to the changes happening around and the unanticipated events. Managing this complexity is a big challenge for business leaders.

Companies can't really afford to ignore complexity; rather, CEOs and business leaders have to embrace it, and they should know how to proactively manage it. This is possible when they understand the basics of complexity management and how it should be managed.

WHAT IS BUSINESS COMPLEXITY?

Business complexity is a state of an organization which functions through large number of interconnected and interdependent stakeholders (such as customers, partners, suppliers, regulators, investors, media and competitors), a complex organizational structure (such as divisions, geographical spread, subsidiaries and joint ventures) and multiple information technology systems.

Business complexities are of two types.

Good Complexity

Good complexity adds value to the enterprise and helps the company grow. This could be through product innovations, personalization, automation and making processes efficient.

Bad Complexity

Bad complexity is value-depleting and slows down the company. It not only impedes growth but also slows down the ability of a company to respond to the market. It also makes the company inefficient and adds to the cost, which at times can be difficult to decipher.

A research done by Martin Mocker and Jeanne Ross at MIT Center for Information Systems Research (CSIR), USA revealed that those companies which were able to create value from product complexity while maintaining simple processes were outperforming others.[1] Managing complexity is about balancing between increasing business complexity to add customer value and decreasing inefficiency in company processes.

So the focus of an enterprise is on eliminating bad complexity.

But before we talk about reducing complexity which does not add value, let's understand the various types of complexities and what you can do about it.

When we talk about differentiating between root cause and symptom, I have seen people mixing causes with complexity. Before getting down into addressing symptoms of complexity, we should step back and understand the big picture. From my experience, I have seen businesses having broadly three types of complexities.

Product Complexity

This is about having products or services which very few people want to buy. The product development and marketing teams overestimate what the market wants and keep generating products which have little or no demand. Have we not seen retail banks churning out myriad types of credit cards without understanding the customer demand for the same? Or let me talk about a personal products company which launched various brand extension and SKUs of hair oils. This confused the customers and many of the product extensions just did not have buyers. As a result, sales dropped by 20 per cent. Product complexity is also sometimes an outcome when companies have a product portfolio which does not align with its strategic ambitions.

Structural Complexity

This happens when a company in its focus on scaling up or to be close to the customer adds new layers and creates complex structures. New regional structures are put in place, independent operating units are created across geographies, additional layers are created and new people are brought on the board. The outcome being there is duplication of roles and sometimes even a lack of accountability. Decision-making takes time, and there are costs associated with coordination to move things through the structural matrix. There are also costs which are not accounted for. People may not have role clarity, and they don't really know who does what.

While many of these actions may make sense in isolation, as they may have been done for business growth or to stay close to the customer, they impede the pace of decision-making and make the company bureaucratic.

Begin the complexity reduction effort by revisiting the operating model of the company and how business units are organized to deliver value to customer. The operating model should align with the business strategy and support in building a differentiating capability for the business. Hence make sure the company is organized to capture biggest growth opportunities and nimbly respond to the market.

Systematically analyze how effectively the company's footprints (locations) are aligned with the overall strategy, customers, suppliers, talent needs and cost structure. Ascertain if there are footprints that are outdated. To understand organizational bloat look at spans of control and management layers. Focus on increasing the span of control or the number of people assigned to a manager and also reduce the layers. Sometimes comparing with what a best-in-class competition does can deliver huge benefits. Also, focus on how a decision gets made in the company and what the barriers in the process are. Make sure that all roles have clear accountability. If there are issues, action items or even costs which are orphans and don't have ownership, please ensure they have one going forward.

Process Complexity

A good process management framework delivers the highest-quality product with the lowest cost. When a process management system of an enterprise becomes complex, there could be large number of activities which don't add value to the customer. The addition of processes and procedures may not only make things bureaucratic but also result in addition of new metrics. As a result, there could also be large number of metrics which no one looks at but still gets measured. The focus should be on designing processes which are fit for purpose and backed with robust metrics. Streamline processes by optimising them to achieve sustainable efficiency and effectiveness. This is achieved by identifying non-value added activities that can be eliminated, combined or automated. Reduce the large number of process improvement projects that may be underway and focus on those that promise biggest return.

WHAT ARE SOME OF THE SIGNALS OF RISING COMPLEXITY?

A business needs to keep an eye on complexity. If kept unchecked, it can impede a company's growth and negatively impact profit margins. The focus should be extra vigilant on excess management layers, blurred accountability, a slowdown in organization agility, non-value-adding processes and cost numbers. However, following are some of the signals of rising complexity which every business leader should keep in mind:

- Costs inexorably rising despite cost containment programmes
- Company finding it difficult to respond to a low-cost competitor
- Difficulty in ascertaining what drives business performance
- Top management having little clue about what's happening in the frontline
- Leaders spending more time focusing on company's processes instead of the customers
- People having blurred accountability
- Drop in sales for which reasons are unfathomable
- Hard to ascertain who is accountable for what
- Decision-making taking a lot of time
- Time, energy and interaction being spent on activities which don't create value

WHAT HAPPENS TO BUSINESS WHEN COMPLEXITY GOES UNMANAGED?

We have seen the scourge of internal complexity in businesses. We all remember the recalls of Toyota cars in 2010 due to unintended acceleration when more than 5 million vehicles were recalled. It was found that one reason why Toyota was slow to understand early warning signals about quality was its highly centralized, engineering-centric communication structure. Also, as *Harvard Business Review* reported, there were issues with the complex pattern of comprehensive data collection and analysis, which prevented it from taking faster action on recalls.[2] In the same year, we had this BP's oil spill disaster in the Gulf of Mexico which was considered to be the largest oil spill in the history of the petroleum industry. Here too, the speed of response was slow because of poor coordination between businesses and functions involved in the crisis.

DON'T GET LOST IN SYMPTOMS

While addressing complexity issues, I have seen companies focusing on symptoms and working on them. For example, a company which in its pursuit to grow its business had expanded across geographies. However, there was an increase in customer complaints about delivery timelines and slow responses. On talking to customers, it was found that they felt that the company had become large and very slow to respond to their needs. Given the noise, the CEO launched a programme to embed customer-centricity across the enterprise. The first thing that they did was to reduce process lead times. Hence, a number of projects were launched. The outcome of this was that there was some improvement in lead times and also employee productivity. However, it was not large enough to impact the customers. The CEO got in touch with my firm. When we started looking at the enterprise, we discovered that the company had not addressed the issue around multiple committees involved in making decisions. While the existing process had become faster, the multiple committees had their own bureaucratic way of doing things. There were also gaps in alignment around committees operating in the corporate office and those in the regions. We focused on two things: We reduced the number of committees, many of which were not required, and helped the company to achieve alignment on focus areas and how things get done. The outcome of these two efforts was drastic. Within a period of four months, there were positive voices of customers on increased organizational agility. Clearly, what the company was addressing was the apparent cause, when what was required was to focus on the root cause.

Remember that excessive bureaucracy, burgeoning meetings, increased amount of coordination, rising costs and slow decision-making often are all symptoms. The focus should be on getting into their root causes.

APPROACH TO REDUCE COMPLEXITY

Figure 22.1 shows a generic approach which could be followed to reduce complexity. Keep in mind that complexity reduction is a

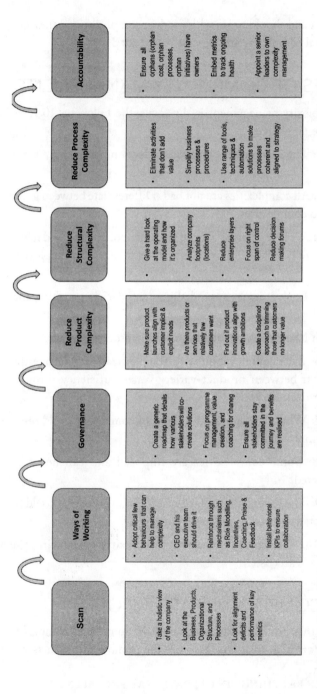

Figure 22.1. A Generic Approach to Managing Complexity

Scan

- Take a holistic view of the company
- Look at the Business, Products, Organizational Structure, and Processes
- Look for alignment deficits and performance of key metrics

Ways of Working

- Adopt critical few behaviours that can help to manage complexity
- CEO and his executive team should drive it
- Reinforce through mechanisms such as Role Modelling, Incentives, Coaching, Praise & Feedback
- Install behavioral KPIs to ensure collaboration

Governance

- Create a generic roadmap that details how various stakeholders will co-create solutions
- Focus on programme management, value creation, and coaching for chaneg
- Ensure all stakeholders stay committed in the journey and benefits are realised

Reduce Product Complexity

- Make sure product launches align with customer implicit & explicit needs
- Are there products or services that relatively few customers want
- Find out if product innovations align with growth ambitions
- Create a disciplined approach to trimming those that customers no longer value

Reduce Structural Complexity

- Give a hard look at the operating model and how it's organized
- Analyze company footprints (locations)
- Reduce enterprise layers
- Focus on right span of control
- Reduce decision making forums

Reduce Process Complexity

- Eliminate activities that don't add value
- Simplify business processes & procedures
- Use range of tools, techniques & automation solutions to make processes coherent and aligned to strategy

Accountability

- Ensure all orphans (orphan cost, orphan processes, orphan initiatives) have owners
- Embed metrics to track ongoing health
- Appoint a senior leaders to own complexity management

holistic effort and should begin with product complexity and then get into structural complexity and process complexity.

10 RULES OF COMPLEXITY MANAGEMENT

When complexity management is the focus, the following 10 rules need to be remembered:

- **Rule 1:** The journey of complexity reduction has to begin from the top.
- **Rule 2:** All complexities are not bad. Differentiate between good and bad complexities.
- **Rule 3:** Achieve enterprise-wide alignment of strategy and make sure there is a clear link with initiatives taken up by employees below.
- **Rule 4:** Look at issues around alignment, decision-making and ways of working.
- **Rule 5:** Make decision-making a simple process.
- **Rule 6:** Balance innovation with standardization. Manage the trade-off between product-variety versus efficiency through standardization.
- **Rule 7:** What may appear as a cause of complexity could often be a symptom.
- **Rule 8:** Some complexities are imposed and can never be eliminated.
- **Rule 9:** The root to a complexity faced by an employee could be product, structural or process complexity.
- **Rule 10:** The key to managing complexity is balancing the benefits with costs.

SOME COMPLEXITIES ARE IMPOSED

Remember that not all complexities are bad. Sometimes complexity is required for value creation. The more the number of products you have, the greater the geographical presence, the number of people you employ, the greater number of business units you create; they all create complexity but help in adding value to the business. These are good complexities. But there could be those which just kill the value and should be eliminated. However, we need to remember that there are complexities which we can't eliminate such as those caused due to regulations, laws or because of the type of business that a company is in. These are imposed complexities and can't be eliminated. For example, a food company would have a requirement of a cold chain which could add to the complexity and can't be eliminated. Or for that matter, a business which gets into banking has to comply with the regulations of the central bank and other regulators.

The focus of a company should not be on shunning complexity and making it as simple as possible. Companies of the 21st century cannot be simple. With the change around us and digital disruptions, it often require complex structures to manage an enterprise. The focus should be on eliminating complexities which make getting things difficult and impede value creation. Companies should strive for simplicity and never allow complexity to go unchecked as this can be a big barrier to growth.

Effective complexity management leads to reduced costs, better returns, and improved employee and customer experience. They also make the company flexible and nimble to respond to the changing market conditions.

REFERENCES

1. Mocker M and Ross J. Rethinking business complexity. MIT CSIR Research, May 2013.

2. Ashkenas R. The C-level job for everyone: Reducing complexity. *Harv Bus Rev*, 28 February 2011, https://hbr.org/2011/02/the-c-level-job-for-everyone-r (accessed 5 February 2021).

Chapter 23

Taking Risks during a Downturn

Robert Woodruff was the longest serving president of The Coca-Cola Company. He led the company from 1923 till 1954.[1] Although he retired in 1955, he remained on the board of directors till 1981. He took over the company when it was bankrupt and made it a global powerhouse. He was an ace salesman and created a large network of bottlers which helped him take Coca-Cola around the world. When he took over the company, the company sold sugar syrups to drug stores and bottlers, but his consulate leadership made the company a global institution. He was among the tallest business leaders in the USA for almost half a century.

This incident pertains to the period of the Great Depression, which started in 1929 and lasted till around 1939. The American and global economy were badly impacted. During the first five years of the depression, the US economy shrank 50 per cent. In 1929, the economic output of the USA was $105 billion as measured by the gross domestic product, and in 1933 it produced $56.4 billion.[2] Unemployment rose, there was mass migration and many businesses perished. There were those who said that the American dream was over. Sales of Coca-Cola started to slow, especially during the winter months. Woodruff knew that as usual strategies would not take the company to greater heights, as he had envisaged. He was a restless man who always wanted businesses to adopt to change. Against all what was happening in the backdrop, he decided to take a bold step. The company decided to change its target audience from the adult looking for a pharmaceutical pick-me-up to the whole family. He went ahead and increased the advertising spend. He raised the budget to $4.3 million, which was a huge money for that time. The money was spent on creating a rosy cheek, chubby, red-suited Santa Claus as we know it today. He hired an artist by the name of Haddon Sundblom with the D'Arcy agency to paint a Santa Claus for their 'The Pause That Refreshes' campaign.[3] The advertisements featured Santa holding bottles of Coca-Cola, drinking Coca-Cola, receiving Coca-Cola as gifts, pausing to read a letter and enjoy a Coke, visiting the children who stayed up to greet him, raiding the refrigerators at a number of homes, etc.[4] It's not that Santa had not been used for advertisements earlier, but they did not deliver the desired outcome. With the new Santa shaped under Woodruff, Coca-Cola sales soared.

Woodruff had made an important choice during a critical moment in the company's history.

TAKEAWAYS FOR OPEX

The normal reaction during a downturn is to play safe and not take risk. When the economy is not doing well and there is uncertainty, business leaders are uncomfortable to do anything beyond business as usual. Having achieved so much in business, there can be a tendency to stop taking risks. However, successful business leaders know that if they are not taking risks, they are not progressing. It is not about doing things blindly and expecting results but about taking calculated risks which have been thought through and where the pros outweigh the cons. Taking risks is sustaining a company's competitive advantage. If you don't take risks, someone else will and blunt your competitive position. No one can be sure if risks will pay off, but one thing is sure that if you don't take risks, you have not tried enough.

It's also important to realize that a downturn is not all doom and gloom. They always bring in new opportunities. Due to an inclement economic condition, the earlier plans might have gone awry. It's time to step back and look at things with a fresh pair of eyes. The choice that needs to be made is between looking at avenues to scale up or hold on to what has been gained. The decision that is taken will be based on the unique challenges of a business. What needs to be kept in mind is that to stay competitive in the long run, it requires to keep innovating and doing things differently.

History is replete with examples of businesses which emanated from recession. Microsoft was launched during early 1975 when the US economy was in a recession caused by the oil embargo imposed by the Organization of the Petroleum Exporting Countries. Apple, as we know today, metamorphosed during the dot-com crash and 9/11.[5] As a matter of fact, the CEO Tim Cook has repeatedly talked about investing during downturns.[6] Companies such as Uber, Warby Parker and Slack were all founded during the recession of 2007–2009 or immediately after that. Alibaba in China was transformed in 2003 when people had self-quarantined themselves due to the SARS epidemic and the company launched its first marketplace for people to shop online. This set the path to its become a global e-commerce giant.

In the COVID-19 pandemic, there have been companies who have been taking risks and innovating. Saral Designs, a start-up in India known for selling low-cost sanitary napkins and the machines that make them, started supplying facemasks. Bengaluru-based nanotechnology start-up Log 9 built the CoronaOven, which is a disinfectant chamber which uses ultra violet-C light to sanitize groceries or masks. Cavin Kare, an Indian FMCG company, repackaged sanitizers and made them affordable by selling sachets for ₹1 ($.013).[7] Heineken created six feet social distancing coolers for Mexican brand Dos Equis. Diesel launched a 360-degree selling platform and virtual showroom, Hyperoom. UK start-up Arrival launched electric buses which help maintain social distance.[8] In China, movie studio Huanxi Media Group could not launch the movie *Lost in Russia* in theatres during the Chinese New Year holiday season. Instead, it struck a deal with ByteDance to live stream the movie, earning $91 million and getting 600 million views in 2 days.[9]

A downturn is a great opportunity for a well-run company.

So what are the questions which can be asked during a downturn?

- Is there a need to revisit our business model?
- Are there new markets which are emerging which can be catered to?
- How is the company equipped to address the changing customer habits/needs with existing or new products?
- Are there any strategies that need to be adopted which will help to mitigate risk?
- Can the business be repurposed to offer something that the customer needs?
- Should the employees be reached out for ideas on what the company should do during a downturn?
- Is there a need to pivot to accurate adoption of digital options?
- Do we need to launch a product or service that help our revenues?
- What sort of messaging do we need to do with customers to show that we are ready for the future?

During a downturn, the primary focus of companies is on conserving cash, cutting costs and delaying capital expenditures. These measures can prevent the company from bleeding. However, to grow in the future, the company has to take risks and take a couple of bold steps.

It has to try a combination of one of the following[10]:

- **Innovate:** Provide products or services which align with changing customer needs.

- **Market share:** Look for ways to increase the market share. This can be expensive if demand is not there and it has to be created.
- **Incentivize:** Provide incentives to relevant parties to much volumes.
- **Partner:** Look for opportunities to partner with entities in the ecosystem.

Remember that taking a calculated risk in a downturn is necessary for survival.

REFERENCES

1. *The New York Times.* Robert Woodruff dies; built Coca-Cola empire. 8 March 1985, https://www.nytimes.com/1985/03/08/us/robert-woodruff-dies-built-coca-cola-empire.html (accessed 6 February 2021).

2. Amadeo K and Estevez E. The 9 principal effects of the Great Depression. The Balance, 30 June 2020, https://www.thebalance.com/effects-of-the-great-depression-4049299 (accessed 6 May 2021).

3. Keough DR. *The ten commandments for business failure.* Penguin Books, 2008.

4. DiSalvo D. Did Coke invent Santa. *Forbes,* 21 December 2011, https://www.forbes.com/sites/daviddisalvo/2011/12/21/did-coke-invent-santa/?sh=e7252791a0c9, (accessed 6 February 2021).

5. Gherini A. 6 iconic companies that succeeded during a recession. *Inc.,* 2 April 2020, https://www.inc.com/anne-gherini/6-iconic-companies-that-succeeded-during-a-recession.html (accessed 6 May 2021).

6. Martellaro J. The Cook's strategy: We believe in investing during downturns. The Mac Observer, 26 January 2016, https://www.macobserver.com/tmo/article/tim-cooks-strategy-we-believe-in-investing-in-downturns (accessed 6 February 2021).

7. Joshi R. Innovators in covid times. *Forbes India,* July 2020, https://www.forbesindia.com/ultimate-120-oppo-innovation/ (accessed 6 February 2021).

8. Covid Innovations. https://www.covidinnovations.com/home/24062020/uk-startup-arrival-launches-electric-buses-that-help-maintain-social-distancing?rq=arrival (accessed 14 Jun 2021).

9. Narayandas D, Hebraic V and Li L. Lessons from Chinese companies' response to Covid-19. *Harv Bus Rev*, 5 June 2020, https://hbr.org/2020/06/lessons-from-chinese-companies-response-to-covid-19 (accessed 6 February 2021).

10. Effilor. Interview with Shiv Shivakumar—What does the future hold? n.d., https://www.effilor.com/lsi-shiv-shivakumar (accessed 6 February 2021).

Chapter 24

What the Tenerife Air Disaster Taught Us

There was an incident which was an outcome of a series of errors and bad luck.

The incident pertains to two charter 747 planes of Pan Am and KLM, which had been diverted to Los Rodeos Airport on the Spanish island of Tenerife together with many other flights. These flights were to land at Las Palmas, on the nearby island of Gran Canaria, where many of the passengers were on their way to meet cruise ships. The flights got diverted as a bomb placed by Canary Island separatists exploded at the flower shop in the Las Palmas airport. The Pan Am had come in from Los Angeles, while KLM had flown in from Amsterdam. Los Rodeos was a fairly small airport with a single runway and a parallel taxiway next to it.

As many flights had been diverted, they were parked wherever they could fit. For any aircraft to depart, they had to go on the runway, take a 180-degree turn and then prepare for take-off. It was also a foggy day, and there was low visibility to pilots.

The KLM lined up on the runway. It was followed by the Pan Am flight. The Pan Am 747 plane was supposed to exit the runway on the third taxiway exit (see Figure 24.1) to allow the KLM to continue its journey to Las Palmas. But it missed this assigned exit due to low visibility and taxied to four instead, keeping it on the runway for much longer than expected. So this put two 747s on the same runway at the same time, invisible not only to each other but also to the control tower.

As Lauren McMah described in a 2019 article published in news.com.au,[1]

As the KLM plane sat at the end of runway 30, in position and holding for takeoff, the Pan Am pilots missed the taxiway they were meant to turn into. They could use the next turn, but it meant they were on the runway for longer. Meanwhile, the pilots in KLM got a route clearance from air traffic control. The route clearance had come unusually late, due to the unusual circumstances of the day. The KLM pilots mistook it for takeoff clearance. Poor communication between both cockpits and air traffic sealed the terrible fate of both aircraft and everyone on board.

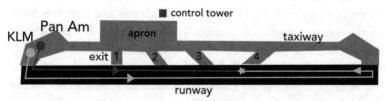

Source: Godfrey K and Xie Q. What happened in the Tenerife airport disaster. *The Sun,* 27 March 2019, https://www.google.co.in/amp/s/www.thesun.co.uk/travel/8722700/air-traffic-controllers-say-roger-deadliest-accident-tenerife/amp/ (accessed 6 May 2021).

Figure 24.1. How the Accident Took Place on the Runway

The Pan Am crew and air traffic control knew Pan Am was still on the runway, and despite efforts to tell KLM, the KLM crew— thinking they were cleared for takeoff, and unable to see due to fog—didn't realise. It was only as the KLM jet started thundering down runway 30 towards Pan Am as it tried to take off that the horrible reality of the situation set in. 'There he is!' Pan Am captain Victor Grubbs yelled, in a cockpit voice recording. 'Look at him! Goddamn, that son of a bitch is coming!'

With that, the two mighty jets collided in a catastrophic crash.

Five hundred and eighty-three people died in the crash. Only a few aboard the Pan Am jet escaped with their lives.

The KLM captain was Jacob van Zanten. He was KLM's top 747 instructor pilot and a celebrity pilot. He even featured in a KLM advertisement. He was KLM's one of the most competent pilots who had 12,000 flight hours to his credit. He had taken off before reaching the green signal from the air traffic controllers. He even ignored his co-pilot's request for clarification. As it was discovered by the Spanish Ministry of Transport and Communication investigation, van Zanten communicated several times with air traffic controllers but ultimately appeared to be immune to their instructions.

The accident was caused by many things such as the fog, interference of the radio transmissions and use of ambiguous phrases, the fact that Pan Am had not left the runway and that the airport was overwhelmed with large aircrafts. As Jon Ziomek mentions in his book *Collision on Tenerife*, an astonishing 11 separate coincidences and mistakes, most of them minor, had to fall precisely into place for this accident to happen.[2] There were several contributing factors such as confusion on the part of both 747 flight crews in understanding taxiing instructions from the air traffic controllers and the captain of the KLM jet did not have control tower clearance when he began his take-off roll.

The crash resulted in many changes in international aviation. The air controller language for international aviation was standardized. Airports now have light systems in place—just like traffic lights for cars—to warn the taxiing aircraft when runways are in use. After the incident, there is now a great emphasis on the importance of exact compliance with instructions and clearances.

WHAT ARE THE LEARNINGS FOR OPEX?

The incident has lot many lessons for the business world. Here, the key ones are being listed.

Overlooking Small Errors

Small errors and problems, if not arrested in time, can quickly become linked and amplified into disastrous outcomes. There are a couple of issues that need to be kept in mind.

First, it's important to build a culture in the company where employees get into the habit of surfacing, speaking up and taking action on small errors. All errors should be captured, and people should never be reprimanded for sharing them. When deep diving on causes for the errors, never get into a blame game. Always focus on the process and why it happened. Let everyone in the company know that small errors and problems, if not addressed, can lead to big problems.

Complex Systems

We live in a connected world. The chances of small problems cascading into bigger problems are all around us. If we look at Bhopal gas tragedy, Fukushima , BP's oil spill or 2008 Financial Crisis, we will realize that these were outcomes of complex and tightly coupled systems which had gone awry.

To understand this better, let's refer to the work of sociologist Charles Perrow. His influential book *Normal Accidents*[3] changed the way how we look at safety and risk. According to Perrow, if a system is 'complex' and 'tightly coupled', failure is inevitable.

So what is a complex system?

A complex system is a web of many intricately connected parts, and much of what goes on in it is not invisible to the naked eye.

What is a tightly coupled system?

A tightly coupled system is one where failure in one can quickly cascade to others, causing a bigger failure. There is little slack for repair.

For example, during the first year of COVID-19 pandemic in 2020, we saw that complex tightly coupled supply chains collapsed due to the closure of Chinese manufacturing.

The other point to note is that sometimes the safeguards to avert a problem can increase the overall complexity of the system. This can have a disastrous outcome.

For example, the Boeing 737 Max disaster would not have happened but for the anti-stall software which was there to make the design safe.[4] Or for that matter, the collapse of the real estate market in 2008 in the USA could not have happened without the derivates designed to control the financial risk.[5]

So what are some of the things that can be done to avoid such failures?

- Reduce system complexity by process simplification, modularity, transparency, installing controls, etc.

- Focus on a transparent design, wherein one gets to see what's happening in the system.

- Perform pre-mortem analysis, where you imagine that there is a failure in future and identify why it happened.

- Build capability within the company to attend to even small errors and failures.

- While working on projects, embed devil's advocate who can be sceptic and can ensure that there is no groupthink.

Abnormal Becoming Normal

There are instances where small errors, mistakes or inept behaviours don't result in immediate negative outcomes. Hence, they don't get the required leadership attention. American sociologist and professor of Columbia University Diane Vaughan has studied organizations where deviations from rules and practices have come to be considered normal. The lack of immediate negative outcomes makes employees continue with them. What's not acceptable slowly becomes acceptable. While reviewing the Challenger disaster, Professor Vaughan came up with a term which she called 'normalization of deviance'. She noted that the root cause of the Challenger disaster was related to the repeated choice of NASA officials to fly the space shuttle despite a dangerous design flaw with the O-rings. Vaughan describes this phenomenon as occurring when people within an organization become so insensitive to deviant practice that it no longer feels wrong. Insensitivity occurs insidiously and sometimes over the years because disaster does not happen until other critical factors line up.[6]

Examples of deviant practices are unsafe practices, not following processes, shutting alarms, breach in infection control (in healthcare) and inept behaviours.

The following are the reasons why deviances get normalized in companies:

- The rules and processes are inefficient.[7]
- People are not aware of the standards. They don't get to know why they deviate from what is acceptable.
- The existing process, procedure and standard are considered counter-productive.
- People are afraid to speak up.
- Actions not taken by leaders when errors are surfaced.

Arresting normalization of deviation requires strong leadership who have to drive it from the top and communicate it to all.

Mistake-proofing Process

Humans are never error-free. Even the best and brightest in a domain with years of experience and training can make mistakes. This is something organizations should know, and they should embed a mechanism to address this issue. Hence, processes, procedures and checklists are needed. You need to mistake-proof processes. This has to be supported by a culture where it's encouraged to challenge the hierarchy and expertise.

The following are areas where mistake-proofing is required:

- When a step in a process is prone to human error, mistakes or defects.[8]
- Where customers can make a mistake which affects output quality. This is true for service processes.[8]
- Where there is a handoff and output needs to be transferred from one person to another.[8]
- When small errors can cause a major problem later down the line.
- When the consequences of a mistake are expensive and dangerous.[8]

Curse of Knowledge

Leaders should be careful of the curse of knowledge. Better informed people have the tendency to not listen to the voices of those who are not experts in the field. Once we know something, it's difficult to imagine not knowing it. The knowledge we have gathered has cursed us. It's difficult to unlearn what one has already learnt. It becomes difficult to get into others shoes, who are not familiar with the subject. While communicating with others, they unknowingly assume that they have the same same background and domain understanding. For example, a Six Sigma Master Black Belt talking about multivariate analysis and design of experiments while discussing a salesforce effectiveness project with a team of sales leaders who have little understanding of complex statistics or a doctor using medical jargon while explaining a disease to a patient. The curse of knowledge makes us misjudge how the other person understands and reacts to something. And they don't realize it.

Chip Heath and Dan Heath in their book *Made to Stick: Why Some Ideas Survive and Others Die*[9] suggest tactics to avoid the curse of knowledge. The following is adopted from their work:

- **Simplicity:** The idea needs to be streamlined enough that the audience can understand it.

- **Unexpectedness:** Adding an element of surprise can focus people's attention.

- **Concreteness:** A concrete idea will be much easier to grasp than something nebulous.

- **Credibility:** If you have credibility with your audience, they are more likely to pay attention to what you have to say.

- **Emotion:** Triggering an emotional response can make a concept more impactful.

- **Stories:** People connect well with stories as a vehicle to illustrate new ideas or concepts.

Let's see how the curse of knowledge can be addressed in a manufacturing company, if there is a breakdown of a machine which requires the involvement of shop-floor workers, machine designers and maintenance staff. The designers may need machine drawings to solve the problem. However, when they decide to engage on the problem, all of them come down to the shop floor and engage in a language that is understood by all the three constituents. Both the designers and the maintenance teams don't use terms that will not be understood by the workers.

Managing a Crisis

Crisis will happen. But do we as businesses have methods to cope with them. It's not possible to anticipate all potential crises. Yet there needs to be planning for the unexpected. Companies need to have a crisis management plan. It should include defining processes which the company should follow when dealing with a crisis. An effectively managed crisis management plan reduces the vulnerability and losses during a crisis. The following pointers need to be kept in mind while preparing for a crisis:

- Identify the various types of crises which can impact a company.
- Ascertain the impact of each type of crises.
- Elaborate a contingency plan for each potential crisis.
- Familiarize employees with their role during the crisis.
- Put together a crisis communication team.
- Appoint a spokesperson.
- Invest in technology and make it an integral part of the company.
- Regularly test the business continuity plan.
- Revisit the plan regularly so that it is up to date and context relevant.

The COVID-19 pandemic has taught us that companies need to prepare for crises they can't possibly predict. These are black-swan events which are impossible to be predicted yet have a huge impact. One solution to this is to perform the disrupter analysis stress test. It is designed to periodically administer a stress test to a large company in order to assess its ability to withstand black swans. It comprises four steps. It quickly and efficiently maps the shape of the enterprise, determines the breadth of potential disrupters, asks the 'what ifs' to determine how severely certain events could stress the enterprise and then implements the contingency plans.[10]

Periphery Issues

When a problem happens, we should not be so engaged with the issue that we forget the issues in the periphery. As Cyril Bouquet pointed in a *Forbes* column in 2009,[11]

> In the case of the Tenerife disaster, the KLM pilot was undoubtedly focused on three important matters: (1) the need to proceed with a quick takeoff (the KLM crew was approaching the legal limit of time it was allowed to fly in a month), (2) the complex

manoeuvres of turning around a 747 on a short runway and (3) floating clouds that reduced visibility in important traffic areas. Because the crew members were so preoccupied, they didn't give sufficient attention to the presumably very important communications coming in from air traffic controllers.

Relaxation

After a period of concentration, when we get into the relaxation phase, we humans can get less vigilant which should be avoided. As the Spanish Ministry of Transport reported,

> Relaxation—after having executed the difficult 180-degree turn, which must have coincided with a momentary improvement in the visibility, the [KLM] crew must have felt a sudden feeling of relief, which increased their desire to finally overcome the ground problems: the desire to be airborne.[11]

Complacence

A business leader should never be complacent. If a certain strategy has worked for an organization, it should not make him complacent. He has to be constantly sensitive to changes happening in the context and periphery.

Also, the leaders should encourage bad news. Create a safe working environment for people to bubble up issues. Encourage your employees to share bad news. How fast it takes for bad news to travel to the top of the company is another indicator of whether we are making it safe for people to share their concerns.

A leader of the company should not be in a state of denial—'It won't happen to us.' They need to have a mechanism to learn from any crisis.

Mindfulness

Train employees on mindfulness to build high-performance psychological skills and help people to understand their emotions and motivations as they erupt.[12] This can not only come handy during a crisis or high-stress situation but also improve concentration. This becomes important in a connected world, wherein we find it difficult to concentrate for a sustained period. We have the urge to check our phone, navigating social media, etc. A short attention span impacts not only our work but also our relationship. Attending mindfulness training and practising it helps in a stress-ridden digital world.

Learn

Learn from others' mistakes. When another organization faces a crisis, it's an opportunity to ask a couple of important questions such as:

- What is the crisis all about?
- Has it been caused by internal forces or external forces?
- Could we have been impacted by such a crisis?
- How would we have addressed the problem if the crisis hit us?
- Do we have systems, protocols and processes to prevent such a crisis?
- What are the things that we need to work on learning from the crisis?

REFERENCES

1. McMah L. What caused the deadliest plane crash in world history. news.com.au, 30 March 2019, https://www.news.com.au/travel/travel-updates/what-caused-the-deadliest-plane-crash-in-world-history/news-story/7456afb4a8c6e57a41a7b27178ff8be4 (accessed 6 May 2021).

2. Ziomek J. *Collision on Tenerife*. Nashville, TN: Post Hill Press, 2018.

3. Perrow C. *Normal accidents: Living with high risk technologies*. Princeton, NJ: Princeton University Press, 1999.

4. Campbell D. The many human errors that brought down the Boeing 737 Max. 2 May 2019, https://www.theverge.com/2019/5/2/18518176/

boeing-737-max-crash-problems-human-error-mcas-faa (accessed 7 March 2021).

5. Amadeo K. Could the financial crisis have been avoided? The Balance, 24 February 2021, https://www.thebalance.com/were-mortgage-crisis-and-bank-bailout-preventable-3305676 (accessed 7 March 2021).

6. Price MR and Williams TC. When doing wrong feels so right: Normalization of deviance. *J Patient Saf* 2018; 14(1, March): 1–2. doi: 10.1097/PTS.0000000000000157

7. Cox C. Diane Vaughan's theory of the normalisation of deviance. 1 January 2020, https://www.pslhub.org/learn/improving-patient-safety/human-factors-improving-human-performance-in-care-delivery/barriers/diane-vaughans-theory-of-the-normalisation-of-deviance-r1284/ (accessed 5 March 2021).

8. Trout J. Poka-yoke explained. n.d., https://www.reliableplant.com/poka-yoke-31862 (accessed 7 March 2021).

9. Heath C and Heath D. *Made to stick: Why some ideas survive and others die.* Cornerstone Digital, 2008.

10. Le Merle M. How to prepare for a black swan. 23 August 2011, https://www.strategy-business.com/article/11303?gko=66cff (accessed 7 March 2021).

11. Bouquet C. The crisis is here to stay. Do you have the key to coping? *Forbes*, 21 April 2009, https://www.forbes.com/2009/04/21/stress-coping-mindfulness-leadership-managing-fixation.html#6c0c99b05779 (accessed 6 February 2021).

12. O'Brien M. New Microsoft study shows reduction in attention span. MrsMindfullness.com, n.d., https://mrsmindfulness.com/new-microsoft-study-shows-rapid-decline-attention-spans/ (accessed 6 February 2021).

Chapter 25

Managing the Third-quarter Phenomenon

The concept of the third-quarter phenomenon has been observed during missions in an extreme environment when people are isolated and confined. They are called ICE (isolated, confined and extreme) conditions. This has been studied in polar and space missions. The term was coined in 1991 by researchers Robert Bechtel and Amy Berning.[1] In the first stage, the crew members are excited and don't think about time. During the second stage, there is boredom and routine sets in. During the third quarter, which happens immediately after the mid-point, the end of the mission can be seen. This is based on the proportion of time and not an absolute number of days, months or years spent. They start thinking about when they will go back to their family, or that the mission may be extended, or that something grave may happen. All these cause anxiety. The mood and morale of teams go down at some stage beyond the halfway mark from the completion of the mission. This has been observed in space missions and also among those who go to poles. There are reported negative and undesirable mood states and change of behaviour.[2] People experience tension, irritability, decrease in morale and interpersonal issues. However, this is not found in astronauts, as they are trained on it and, unlike explorers in Antarctica, they are able to connect with family and psychologists 24 × 7 in mission control from the space station.

There were similar examples during the lockdown which happened during the pandemic. After the initial phase of binding exploration, people got into a dull rhythm of togetherness in confines. What started bothering them was whether they would have jobs, would their children go to school and so on. People reported increased battles with their spouses and children over trivial things. When people don't have social interactions, these problems can occur.

TAKEAWAYS FOR OPEX

Although organizational transformations don't have any of the ICE conditions, they too have 'third-quarter phenomenon'. This happens with the following individuals:

1. Those who are a part of the core transformation team
2. Those who are impacted by the change

Let's look at both of them.

Those Part of the Core Project Team

OPEX transformations can be very stressful. This is especially true when a tight schedule of a project does not give much time for socialization. People come to the office in the morning and leave late at night. Sometimes, the transformation could take them to a different location and would require them to the stay away from their families for a long time. They spend the whole day to accomplish the milestones. They are in a pressure cooker sort of environment. Given the punishing schedule, they don't get time to socialize with others. It's almost like being cocooned with a set of people. I have seen the 'third-quarter phenomenon' here too. Somewhere after the mid-point of the project, one sees this happening.

The initial excitement of the project is over, and the team has now been sucked into completing the phases of the project. Having been cocooned together for some time, they start losing the initial enthusiasm. The end date of the project is visible to all, and they realize that they have completed half the journey. What worries them is that more than 50 per cent of the time is over, and the results are still not visible. What also bothers them is that so much hard work has gone in and what if they don't achieve the desired outcome.

The other thing which needs to be kept in mind is that in the first half of the project, the team is focused on the voice of the customer, defining the problem, scoping, process dissection, data analysis, cause analysis, identifying countermeasures and so on. The implementation of the countermeasures happens in the second half. This is hard, and they start feeling the pains of change. Those impacted by change resist the new ways of working and push back. All these results in demotivation and irritation. Project team members get angry over small issues, and there are times when they blame each other. Clearly, the leader of the business improvement team members should be able to sense and manage these mood swings to avoid the project getting derailed. This requires strong leadership and the ability to project optimism, despite all the challenges that the transformation may have.

Those Impacted by the Change

When a transformation is launched, there is a lot of hype. Project launches, town halls and alignment sessions keep the enthusiasm of all those impacted by the change. They are told about the purpose of the project, what's going to be the impact on the company and how it will impact their team and them personally. They are kept engaged by the communication from the transformation team. They may have concerns and doubts, but it still has not hit them. It's in the second half of the transformation when the rubber meets the road. People start getting impacted by change. They resist new processes and find new ways of doing risky things. They find it difficult to adopt the new ways of working. This is when they start to resist the change and find ways to avoid it. They call the transformation as another of those initiatives from the management which will not deliver any results. There will be voices which will question the judgement of the management. Others will question the vision that the project has set out to achieve. This is the phase when people are very cynical about the transformation. Change management professionals call it the valley of death. If not addressed, this can quietly kill the transformation. This will test the leadership of the transformation team and the senior management. They have to proactively address all the concerns and patiently hear all the people out. What also works is to repeatedly share the vision of the project and how it will make things better. You have to share success stories, recognize people for adopting new ways of working, build capabilities and sometimes even remove people who act as blockers despite all the efforts to take them on board.

Managing the 'third quarter' in an operational transformation is a key leadership challenge, which has to be navigated with lots of sensitivity, drive and care. Leaders need to demonstrate compassionate leadership. Talk to team members regularly. Share with them the bigger picture, the larger vision and how an individual's work connects with the big picture. Emphasize why what they are doing is significant. Astronauts aboard spaceships are acutely aware of their lofty goals and how their work fits into that. So even when the task is mundane—such as practising putting away tools one more time—they have a clear sense of how that work fits into the bigger picture.[3] To manage the phase when they are emotionally down, the leader should be available to provide support when the team members need it. And most importantly, they should weave in light-hearted moments so that employees can restore their energies.

REFERENCES

1.   Bechtel RB and Berning A. The third-quarter phenomenon: Do people experience discomfort after stress has passed? In: Harrison AA (ed.) *From Antarctica to outer space*. New York, NY: Springer, 1991, 261–265.

2. Van Wijk CH. Coping during conventional submarine missions: Evidence of a third quarter phenomenon? *J Hum Perf Extr Environ* 2018: 14(1).

3. Contractor N and DeChurch L. What astronauts can teach us about working remotely. 29 July 2020, https://insight.kellogg. northwestern.edu/article/remote-work-lessons-astronauts (accessed 6 February 2021).

Chapter 26

Learnings from the First Space Mutiny

The Skylab missions were launched in the early 1970s to ascertain and prove that human beings could live and work in space for a long period of time. The other objective of the mission was also to expand our knowledge about the solar system by being in space. The Skylab space station was launched on 14 May 1973. It was called Skylab 1. Till the project got over in February 1974, it operated three missions which delivered three successive crews of astronauts through missions which were called Skylab 2, Skylab 3 and Skylab 4. The three missions lasted for 28 days, 59 days and 84 days, respectively. The missions created and established human's endurance in space. The incident which is being discussed happened in Skylab 4, which had astronauts Commander Gerald P. Carr, Science Pilot Edward G. Gibson and Pilot William R. Pogue. When Skylab 4 blasted off to space on 16 November 1973, NASA had thought to get work done as efficiently as the previous astronauts. The crew members had a very regimented schedule. All the asks of the astronauts were detailed out.

Things got off to a bad start when William Pogue developed space adaptation syndrome, which results in illusions, loss of knowledge, nausea and vomiting. The crew members hid this with the mission controllers on the Earth which they later discovered. Unlike the crew members of Skylab 3, these crew members were rookies, but the mission controllers expected the same level of productivity as the earlier veterans.[1] NASA's plan called for a total of 6,051 work hours between the three men. This was basically a 24-hour schedule. Besides the medical and scientific experiments, there were loading and unloading gears and making observations of the Sun and Earth as well as the Comet Kohoutek. On top of all that, there were four spacewalks at a combined total of about a day in length.[2]

The schedule was so dense that the crew could not take it. It was so regimented that the astronauts found it hard to find time to go to the toilet and to eat. They also had to limit their sleep breaks. They complained of being pushed too hard while those on the ground in Houston complained that they were not doing what they were supposed to do. The astronauts who were on the ground at the mission control also felt that the schedule was too punishing. As Gerald P. Carr recalled in the book *Homesteading Space: The Skylab Story* written by David Hitt in 2008, an 'us versus them' mentality began to set in, with ground controllers and astronauts becoming more and more aggravated with each other. As Lead Flight Director Neal Hutchinson mentions in the book, 'Of course as we continued to press [the astronauts], more mistakes began to be made, more than we had seen with the other crews.'[3]

On 28 December 1973, they announced that they were going on a strike and turn off their communication with ground control. They spent time relaxing and looked out of the window and did not do much. They resumed communication with NASA after spending one day[1] doing things at their pace.

---

[1] There is a confusion on the time that they switched off communication. Some writers say that it was 90 minutes, while others say that it was 1 day.

When the Skylab communication came online, the staff in mission control were much more willing to have a discussion around their schedule. The crew had a heart-to-heart conversation with mission controllers and asked for more time to rest, a less densely packed schedule and more control over when and how they did things. Mission controllers in Houston agreed to afford the crew full rest and meal breaks and replace its minute-by-minute schedules with a list of tasks to be completed, leaving it to the crew to manage its own time.[4] The productivity of the astronauts rose after this, as they were given the freedom to decide how they went about their schedule.

The mission carried on for several weeks, and they were able to complete a large amount of work. None of the three astronauts returned to space again. The Skylab orbited till 1979 when it decayed.

This was essentially an industrial action which was followed by negotiations with 'management'. The only difference is that it took place in outer space. What bubbled up was that those in mission control and the astronauts space did not work towards a jointly held objective.

The usually staid communiqués between NASA's mission control and orbiting astronauts, which convey the impression of jointly held objectives and cooperation, were replaced by considerably more tense and fraught communications.

WHAT ARE THE LESSONS FOR THE WORLD OF BUSINESS?

The Skylab 4 story provides quite a few lessons for those working on business improvement. Following are the things which we need to keep in mind:

- While making a blueprint for a business improvement plan, don't make it so detailed that the team members find it claustrophobic. Set targets and let teams decide how to execute them.

- Allow teams to decide their own schedules. This needs to be kept in mind as more people are working from home in a post-COVID-19 world.

- While selecting people for business improvement, you need to remember that you need people who have the right emotional intelligence, are patient and have good communication skills.

- Those involved in OPEX should be ready to do lots of boring stuff. They can't just expect to do things which make them visible such as presenting to senior leaders, running workshops or communicating in town halls.

- Create a safe working environment so that members willingly bubble up concerns, issues and challenges.

- Never reprimand your team members when they come back with thoughts, ideas and suggestions on how things should be done or why they can't do something.

- If people are falling back on execution/tasks, it's important to patiently understand why they have failed on the planned schedule.

- The leaders and change agents who act as catalysts for business improvement should encourage employees to open up and share their concerns.

- The core team driving business improvement should be a mix of genders. As per a London Business School study, a mixed team was more likely to experiment, share knowledge and fulfil tasks, regardless of whether the team leader was a man or a woman.[5]

- Transformations can be taxing; hence, nudge people to use their free time on doing things which help them to unwind.

- If people have personal issues, hear them out. Don't always make them adjust. Listening to them you may realise that they have a perspective. For example, in the Skylab 4 mission, two of the astronauts grew beard when in the space station. This made the mission control team very uncomfortable. They branded them as lazy. They could not influence them to change their behaviour.

- Don't treat members of the team as expendable if not on schedule. Trained and accomplished individuals in a team are likely to push back when placed in an artificially controlled, too-tightly regulated environment.[6]

- When discipline is enforced on remote team members (including those working from home or who are based in a distant geography), they can assert their resistance and even become combative and have unvarnished conversations. Minute-by-minute monitoring is no way to do business.

- Conflict helps to sort out issues. Hence, encourage team members to bubble up all conflicts. If the astronaut did not have conflict, they would have to go through an arduous schedule.

In Chapter 29, we will delve more into how conflicts should be managed in OPEX efforts.

REFERENCES

1. Adler D. Was there really a 'mutiny' aboard the Skylab space station? *Astronomy*, 12 June 2020, https://astronomy.com/news/2020/06/was-there-really-a-mutiny-aboard-the-skylab-space-station (accessed 6 February 2021).

2. Eschner K. Mutiny in space: Why these Skylab astronauts never flew again. *Smithsonian Magazine*, 8 February 2017, https://www.smithsonianmag.com/smart-news/mutiny-space-why-these-skylab-astronauts-never-flew-again-180962023/ (accessed 6 February 2021).

3. Hitt D. *Homesteading space: The Skylab story.* Lincoln, NE: University of Nebraska Press, 2008.

4. Hiltzik M. The day when three NASA astronauts staged a strike in space. *Lost Angeles Times*, 28 December 2015, https://www.latimes.com/business/hiltzik/la-fi-mh-that-day-three-nasa-astronauts-20151228-column.html (accessed 6 February 2021).

5. Ward L and Carvel J. Best ideas come from work teams mixing men and women. *The Guardian*, 1 November 2007, https://www.theguardian.com/uk/2007/nov/01/gender.world (accessed 6 February 2021).

6. Chopra S. On strike in outer space. 23 October 2013, https://openthemagazine.com/essays/true-life/on-strike-in-outer-space/ (accessed 6 February 2021).

Chapter 27

Understanding the Blackbox of Culture

Organizational culture and OPEX go hand in hand. A successful OPEX effort takes care of issues around organizational culture. Over the last three decades, I have myriad experience on how culture plays a role in embedding OPEX. Some have been good and some not. For many, culture is a soft mushy thing which has to be taken up by the human resources folks. In the initial days of my career, I also thought the same. The reason why I believed it was that no one had explained to me what culture is all about. To me, it was one of those amorphous things which many people talk about yet never made it explicit of what it was made up of. It was only when one of my OPEX efforts failed did I realize that this thing called culture can kill an enterprise despite all positive intentions. It was then that I realized the role of corporate culture in enterprise performance. Confronting culture issues superficially does not work. Tinkering a few things here and there has little impact. What's required is that culture has to move from human resources to the table of the CEO and even the board.

The other thing which is worth noting is that so many people talk about companies such as Toyota, Disney World and Zappos. Books have been written about what they do. People have visited these organizations, observed what they do and even asked questions. Yet they are never able to copy them. They may implement their tools and techniques, but they are not able to create another Toyota, Disney or Zappos. The differentiating element is culture.

Culture does not get built by high visible road shows, high decibel town halls, flashy communication campaigns or posters. It's always an outcome of tangible actions which emerge from the thorough understanding of its anatomy.

So what has been my learning around culture? I have been hugely influenced by the works of Edgar Schein, Professor Emeritus with MIT Sloan School of Management, and author of many bestsellers including *The Corporate Culture Survival Guide* and, his most recent book, *Humble Inquiry: The Gentle Art of Asking Instead of Telling*; John Kotter; James Heskett; Shalom Schwartz; Geert Hofstede; and many others. Here's my take which I believe everyone associated with OPEX professionals should know.

NEVER BEGIN BY CHANGING THE CULTURE

While embarking on an OPEX journey, don't first target to change the culture. The first thing to do is not to define the culture but the problem which you are trying to solve. Having defined the problem, it's time to ascertain if the existing culture will enable achieving the goal which you have set out for yourself. Then one should ask the behaviours which are required to achieve the OPEX goals. What behaviours are present and what are not. As Edgar Schein mentioned in an interview with *Forbes*,

> Managers today understand the importance of culture as a factor in whether a company performs well or not. But many of them mistakenly believe they can arbitrarily decide whether or not you will have a good culture. They still don't understand that culture is a product of years of learning and experience, not something you implement.[1]

So if you think that you can change the culture before embarking on an OPEX journey, you will not be successful. This is because the existing culture in a company has been gathered from the leaders and founders who have worked there in the past. In a company which has been running for some time, you can't just fly in and change the culture as there are behaviours which they have internalized over the years. So when a leader comes in and tries to impose a new set of behaviours, they will resist it. So if there are people who don't align with the new behaviours, there would be a conflict. When there is a conflict, you see things not moving. As Schein said to *Forbes*,

> The leader will win in such conflict only by firing large numbers of the carriers of the old culture, as turnaround managers usually do. The new leader can then start [fresh] by imposing new values and behavior patterns. But this is not a new culture until it succeeds for a number of years and becomes internalized by the employees. So you can talk about *destroying* an old culture, but you cannot create or *impose* a new culture, only new values and behavior patterns.[1]

Edgar Schein further gave the example of Louis Gerstner when he joined IBM. As he said,

> [Gerstner's] success was based on figuring out what the culture was that had led to IBM's success. He noticed that the company had drifted away from some of the elements of that culture and he found a way to revive it. He worked on the culture by reviving and reinvigorating the best elements of what was already there, not by 'changing' the culture.[1]

There are important takeaways for those catalysing OPEX:

- When you embark on a journey of OPEX, don't try to change the culture. This is especially true if the company has been there for some time.

- Ascertain the existing culture.

- Focus on the problem you are trying to solve through the OPEX effort.

- List the elements of the culture which will enable your journey and what would derail it.

- Works towards embedding values and behaviours which will accelerate the journey.

DON'T OVERSIMPLIFY CULTURE

I have seen many practitioners defining culture simplistically as 'way things get done here'. I think it's over simplifying a complex concept.

The problem with oversimplification is that you may miss the essence of what the key drivers of building an organizational culture are.

Actually, culture is a very complex subject.

I like the way Edgar Schein defines it. In his book *Organizational Culture and Leadership*,[2] he defines culture as follows:

> Organizational culture is the pattern of basic assumptions that a given group has invented, discovered, or developed in learning to cope with its problems of external adaptation and internal integration, and that have worked well enough to be considered valid, and, therefore, to be taught to new members as the correct way to perceive, think, and feel in relation to those problems.

He demystified the above in an interview to CultureUniversity.com.[30] He said, 'Culture as the sum total of everything an organization has learned in its history in dealing with the external problems—which would be goals, strategy, how we do things—and how it organizes itself internally.' This defines how we're going to relate to each other, what kind of hierarchy exists, etc. 'These early learnings, if they are successful, become the definition but it's always something that's been learned. It's not something that just can be imposed or that's just there.'

According to John Kotter and James Heskett, the culture has two parts: (a) the pattern of shared values and beliefs which helps individuals understand organizational functioning (invisible) and (b) those conventions which provide them with norms of behaviour (visible).[4]

According to Boris Groysberg et al.,

> Culture is the tacit social order of an organization: It shapes attitudes and behaviors in wide-ranging and durable ways. Cultural norms define what is encouraged, discouraged, accepted, or rejected within a group. When properly aligned with personal values, drives, and needs, culture can unleash tremendous amounts of energy toward a shared purpose and foster an organization's capacity to thrive.[5]

Further, Boris Groysberg, Jeremiah Lee, Jesse Price and J. Yo-Jud Cheng[4] talk about the following generally accepted attributes about culture:

- **Shared:** Culture is a group phenomenon. It is not a characteristic of an individual. It comprises shared beliefs, values and assumptions.

- **Pervasive:** Culture permeates the entire organization across levels. It manifests in collective behaviours, physical environments, group rituals, visible symbols, stories and legends.

- **Enduring:** Culture directs the thoughts and actions of groups over the long term. It develops through critical events in the collective life and learning of a group.

- **Implicit:** It's kind of a silent language. Despite its subliminal nature, people are effectively hardwired to recognize and respond to it instinctively.

KNOW THE KEY BEHAVIOURS

We have talked about it earlier. As a part of OPEX transformation, it's important to identify the key behaviours which will enable the transformation and have the greatest impact. But how do you know about this? There was this manufacturing company wherein the new CEO wanted to embark on an OPEX transformation. When I met him, he told me that he wanted to change the culture as things didn't seem to get done there. I asked him about the problem he was trying to solve. He told me that they were facing major issues with the customers.

Quality issues were going up and consumer issues were the problem of technical services. He said that the employees needed to collaborate more and come out of their functional silos. When I asked him what he would like to change, he said that he would like all problems to be resolved by a cross-functional team. So while quality issues should go down, he would like members of all functions involved in the effort. And if there was a consumer issue in future, it would not be the baby of technical services but a team comprising sales, marketing, production, quality, technical service and product development should be looking into it.

Based on our analysis, deliberation and observations we recommended that the company needed to embed two behaviours comprising collaborating more across functional boundaries and employees needed to take extra steps to meet and address customer issues and problems. So how did the CEO take this forward? He announced that addressing consumer issues would be the responsibility of the cross-functional team comprising sales, marketing, production, quality, technical service and product development. They would also be responsible for resolving the issue. Also, they would be collectively rewarded on how the team delivers on the issues. It would no more be the baby of one function. He did not leave it there. He came out with a 'ways of working document' which had 'collaboration' and 'customer-first' as two of the key elements. It elaborated in detail what these meant in day-to-day working and how these could be practised. Top management started acting as role models on the two new behaviours. Leaders looked for employees who demonstrated these behaviours. They recognized their actions in town-halls in front of all employees. These individuals then became the culture catalysts who started priming other employees to demonstrate these behaviours. The top management took every opportunity to role model the behaviours which included things like the executive team members participating in problem-solving (root cause analysis) sessions on customer issues. They also ensured that the two values 'customer-first' and 'collaboration' were integrated with the KPIs of performance management. These were supported with training sessions the strengthened these values. The organization even declared a war on silos and even carried out changes in organization structure to ensure various customer segments were responded in time. All these helped to embed the two values over a period of 14 months.

CHANGE BEHAVIOUR TO CHANGE THINKING

Many of us are from a school of thought that if you have to change culture, first focus on thinking of employees. Once the thinking changes, behaviour will change. The thought here is that change of thinking will result in change of values and attitude, and this may gradually result in people doing the right things. As Ralph Waldo Emerson had said, 'The ancestor of every action is a thought.'

However, there are others who would say that we should focus on behaviour first and this will gradually change the thinking. As John Shook mentioned in *MIT Sloan Management Review*, 'The way to change culture is not to first change how people think, but instead to start by changing how people behave—what they do.'[6] The reason why this happens is that when people are told to behave in a certain manner which is not in alignment with their thinking, they slowly change their thinking to avoid seeing themselves as a hypocrite.

So as someone focused on OPEX, which of the two should you adopt? Well, my view is that most of the time we should focus on changing behaviour. The reason is very simple. Changing one's thinking can be very difficult. Thoughts and beliefs are extensions of our identity. When someone tells us to change them, people can have strong reactions. Sometimes they may further harden the very thinking or the belief that you are telling them to change. After all, we are attached to our beliefs and extension of our personality. Hence, it results in adverse outcomes.[6] Also, it's never easy to translate intention into actions.

However, there are times when changing one's beliefs does change behaviours. For example, when Tim Braganza (actually name hidden), in plaster and sitting on a wheelchair, told his colleagues about how he had fractured his legs and ribs after he fell from a spray drier in a food factory—he had not followed the laid-down safety practices and not worn helmets and other safety gears—the fellow employees listening to him could viscerally connect with his pain. The immediate reaction one could see after Tim's address was that employees started wearing safety gears. This was a great example of how belief can be changed by an event or address or a speech or emotionally charged slogans.

The approach that you take depends on the context. But what works most of the time is to focus on behaviour and thereby changing the thinking. You can be sure of faster outcomes. Taking the 'thought to behaviour' route takes time. It can also require a lot of energy and resources.

REACH OUT TO EMPLOYEES

Employees are a great source in the company to let you know what needs to change in the organizational culture. More often than not, they will tell you the good and the bad about the existing culture. Their thoughts, ideas and observations will provide you sufficient meat on what to work on. One of the approaches to do this is to meet employees in small groups and ask them. What this also does is that you get a sense of what will work and what will not when you will embed the new behaviours. Probably the biggest benefit in seeking inputs is that employees will have a much better buy-in. This is because they have been a part of the co-creation.

In his book *Delivering Happiness,* Tony Hsieh talked about how he went about defining the corporate culture of Zappos. As a part of the process, he asked for every employee's input on what the company's core values should be. Then, after Zappos had come up with a list of those values, everyone was asked to change one thing in the company's policies, documents and processes to make them more aligned to the new values.[8] This approach works even if a company has been in existence for a long time.

CEO SHOULD BE IN THE DRIVER'S SEAT

It's true that a successful culture change happens when everyone is involved in it. However, what is critical to note is the role of the

CEO. He has to be closely involved in the elements of culture which he wants to change. So if a CEO does not believe that his success and the success of the OPEX transformation depend on culture change, things may not change. Typically, the culture change in an OPEX transformation will require a change of behaviour on the part of the CEO and the entire senior team. We got a sneak peek into this earlier example. These behaviours have to be role modelled by them so that everyone in the company realizes that top management means business. Beyond this, if there are resources which are required, the CEO willingly provides them. This includes not just money but also his time. For example, as a part of an OPEX transformation, a CEO of a packaging company made 'build relationships' as an additional value in its existing set of values. This was about connecting with customers, partners, consumers, communities and leveraging each other's strength to drive success. To make it happen, the CEO made sure to give top priority to any matter pertaining to these stakeholders. Be it a partner grievance or an investment for a better service experience, he made sure it got priority. He also made sure that decisions were taken keeping these stakeholders' interest in mind.

STRENGTHEN THE ENABLERS

Just trying to change behaviours of employees without strengthening the enablers will not work. If new behaviours have to be embedded, the elements of the context need to work in sync to shape the behaviours. They are also needed to sustain the desired culture. What's critical is to understand the interplay between the elements and how they can be used to amplify the desired behaviour. So key enablers that we need to focus on are as follows:

Performance Management

What gets rewarded gets done. It's important to design your performance metrics in a way that it encourages the right behaviours. A poorly design compensation mechanism can run the other efforts to build the desired culture in the company. For example, when a financial service company into mortgages decided to embed a 'quality-first' mindset, it decided to change the way the sales team got compensated. Earlier, their incentives were based on the number of applications sourced. This was irrespective of whether the customer was eligible for the home loan or not. After the 'quality-first' focus, the new incentives were based on the 'quality of accounts'. This forced the sales teams to get accounts from the right customers and those who were eligible for mortgage. This initially brought down the number of accounts sourced by the sales team but ensured that only good quality-clients were sourced. This reduced the rejection of accounts as only good-quality accounts were sourced. It also demonstrated that the company was focused on customers and spent time understanding the customer profile before pitching for a home loan. It also resolved the earlier problem of raising false expectations. It was now getting applications of only those customers who were eligible to get a home loan.

Process

Processes should enable a culture which is being tried to be embedded in the company. One key thing which needs to be remembered is that processes which are implemented without keeping the culture in mind can undermine the culture which you are trying to embed in the company. The processes should also demonstrate the elements of culture. For example, if customer focus is one of the values of the company, the company should focus on just not external customers but also internal customers. The company should make the process easier for not only external customers but also internal customers. For employees to feel that the company is serious about it, the various employee-related processes should be hassle-free and convenient.

Talent Management

Management of talent comprises hiring the right person, developing them, leveraging their capabilities, making sure they are engaged and giving them an opportunity to grow in the company. The people who are hired should not demonstrate behaviours which are consistent with the organizational culture. When their performance is gauged, it's just not on KPIs but also how effectively they demonstrate the value of the company. When employees are looked for leadership roles, fitment with cultural attributes is an important deciding factor.

Organization and Workplace Design

The organizational structure and workplace design should enable and support the values and behaviours which are a part of the culture. So, for example, if 'openness' is one of the key elements of the company's culture, the company should design workplaces wherein the conference rooms are made of glass, the workplace has an open-office plan, etc. Office space reveals how employees interact, which is a key element of organizational culture. The office environment should reinforce the elements of the culture. Similarly, a company's organizational structure should strengthen the components which make up the culture. For example, when a fintech company wanted to have a 'risk-based culture', it reorganized itself and made the chief risk officer report to the CEO. This was to indicate to the company that 'risk management' was a critical function of the company.

Resources and Tools

The company needs to make tools and resources available for the employees to navigate and support the behaviours which you want them to demonstrate. When a pharma company wanted to include collaboration as a cultural element, it bought a digital collaboration management solution for businesses around the globe to manage projects, communications and workflows. This provided a great opportunity for them to cross-pollinate and collaborate on projects. Similarly, when a food company embarked on creating a quality culture, it bought an IT system which provided all the metrics and dashboards for quality and process performance in one place for everyone to access. This helped to track performance without hassle, which was earlier done manually. Sometimes tools can be coaching sessions for navigating the conflicts which may emerge because of new values which are in contradiction to a person's personal beliefs.

CULTURE SHOULD ALIGN WITH BUSINESS STRATEGY

The culture and strategy of an enterprise should be in sync. In fact, the culture should enable the execution of the business strategy. When the culture aligns with strategy implementation, an organization can operate more efficiently and achieve better results. A Korn Ferry study found that businesses that align culture with strategy and engage and enable their people to deliver see a 117 per cent greater return on investment than those that don't. They get a 145 per cent higher return on their assets and a 56 per cent greater return on their equity too.[8] For example, when a restaurant chain adopted a strategy of differentiating through legendary services, its cultural elements came in handy. One of the key elements of the company was flexibility. This was of great help to them. The staff had the freedom to do what it felt for the customer so long as it took care of the customer. For example, when a loyal customer walked into their store for a meal, there were often times when the staff gave away free drinks or free hors d'oeuvres. Once when a customer walked into a store and found that he had lost his credit card, the store manager told him that the food was on them and the customer did not have to worry about payment.

DEMONSTRATE THROUGH MINI-WINS

To give credibility to the role of the new culture, it's important to demonstrate how it can deliver benefit to the company. If these are not done, employees would tend to think that it is another of those fuzzy concepts from the management which have little value to the real value. They can grow cynical and withdraw from participating in it. Hence, it's recommended to create pilots which can demonstrate the impact of the new behaviours. What such pilots also do is that they provide an opportunity for coaching and handholding on the new behaviours.

When a multilateral bank embarked on a journey to strengthen the power of cross-functional participation, they hired my firm to help in the effort. The organization had done very well, but the president felt that the company could achieve much more if the cross-functional working became a part of the culture. To demonstrate how to make it happen, we put together a cross-functional team to work on improving the efficiency and effectiveness of the finance team. The teams met every day for the next 30 days and looked at all the finance processes in detail. It decided to focus on reducing one of the key pains faced by the top management. It took more than 60 days to prepare the quarterly financial statements. The outcome of the bootcamps was that the time taken to prepare the financial statements came down from 60 days to 10 days. This success was widely showcased in the company as the power of cross-functional mind. This effort helped employees to understand what cross-functional working was and how it needs to be done. It also provided a safe environment for the leaders to hone their skills under a coach. At the end of the pilot, all participants unequivocally said that it changed their thinking about what could be achieved when a diverse set of people think beyond their function and focus on a larger organizational objective.

REFERENCES

1.   Duncan RD. Culture, leadership, performance: How are they linked? *Forbes*, 23 October 2018, https://www.forbes.com/sites/rodgerdeanduncan/2018/10/30/culture-leadership-performance-how-are-they-linked/#2343e1455e44 (accessed 7 July 2021).

2.   Schein E. *Organizational culture and leadership*. 3rd ed. San Francisco, CA: Jossey Bass, 2004.

3.   An interview with Edgar Schein https://www.humansynergistics.com/blog/culture-university/details/culture-university/2014/03/03/

culture-fundamentals—9-important-insights-from-edgar-schein (accessed 15 Jun 2021).

4. Kotter J P and Heskett JL. *Corporate culture and performance.* New York, NY: Free Press, 1992.

5. Groysberg B, Lee J, Price J, et al. The leader's guide to corporate culture: How to Manage the Eight Critical Elements of Organizational Life. *Harv Bus Rev* 2018 (January–February).

6. Shook J. How to change culture: Lessons from NUMMI. *MIT Sloan Management Review* 2010; 51(2, Winter), https://www.lean.org/Search/Documents/35.pdf (accessed 7 May 2021).

7. Smith K. Don't change beliefs, change behaviors. *Forbes*, 11 August 2019, https://www.forbes.com/sites/khalilsmith/2019/08/11/dont-change-beliefs-change-behaviors/?sh=70c779bc2820 (accessed 6 February 2021).

8. Hsieh T. *Delivering happiness: A path to profits, passion, and purpose.* New York, NY: Grand Central Publishing, 2010.

9. Korn Ferry. *The truth about strategy execution: Why successful CEOs focus on culture*, https://www.kornferry.com/solutions/organizational-strategy/cultural-transformation/cultural-transformation-insights (accessed 6 February 2021).

Chapter 28

Demystifying Robotic Process Automation

In this century, OPEX is not possible without intelligent automation. In a post-COVID-19 world, there has been a heightened need for companies to adopt digital solutions to remain competitive and relevant in the marketplace. For CEOs, business owners and C-suite, intelligent automation is no more a question of 'whether' but 'how'. During the pandemic, did we not see that businesses which had already embarked on a digital journey earlier could quickly pivot their distribution model to deliver products directly to customers when they were confined to their homes due to lockdowns?

But what is intelligent automation?

In the book *Intelligent Automation*, authors Pascal Bornet, Ian Barkin and Jochen Wirtz provide a comprehensive definition which is as follows:

Intelligent Automation is a concept of leveraging a new generation of software-based automation. It combines methods and technologies to execute business processes automatically on behalf of knowledge workers. This automation is achieved by mimicking the capabilities that knowledge workers use in performing their work activities (eg: language, vision, execution and thinking & learning). The goal of using IA is to achieve a business outcome, through a redesigned automated process, with no or minimal human intervention.[1]

It helps to achieve the goals of OPEX of cost efficiency, process lead times, enhanced compliance, employee experience, customer experience, better quality and even resilience.

Intelligent automation is also called Hyperautomation (by Gartner), Integrated Automation Platform (by Horses for Sources) and even Cognitive Automation.

The scope of intelligent automation includes the following:

• Smart workflow

• RPA

• Data

• Machine learning

• Natural language processing

• Computer vision

In this chapter, I am focusing on RPA, as it is a critical tool which is being widely used by businesses.

Process optimization is an integral part of OPEX. When we talk about process optimization, we can't afford to overlook RPA.

However, there are two things which we need to be kept in mind while adopting RPA. Don't think it to be a machine or a robot taking over your task, as some may think. They are non-physical digital robots. They are entrusted with the task of automating a specific task.

Get the implementation of RPA right in an OPEX effort. I know an organization which embarked on RPA implementation across their large finance shared service centres. The initiative was started with a lot of pomp and show. A small team was put in place to make it happen. The efforts were underway for almost a year and a half but reaped little benefits. What came out later was that the team which was driving RPA wasn't clear on the fundamentals to make it happen. They had not only picked the wrong processes but also not addressed issues around audit trails and change management associated with RPA. Finally, they had to abort the programme.

Hence, it is imperative to get a good understanding of what RPA is, what it can do and what it takes to implement it. As a matter of fact, if you are into OPEX, you need to know the basics to ask the right questions and make sure things get done in the right way. Let me share with you some fundamentals of RPA.

WHAT IS RPA?

It is a tool which helps to optimize a business process by using a software (called robots) which automates the tasks done by humans. These software robots mimic what humans do and automate repetitive manual tasks. They take away physical tasks which don't need knowledge, understanding or insight.

This is achieved by codifying rules and instructing the computer or the software to act. They also act as software workflow tool and route the output to the next step in the process. The processes which are taken up don't have the scale or value for a full-blown IT transformation. What RPA does is to improve the efficiency of the processes without their fundamental redesign. What's good about RPA is that it can be done with short time frames and incorporated into legacy systems of the enterprise. Hence, it does not require the eradication of legacy systems; rather, it helps to up their game. It also does not require complex system integration.

What RPA does is to free up humans to do tasks which require emotional intelligence, reasoning, judgement and interaction with customers.

WHAT ARE THE BENEFITS OF RPA?

The following are the benefits of RPA:

- It helps to reduce cost. I have seen cost reduction anywhere between 20 and 40 per cent.

- It enhances the quality and accuracy of a process. Data entry and manual errors also go down.

- It helps to improve cycle times and employee productivity.

- It ensures consistency. The same task is performed time after time every time.

- It enables compliance. Its actions are maintained through activity logs which can be used for subsequent audit trails and can be later monitored and reviewed.

- Employees don't need to do boring repetitive work and can spend time in more engaging work. This positively impacts employee morale.

- It helps to reduce operational risk as the rate of errors goes down.

- Existing IT systems do not need to be changed.

- It eliminates the labour-intensive approach of data extraction, as it interacts with existing systems and extracts data.

- The bots don't take rest, and there are no sick days. They can work 365 days a year.

- It can help to scale up and scale down, as and when required.

- It is relatively inexpensive to implement as compared with other automation technologies and can deliver quick results.

- It helps to reduce lead time of processes.

- It helps to improve business efficiency, effectiveness and data security.

- It can reduce outsourcing, as RPA is comparatively cheaper.

WHAT CAN RPA DO?

The type of tasks which get automated through RPA are as follows:

- Open, read and create mails
- Extract and enter data from and into documents
- Log into enterprise applications
- Move files and folders
- Process and update forms
- Pull data from the internet
- Copy and paste
- Merge, consolidate and archive
- Fill in forms
- Read and write databases
- Obtain human input via mails or workflows
- Make calculations
- Track, monitor and archive
- Format and report
- Download, update and upload files
- Conduct periodic analyses, perform calculations and prepare analytics reports

WHAT PROCESSES ARE CANDIDATES FOR RPA?

All processes are not suitable for RPA. It's important to understand the processes which are best candidates for RPA. The following is the list for you:

- Pick up processes which are highly manual and repetitive processes have high volumes and high frequency and have low exception rate.

- The processes should have repeatable, predictable interactions with IT applications.

- The processes should be rule based wherein decision-making is based on standardized and predictive rules.

- They should be well-defined, documented and stable. They should happen in the same way every time.

- They should have few exceptions.

- They should have an impact on cost and/or revenue.

- They should have issues with delivery of product or service to customers.

- They should require irregular manpower where people need to be hired for to cater to peak demands.

- They can be executed without human intervention

- The triggers and input data to the processes should be in standard electronic format and readable such as Excel, Word, email and readable PDFs. They should work on digital inputs rather than analogue inputs.

- The processes should be stable and not be under any transition or change.

WHERE CAN IT BE APPLIED?

RPA can be applied across functions such as human resource service, finance operations, supply chain, IT services, banking operations, internal audit, tax and information technology.

Examples of processes where RPA can be applied are data entry, payroll, benefits and administration, procure to pay, order to cash, sales order, collections, inventory management, demand planning, batch processing, password unlock, server and app monitoring, IT routine maintenance and monitoring, email processing and distribution, account closure and opening, account audit request, foreign exchange payments, energy consumption and procurement, payment protection measures, data cleansing, data analytics, etc.

Table 28.1. Processes for RPA in Finance, HR and Supply Chain

Finance	Human Resources	Supply Chain
• Customer data management	• Resume screening and shortlisting	• Order processing
• Invoice processing	• Offer letter administration	• Inventory management
• Maintain general ledger master data	• Employee Onboarding	• Automation of emails
• Payment processing	• Employee data management	• Shipment, logistics and transportation management
• Perform fixed asset account	• Induction and training	• Supply and demand planning
• Intercompany transactions	• Attendance tracking	• Customer service
• Legal and external reporting to regulatory bodies	• Payroll	• Selection of vendors
• Receive and compile reimbursement requests	• Travel and expense management	• Onboarding of vendors and partners
• Period-end processing and reporting	• Human resource reporting	
	• Employee exit	

Note: This is a partial list of processes which are amenable to RPA.

Table 28.1 shows examples of processes in finance, human resources and supply chain which is amenable for RPA.

THINGS TO REMEMBER

The following is a list of things which need to be kept in mind while deploying RPA:

- Don't take up a complex process on the first go. Begin with a one. Complexity includes a number of systems involved, frequency of human intervention and number of tasks to execute the task. This will help to understand what RPA can deliver.

- Let a member of C-suite own the RPA implementation so that it gets top management's required focus.

- Embed change management practices, as it would require the employees to adopt to automation and new ways of working.

- Build a centre of excellence which can build, embed and grow RPA capability firm wide. This team develops the business case, calculates the potential benefits (including ROI) and tracks deployment and how they progress against milestones.

- Install a governance mechanism so that the bots can be managed.

- Involve the chief information officer from the very outset, as you would need his help later on.

- Remember the following rules of thumb. A process is a good candidate for RPA when

  - There is a requirement for high-degree consistency and accuracy.

  - Tasks are repetitive and manual .

  - There is a need for data entry, data manipulation and report generation.

  - Data need to be gathered from multiple fragmented systems

- When processes and rules are updated, ensure that the bots are tuned and updated.

- Embed the people strategy with RPA deployment so that employees can be reskilled and redeployed.

- Deploy all RPA efforts through the COE and shun local deployments.

- Make sure that RPA is driven by business imperatives and target multiples metrics such as productivity, speed, quality, regulatory compliance and employee engagement. Don't just implement RPA to reduce the headcount.

- Maximum benefit is reaped when RPA is looked at as a part of larger automation and digitization efforts comprising RPA, artificial intelligence (AI), image recognition, natural language processing, analytics and so on.

ROLES OF RPA CENTRE OF EXCELLENCE

The following are the roles of RPA centre of excellence:

- They own the deployment of RPA in the company.
- They work towards getting enterprise alignment and support
- They look for opportunities for automation through RPA
- They create the business cases for RPA projects
- They govern and manage the RPA projects
- They provide day-to-day support and answer all queries
- They help to create awareness around RPA—what it can do and what it can't. They also provide technical training to users
- They create a communication plan around RPA
- They help to manage change and work with human resources in the deployment of resources
- They provide first-level support for users in the event of malfunctions or minor modifications
- They monitor investments and expected gains

DIFFERENCES BETWEEN ATTENDED AND UNATTENDED BOTS

Attended and Unattended bots operate differenly. Their differences are decided based on the relationship beween the bots and the human operator. Let's demystify them.

Attended Bots

These are bots which work alongside human beings and perform activities based on their request. These are commonly used for front office activities and typically used when full end-to-end processes can't be automated. They are woven into the employee processes.

These are also used in contact centres for answering customer queries. They help in providing order status to customers. They also enable contact centre representatives by providing 360 degree view of customers which include age, profile, past transactions, past queries and so on. They also help in running multiple applications at the same time. This is very useful when a customer calls up a contact centre and the representative needs to look up various applications to respond to customers immediately.

Unattended Bots

They typically execute tasks without the involvement of a human operator. They are triggered by events which can also be scheduled.

The human operator gets involved when some troubleshooting is required.

Used mainly for back office functions, these bots are stored in servers and are used when end-to-end automation has happened.

INTELLIGENT AUTOMATION BY MARRIAGE OF RPA WITH AI

Over the years, service providers are becoming innovative and providing myriad solutions to customers, which combines RPA with AI. This has also been called cognitive or augmented RPA.

Here, the RPA uses AI capabilities such as machine learning and natural language processing. This happens in three ways:

- **RPA output feeding with AI:** RPA produces standard reports, and AI capability helps to add comments.

- **AI triggering RPA action:** The AI module interprets an email sent by a customer and triggers an action which is to be performed by an RPA module.

- **AI and RPA action are combined:** For example, there is an observation software installed on the computer. This mimics the tasks performed by a human operator and can then reproduce them.

RPA does eliminate jobs. This is a challenge which companies have to manage. They have to work towards reskilling employees so that they can transition to new jobs.

REFERENCE

1.   Bornet P, Barkin I and Wirtz J. *Intelligent automation.* Singapore: World Scientific Publishing Company, 2020.

Chapter 29

Embrace Conflict to Solidify Outcomes

Steve was an operations leader or chief of operations. He was responsible for the technology, operations and innovation of a financial services company. His focus was on running banking operations like a factory and ensuring things get delivered fast and cheap to the customers. He embarked on an operational excellence transformation. To achieve this, he brought on board a host of OPEX experts who tirelessly worked on the processes to weed out waste and make them efficient and effective. He also adopted RPA and other myriad technology solutions to make processes better so that they could deliver flawlessly what the customers wanted. He also installed a solid programme management framework to make sure that all the initiatives worked in sync to deliver the outcomes without much noise.

However, one thing he did not encourage was debates and arguments while all these were getting implemented. For him, these were distractions which had to be avoided at all cost. He pushed the idea that debate and arguments derail and delay projects. He was of the opinion that employees have been trained on improvement methodologies such as Six Sigma, Lean and TOC and have been enabled through technology. They have to just follow the relevant structured approach and get results. In any meeting, if anyone challenged any of the recommendations, he would come heavily on them and call them time wasters. Since every project had a coach, his view was that any doubt or disagreement should be taken with the coach beyond the meeting room. He did not want anything which could derail the timelines which he had committed to the CEO.

The OPEX transformation happened; the operations team did see some benefits but clearly it did not deliver the cost/income ratio targets which he had promised to the CEO. As a matter of fact, it came up later that some of the obvious low-hanging solutions had been missed. Many employees observed that they wanted to share it but did not do it because of the fear of being reprimanded. No one wanted to cross the path of the chief of operations for whom conflicts were speed breakers in a journey of OPEX.

I have come across professionals for whom conflicts are a clear taboo. They would go all out to avoid and arrest it. For them, it generates an image of disgruntled employees, frazzled staff and project getting derailed. For them, any form of conflict hurts rather than enabling the employees. They would say that conflict corrodes the workplace, kills trust and impacts employee engagement. These individuals have all the technical qualifications in areas such as Six Sigma, Lean, Agile, TOC and RPA. Their belief is that harmony gets the best results in OPEX.

They are wrong to think that you can get the best by not rocking the boat and just going along. Contrary to what Steve tried to propagate in his team, the OPEX teams should be built on a culture which embraces conflicts. All ideas and points should be passionately argued upon, irrespective of what they are, from where they are and who has raised them. Leaders involved in OPEX need to be comfortable with conflict as it is a powerful engine for better solutions and progress.

Conflict triggers reflection and brings about positive improvements. Divergent thoughts provide an opportunity to explore and find out some original thinking which could be beneficial to the transformation. When there is a conflict in open, everyone is alert and unspoken rules and assumptions get questioned, which makes the ideas and solutions more robust.

CONFLICT DEFICIT AND ITS CAUSES

When conflicts are dodged, deflected, deferred and ducked, the outcome is conflict deficit. This could be as simple as an observation which was not made during a process solutioning exercise or a feedback which was not provided when an automation UAT was underway or not challenging an idea with thoughts which you strongly felt would cause the efforts to fail.

Conflict deficit happens in many ways. The first approach to avoid the conflict is by not raising the issue in a meeting or deflect it by saying that you will discuss it after the meeting by which the issues go off the radar. The second way towards conflict deficit is by avoiding people who will ask the tough question. You go ahead and take the decision without involving those who you think could derail the process. The common strategy adopted here is surrounding yourself with only those people who will agree with you. The third way to conflict deficit is harping in a meeting that relationships are very important and you don't want anyone to raise issues which will spoil them. In turn, you try to bury any potential opposing views which may get surfaced. The fourth approach is that even if a difficult question is asked or someone tries to oppose your idea, you try to get away from the distressing part of the conversation. Just when the crux of the matter is about to be discussed, you take the discussion in a direction which makes people forget it and it is never discussed. The fifth approach to conflict deficit is when a leader forces decisions and actions without taking on board those impacted by it. The leader has a 'I know it all' mindset and wants to get his way on everything. Sometimes the leader is not even aware of the consequence of his actions and actually believes that this is the right thing to do. But without proper buy-in, those impacted or involved in implementation do the work half-heartedly and this throws up in the quality of work. You can never succeed in an operational excellence transformation with a dictatorial leadership style. The sixth reason for conflict deficit is that members don't want to raise issues which can question a person in power as they don't want burn the bridges or fear retribution. The seventh reason for conflict deficit is when members quickly agree with the group and don't share their voices as they fear social rejection and ridicule.

What happens in a conflict deficit workplace is that it stifles innovation. Since divergent views are never discussed, the solutions discussed are often half-baked. And most importantly, it does not help to get buy-in as people's ideas are not taken on board.

TYPES OF CONFLICTS

Figure 29.1 summarizes the types of conflict I have seen in a workplace while on a journey of OPEX.[1]

IDENTIFYING HEALTHY AND UNHEALTHY CONFLICTS

As an OPEX professional, you need to welcome healthy conflicts while shunning unhealthy conflicts. So how do you find about it?

Healthy Conflicts

Healthy conflicts focus on the issue or idea in hand. These are marked by inquisitiveness and bereft of heated emotions. What you see here is an assertive behaviour which is aimed at addressing the idea at hand.[2] The types of voices which you hear are as follows:

- 'Let me push back on this action....'

- 'Have you looked at the idea in this way...?'

- 'The action needs to be solidified with....'

Type of Conflicts	What are they	Example	Recommendation
Relationship Conflict	This happens when people have differences due to inter-personal issues and dislike each other. This happens when there is history of past differences. Both of them feel threatened by each other and tend to harm each other. They make personal attacks that tends to defile the work environment.	Arjun and Dolly have had a history of personal dislikes. During a process transformation review meeting when Dolly shared an idea, Arjun not only debunked it, he went on to make sarcastic remarks on her ability to drive change.	Relationship conflict has no place in a journey of operational excellence. Leaders should come heavily on those who resort to these conflicts.
Task/Issue/ Intellectual Conflict	This happens when people debate, discuss and argue over ideas and tasks & actions in hand. The discussion is based purely on ideas and does not impact their personal relationship. While they debate and argue, they do it in an atmosphere of mutual respect. Such conflicts are a must in problem-solving.	While working on a operational excellence project, Tim makes it a point to hold meetings at regular interval wherein all stakeholder are called in to question and poke holes on the work done so far.	Business leaders should encourage teams to fight, debate & discuss issues at hand. They should remember that when everyone agrees in a group, and there is no conflict, quality of solutions will suffer.
Value Conflict	This happens when there is fundamental difference in values between two people. The value could be around religious beliefs, norms, ethics and so on. While these may not be common in an operational excellence transformation but they do crop up sometimes. They can come up during discussions pertaining to policy design, client etc.	As a part of an operational excellence effort a retailer refused to do business with vendors who had a history of using child labour despite it having some of the finest processes and great set of managers.	To address this issue it helps to sit down with the other person and accurately understand the other's view point.

Figure 29.1. Types of Conflicts

Unhealthy Conflicts

Unhealthy conflicts are personal and tend to demean the person. You shall see finger pointing, hurting feelings and negative emotions. Sometimes unhealthy conflicts can take a passive form, wherein the person shakes head during a meeting but later complains or gossips about it. What you see here is aggressive behaviour, harsh language, sarcasm and a lack of acceptable manners.

The type of conversation which you would hear would be as follows:

- 'You lack insights to drive this project.'
- 'This is another of those sick solutions from Tuhin which never work.'
- 'You think you can deliver this solution? I don't think you have the ability to.'
- 'How can a disorganized person like yourself talk about workplace organization?'

SIXTEEN WAYS TO CREATE A WORKPLACE WHICH ENCOURAGES CONFLICTS

The following is a list of 16 things you can do to build a culture wherein conflicts are embraced:

1. Encourage employees to adopt a 'I don't know' mindset. When they don't know something, they should willingly say, 'I don't know.' By admitting to people that 'I don't know', we can engage in discussion and talk about problems.[3]

2. Kill stereotypes such as 'engineers are better problem-solvers', 'creative people are difficult' and 'technology people are disorganized'.

3. Make the workplace psychologically safe for employees to voice their opinions and engage in disagreements, criticisms and non-defensive behaviours in response to criticism.

4. Proactively call all those impacted by your projects and tell them to poke holes.

5. Tolerate a high degree of conflict so long that it does not turn personal.

6. Practice red teaming, which has been picked from the US Army, and is about role planning the adversary or alternate points of view. It is the practice of rigorously challenging and dissecting plans, policies, systems and assumptions by adopting an adversarial approach. There are two teams who are involved in the process. The red team who play the role of an adversary while blue team which defends the organization. This approach builds capability to challenge plan, operations and organizational capability.[4]

7. Teach people the difference between intellectual and interpersonal conflicts.

8. Educate teams to manage rejection and the art of managing resistance.

9. Come heavily on those executives and managers who indulge in relationship conflicts. Explicitly state that 'playing below the belt' is not allowed.

10. Train the teams to manage their emotions, especially when someone challenges their ideas and the willingness to revisit the idea with a fresh pair of lens.

11. Pair together individuals with different work styles and abilities and tell them to create something meaningful, for example, making a Six Sigma Master Black Belt pair up with a brand manager.

12. Teach employees the listening skills. This is about listening to the others to understand their perspectives and also listening to one's own self to understand one's instincts during difficult situations.

13. Use humour to make people focus on the issue in hand and facts and not get into personal attacks. Share jokes in meetings and use humour to diffuse situations which get personal.

14. Educate employees on assertive communication and how it's different from aggressive communication. Coach them on the art of receiving and giving constructive feedback.

15. Perform a project pre-mortem to identify what can go wrong in a project. This is about imagining that the project has already failed and giving an opportunity to all, especially the dissenters and those who have concerns to speak up.

16. Shun decision spin. This happens when a company's planning and decision-making processes involve a lot of meetings, discussions, committees, PowerPoint decks, emails and announcements, but very few hard and fast agreements.[5]

It is true that all disagreements don't lead to better decisions or actions. However, it sends out a signal to all to be open and think in divergent ways, which can help in better problem-solving. You are not a good leader for operational excellence if you don't encourage those around you to speak their minds, share openly whatever will work and whatever will not, and allow them to openly share their views.

Clearly, I have seen some of best solutions coming from a group which had individuals who didn't think alike. Not surprisingly, Apple was built by two personalities who were very different. Steve Jobs was the visionary salesman, while Steve Wozniak was a great inventor.[6] Their diverse skills complemented each other and went on to build Apple as we know it today.

Best outcomes of OPEX don't come from harmony but when divergent views are brought to the table and vigorously discussed and debated. However, you should know when to encourage a conflict. The following are some of the situations where conflicts should be allowed:

- When an idea is at its infancy
- When doing a root cause analysis
- When solutions to a problem are being discussed
- When action planning is being done
- When working on new policies

- When you have completed brainstorming and want to discuss an idea
- When working on an OPEX road map
- When doing strategic planning
- When deciding on a team and its members
- When deciding on a technology solution

Once things have been agreed, there should not be any room for any more disagreements. Remember that once a path has been chosen, disagreements can be destructive.

Conflicts solidify an OPEX journey. Embrace them to make a meaningful difference.

REFERENCES

1. Shonk K. 3 types of conflict and how to address them. Harvard Law School Blogs, 17 September 2018, https://www.pon.harvard.edu/daily/conflict-resolution/types-conflict/ (accessed 7 February 2021).

2. Davey L. *The good fight: Use productive conflict to get your team and organization based on track.* Vancouver: Page Two Books, 2019.

3. Stackpole B. Why Pixar founder Ed Catmull wants you to 'fail the elevator test'. *MIT Sloan School News*, MIT Management Sloan School, 8 May 2019.

4. Longbine DF. *Red teaming: Past and present monograph.* Fort Belvoir, VA: Defence Technical Information Centre, 2008.

5. Ashkenas R. When an inability to make decisions is actually fear of conflict. *Harv Bus Rev*, 4 June 2014, https://hbr.org/2014/06/when-an-inability-to-make-decisions-is-actually-fear-of-conflict (accessed 7 February 2021).

6. Lovric D and Chamorro-Premuzic T. Too much team harmony can kill. *Harv Bus Rev*, 28 June 2018, https://hbr.org/2018/06/too-much-team-harmony-can-kill-creativity (accessed 7 February 2021).

Chapter 30

Why Employees Don't Follow Processes

Processes are an integral part of all enterprises. They are required for not only executing day-to-day work but also ensuring consistent delivery of products and services to the customers. Instituting processes is also an integral part of an OPEX transformation. If processes don't get embedded properly, the gains will not get sustained. The processes need to be instituted, modelled and followed properly so that the gains are sustained over a period of time. A company cannot remain operationally excellent if processes are not consistently followed and adhered to.

To demonstrate their commitment, they get certifications such as ISO 9001 (Quality Management Systems), ISO 22000 (Food Safety Management Systems), IS0 27001 (Information Security Management Systems) and so on. However, despite all these efforts, there are still countless incidents of employees going rogue and not following them. Sometimes these non-adherences have a detrimental impact on customers, cause regulatory violations and even sully the company's reputation. We've all heard of product recalls, rodents in foods, quality issues in pharma products and what not. One major reason for such failures is employees' non-compliance to processes.

This non-compliance manifests in various ways[1]: not following stipulated steps, skipping steps, accidental omissions, performing activities without authorization, doing additional activities, etc.

Whenever such incidents erupt, the typical reactions of business leaders are to put together a task force, come up with technical reasons (which don't look at human psychology), fire those associated with the process or send employees for training. However, I believe that they could take far more constructive steps if instead of jumping to action they try to understand why employees did not follow the laid-down processes. This will not only give clarity on the right action to take but also ensure that similar cases do not occur in the future. As someone who has been involved with operational excellence over the last 30 years, I can tell you with confidence that addressing the following issues will reduce the incidences of non-compliance.

So following are 10 reasons why employees default in the following processes.

1. **Not believing in processes:** When there is a mismatch between what one believes in and what one is told, it causes an inner conflict or cognitive dissonance. For those not familiar, cognitive dissonance is a mental conflict when the beliefs and actions of an individual don't align. It also occurs when an individual holds two conflicting beliefs. To reduce the mental discomfort, they alter the beliefs or the actions and get back the balance.

When a manufacturing company embarked on implementing a new ordering process, the staff were not keen on adopting it. This is because they believed that the new process would make their life more cumbersome when in reality it was the other way round. This created a dissonance between what they believed in (cognition) and what they were told to do (their actions). This was the reason for employees not following the new process.

This is where communication plays a role to convince people 'why' they need to do what they need to do.

2. **Not seeing the impact of their work on customers:** This is especially true about employees who work behind the scenes in production factories, back offices, warehouses, etc., far away from the sight of the customer. These employees go to work, just do the piece of work entrusted to them and after that they have no connection with the customer's experience. Hence, they could be oblivious of the customer's needs, pains and concerns. Sometimes employees are a bit lax about process adherence because they don't think or realize about their work's impact on customers. Hence, it becomes imperative to tell them that they are doing work not just for the next person in the process but also the end customer. They need to be told how their work impacts the customer who finally pays for the product or service.

3. **Not having a sense of ownership:** When those running the process are involved in its design, they have a sense of ownership. They know that their inputs and concerns have been addressed, take extra care and are more disciplined. This reduces the chances of non-adherence. So next time you dump a process onto an employee and tell him to follow it, remember that his ownership will be minimal and there could be chances of his not following it. Try to design processes in collaboration with employees instead. Also, when those running the process provide inputs on problems and opportunities to make it better, the design team should immediately take it up for action. In case the recommendations are not implemented, it should be communicated to the person who gave the suggestion with clear reasons as to why it was not done.

4. **Thinking they can get away with laxity:** If there's a lack of punitive action against employees who have been careless or have violated processes wilfully, it will embolden other workers to be non-compliant. They will feel that they can also get away with it. Try to institute a culture wherein the employees know that the consequences of not adhering to a process wilfully can be serious. Give them adequate

opportunity to share their concerns about the process. But once it's agreed, make it clear that they need to adhere to it as agreed. What can also be done is to include the outcome of the process in their performance scorecard. When a person is caught not following the desired process, ascertain the reason why it happened. If it's wilful negligence, let the punitive action taken by the organization known to everyone in the team.

5. **They want to innovate:** Sometimes process non-compliance happens when employees want to innovate the existing way of doing work—their behaviour has a positive motive. Nonetheless, while an entrepreneurial mindset is to be encouraged, employees need to be told what is allowed and what is not. If they want to change or better the existing process, it should go through a formal authorization process. Hence, organizations need to install a process for process change.

6. **They are not trained:** When employees are not trained in a process, there can be mistakes. Training people on the process is a critical element for process compliance. Of course, when there are process violations, you will often hear of executives sending their employees for more training as if 'lack of training' is the only cause for process non-compliance. But yes, it is one cause out of many. Training people on processes happens in the classroom and while performing the task. The latter happens with a mentor, who coaches, mentors and guides the actions.

7. **Not seeing the impact on the big picture:** All employees want to do something meaningful and see their work having a positive impact in the company. As we have learnt from Austrian psychiatrist and holocaust survivor Viktor Emil Frankl, if people find meaning in their work, they will go above and beyond to accomplish it.[2]

The worst thing that can happen to an employee is to feel that his work is not meaningful for the company. This can lead to their being disinterested in work and being frivolous with process compliance.

8. **Employees are disengaged:** A Dale Carnegie study found that engaged employees feel enthusiastic, inspired, empowered and

confident. It further found the drivers of engagement to be their relationship with the boss, belief in senior leadership and pride in working for the company.[3] When employees are disengaged, it can lead to process non-adherence. OPEX leaders should understand the drivers of employee engagement. This includes alignment with organization purpose, connect with strategic objectives, trust in leadership, pride in the organization, investment in people development, a good relationship with supervisor, adequate support to do their job, autonomy to do their job, high trust environment, recognition and appreciation and so on.[4]

Engaged employees also challenge the process to make it better with their critical thinking.

9. **Complicated processes:** There is this theory in evolutionary biology which is called principles of least effort. It states that human beings will naturally choose the path of least resistance. The principle was first articulated by Italian philosopher Guillaume Ferrero in an article in 1894, though this was studied in detail by George Kingsley Zipf, who wrote *Human Behaviour and the Principle of Least Effort: An Introduction to Human Ecology*, which was published in 1949.[5] We humans tend to take the option which has the least resistance even if this may not be the best option.

It's human nature to take the path of least resistance. This will include the amount of thought, time, energy, steps, activities or even key strokes which may be required in the process.

So if an operator sees that a process is too complicated, he may try to take shortcuts and do what does not require effort. Humans like to take the path of least resistance, and this may mean violating processes which are too complicated. Hence, process designers should know how the least effort principle is incorporated as a part of designing the process.

What needs to be kept in mind is that if you want people to follow processes, keep these simple and easy to execute. For example, if a process requires a sign-in, make the user signup/login page as seamless and effortless as possible, or using icons instead of a detailed description as the brain processes icons much faster than the description.

10. **Managing deviations demanded by customers:** There may be occasions when employees need to deviate from the laid-down process to meet the demands of internal or external customers. This is definitely supposed to be the norm but an exception. To handle such situations, organizations should also have processes for workarounds or deviations from the normally followed steps. Often these are overlooked as the deviations are far and few. A company aspiring to be operationally excellent should have a process for managing exceptions or process of handling waivers.

REFERENCES

1. Andrade E, van der Aa H, Leopold H, et al. Factors leading to business process noncompliance and its positive and negative effects: Empirical insights from a case study. Twenty-second Americas Conference on Information Systems, 2016, http://www.henrikleopold.com/wp-content/uploads/2016/05/NoncompliancePaper_Camera-Ready.pdf (accessed 8 February 2021).

2. Frankl VE. *Man's search for ultimate meaning*. Ebury Digital, 2011.

3. Sood F. Employee engagement: It's time to go 'all in'. Dale Carnegie, July 2016, https://www.dalecarnegie.com/en/resources/employee-engagement-making-engagement-a-daily-priority-for-leaders (accessed 8 February 2021).

4. Marone M. Every manager's guide to the fundamentals of employee engagement. Dale Carnegie, 5 March 2020, https://www.dalecarnegie.com/blog/managers-guide-to-employee-engagement-strategies-2/ (accessed 8 February 2021).

5. Ferrero G. L'inertie mentale et la loi du moindre effort. *Revue Philosophique de la France et de l'Étranger* 1894; 37: 169–182.

Chapter 31

Perfect Your Brainstorming Techniques

For business improvement professionals, 'ideation' is an integral part of their problem-solving efforts. When I started my journey as an improvement professional in 1991, ideation meant sitting together in a group and being a part of the brainstorming session. The approach followed was always a team sport. What we learnt from the technique was that it is a group process and we need to leverage its power. The other thing that we learnt was that while brainstorming, no one should criticize others' ideas; we should build on others' ideas and the focus should be on quantity. This was meant to be conducted in a group setting of approximately 5–12 people. So if anyone had to ideate, the recommendation or approach taken was to get into a room and do a brainstorming session. I still remember that in the mid-1990s, I used to hear business leaders talking about brainstorming as if it was a panacea for new ideas and problem-solving.

Brainstorming as a concept was not new then. It was introduced by Alex F. Osborn in 1953 in his book *Applied Imagination: Principles and Procedures of Creative Thinking*.[1] Osborne was an advertising professional and had co-founded an advertising agency called Batten, Barton, Durstine & Osborn, Inc. (BBDO). As a matter of fact the agency claimed that the agency generated, in 1956, 34,000 new ideas from brainstorming sessions out of which 2,000 ideas were deemed to be of superior quality and worth investing in. Osborne even claimed that brainstorming produced 50 per cent more ideas versus individuals working on their own. Since its invention, companies the world over have used this tool for generating ideas.

Over the last three decades, I have also used it on a number of occasions. However, one thing that I always felt was that the process delivered much less than what it claimed to deliver. Although I always found the process to be very democratic and it provided an opportunity for a diverse set of people to contribute to an improvement effort, the end promise of brainstorming of getting 'lots of great ideas' always seemed to be illusory. Not only did it deliver a lesser number of ideas, the volume of ideas was never as I would have liked. The outcomes were often banal thought bites and good ideas getting lost in the process. Research done over the last couple of decades has also not found any evidence that brainstorming produces superior ideas or more quantity of ideas. These two were the stated claims of Osborne. As psychologist Adrian Furnham of the University of London mentioned, 'Evidence from science suggests that business people must be insane to use brainstorming groups.'[2]

It was only in the last decade that I seemed to have found the answer. Thanks to the work done by experts such as Leigh Thompson, Adrian Furnham, Susan Cain and Melissa Schilling that we now seem to know why brainstorming does not work.

Following are the reasons.

MYTH ABOUT GROUP

We as humans always believe that groups deliver best results. This emanates from our belief in the power of synergy and cross-pollination. Many workplaces also push this idea that in teams we can get things done. There is nothing wrong with this statement; it's only that we don't qualify it telling that it is contextual. We also tend to believe that whole is great than the sum of the parts which do not work in brainstorming. As psychologist Adrian Furnham said, 'If you have talented and motivated people, they should be encouraged to work alone when creativity or efficiency is the highest priority.' A meta-analytic review done by Brian Mullen et al. of over 800 teams found that individuals are more likely to generate a higher number of original ideas when they 'don't' interact with others.[3] What they also found was that there was productivity loss when brainstorming was done (a) in large teams, (b) in presence of a supervisor and (c) and people spoke out their ideas instead of writing. Research done by Leigh Thompson found that nominal groups outperformed real groups in terms of quantity as well as quality. In one of the studies done by her, the nominal groups generated over 20 per cent more ideas and 42 per cent more original ideas.[4]

Clearly, there is enough evidence to establish that brainstorming in a group does not deliver the results in terms of quality and quantity.

FEAR OF GETTING JUDGED

When people speak out their ideas, they have this fear that they could be judged by others for their competencies. We all would have experienced this in ourselves. When human beings are told that they will be judged during the brainstorming session, they come up with much lesser ideas and much lesser novel ideas. So both the quality and quantity get impacted. This was also established in the research done by Michael Diehl and Wolfgang Stroebe, which found that evaluation apprehension reduced productivity in individual brainstorming.[5]

What actually happens is that for the fear of not getting judged, they tend to self-censor themselves and don't fully open. Their overcarefulness impacts the process of ideation and quality of ideas.

GROUPTHINK

We humans don't want to suggest ideas which others may not agree with. This is because group members want and value harmony and don't want to go against the larger views of the group. As Gregory Berns et al. of Emory University found, when we take a stance different from the group's, we activate the amygdala, a small organ in the brain associated with the fear of rejection.[6] Our body continuously picks sensory data through our eyes, ears, tongue, skin, hands stomach etc. Things work fine till we pick some threat when our amygdala gets activated. It communicates with our body through our nervous system and there is the release of hormones and neurotransmitters to aid in our fight-or-flight response, potentially saving our lives. This even happens when theres is lack of conformity which the brain picks as dangerous. Hence, it appears that our brains consider lack of conformity dangerous. Professor Berns calls this 'the pain of independence'.

This is felt when we remain uninfluenced by the peer pressure and stick to our views. This is the pain of independence in action and one more reason why brainstorming does not give desired outcomes. Hence, people go with the group as they don't want to experience that discomfort.

'DO NOT CRITICIZE' IS A COUNTERPRODUCTIVE STRATEGY

A research done by psychologist Professor Charlan Nemeth, in 2003, at the University of California at Berkeley, found that teams given no instruction about 'do not criticize' perform less than the teams which were instructed to debate on the ideas. They found that teams which were told to debate generated 20 per cent more ideas.[7] What Nemeth concluded was that when people get questioned on their ideas, it stimulates them to engage better and come up with other ideas. The debates push them to reassess their positions and come up with better and newer ideas. So Osborne's thinking that criticism inhibits creative ideas has had a counterproductive impact.

When people are criticized, they think deep within to come up with alternatives which you may not expect.

COGNITIVE FIXATION

This is the phenomenon which happens when people are exposed to other members' ideas and are not able to come up with their own. Research done by Nicholas Kohn and Steven Smith, at the University of Texas at Arlington and Texas A&M University, found that this had an impact on brainstorming. As they wrote in their 2011 paper, 'Exchanging ideas in a group reduced the number of domains of ideas that were explored by participants. Additionally, ideas given by brainstormers conformed to ideas suggested by other participants.' [8] What they also found was that taking a break improved the quality of ideas both in the quantity and variety of ideas. Clearly, cognitive fixation makes people focus on other's ideas and they don't come up with their own.

PRODUCTION BLOCKING

This happens in a brainstorming session when one person is speaking an idea and the other people are not able to provide their creative inputs. This specifcally occurs when only one member is allowed to speak at a time and others are prevented from sharing their ideas. This results in other members forgetting the idea about which they were thinking or they may have got distracted or just that they did not get time to think about an idea. This phenomenon is called production blocking. This may happen more when the size of the group increases.

SOCIAL LOAFING

This is the phenomenon which happens when members put less efforts into a work taken by a group. This occurs as they think that their contribution will not be evaluated. They also do it as they believe that the work which they are doing is not meaningful. They also do it because they believe that there are others in the group who will do it. This is almost like being a bystander. During a brainstorming session, this can manifest as people participating superficially or not thinking enough to come up with quality ideas.

REGRESSION TO THE MEAN

Regression to the mean is the natural tendency of extreme scores to come back to their mean scores. This phenomenon was first observed by a Victorian era polymath, Sir Francis Galton. He wrote about it in 1886 in the *Journal of Anthropological Institute*.[9] He had measured the height of 930 adult children and their parents and calculated the average height of the parents. He noted that when the average height of the parents was greater than the mean of the population, the children tended to be shorter than the parents. Likewise, when the average height of the parents was shorter than the population mean, the children tended to be taller than their parents. Galton called this phenomenon 'regression towards mediocrity', and it is now known as regression to the mean.

Statistically speaking, it means that it's a process by which a measured observation which obtains an extreme value on one assessment will tend to obtain a less extreme value on a subsequent assessment and vice versa.

During brainstorming, even the performance of talented individuals finally matches up with those who are less talented. This is called the tyranny of the average. The quality of ideas that emerge deteriorates.

THE ANTIDOTES

So how do you address some of the concerns mentioned above? What are some of the points which you need to keep in mind when ideating?

Think Individually

Let people think individually. Then let them meet to combine and develop on the ideas. Research done by Donald Taylor, Paul Berry and Clifford Block has shown that letting them think independently and then letting them meet to combine and build on their ideas not only produces more number of ideas, but the quality of ideas is also better.[10] What these researchers found was that group participation inhibits creative thinking.

Brainwriting

This is not a new technique and has been there for some time. The technique of brainwriting which can come handy is the 6–3–5 technique. This requires six people sitting together. They are given a sheet of paper which has three columns and five rows (see Table 31.1). Each one of them first writes three ideas within five minutes. Then each participant passes on the sheet to the next person. The next person builds on the earlier person's ideas or comes up with new ideas. This passing is done five times. You soon get $6 \times 3 \times 5 = 90$ ideas. Then the group can sit together and evaluate the ideas. This approach does not require a facilitator. The creative potential of people from different domains can be explored. Before shortlisting ideas, one needs to look at many ideas. This approach allows this to happen. As a part of the process, it's conveyed in the very beginning that there won't be any evaluation till everyone has generated their ideas. As a result, it does not worry people of getting judged or concern them of their idea being shut down. This process ensures that even people who want a quick close of the ideas need to wait till ideas are developed.

There could be other versions of brainwriting as well.

Table 31.1. Template for 6-3-5 Approach to Brainwriting

Problem Statement: _____

Name	Idea 1	Idea 2	Idea 3
Ted			
Cooper			
Mary			
Satish			
Tom			
John			

Meet to Debate and Criticize Ideas

After the individuals have come up with their ideas separately, let them come together to evaluate those ideas. The objective of this meeting should be to criticize and debate on the ideas that each one of them had brought with them. As we discussed earlier, Charlan Nemeth of the University of California at Berkeley had found that debate and dissent result in not only more number of ideas but also better ideas.

Conflict indicates the diversity of idea. When you debate and dissect ideas, the ideas get strengthened and the medley of different ideas evolves into a strong concept. Debate and discussion are imperative when ideas are being developed. What debate does is that it pushes people to reassess what their ideas are and think deep about them. Also, it forces people to think beyond the obvious and come out with what is not obvious and predictable.

David Burkus in a *Harvard Business Review* article talks about how Alfred Sloan used dissent during decision-making at GM. In one such meeting, where an important decision was being made, he closed the meeting saying, 'Gentlemen, I take it we are all in complete agreement on the decision here?' He then waited for the reaction. When all those present nodded in agreement he said, 'Then, I propose we postpone further discussion of this matter until our next meeting to give ourselves time to develop disagreement and perhaps gain some understanding of what this decision is about.'[11]

Best ideas emerge when teams are brutally critical about them. This only works when team members participating are not worried about the idea to be perfect and don't mind to accept if they were wrong. And when this happens, it reduces the cost of wrong decisions.

Practise Plussing

This is a concept which has been picked from Pixar. While working on movies, they use criticism to build on their work. So anytime someone gives feedback or criticizes others' work, he adds a 'plus'.

In his book, *Little Bets: How Breakthrough Ideas Emerge from Small Discoveries*, Peter Slims gives an example. An animator working on *Toy Story 3* shares her rough sketches and ideas with the director. 'Instead of criticizing the sketch or saying "no," the director will build on the starting point by saying something like, "I like Woody's eyes, and what if his eyes rolled left?"[12]

So what is plussing?

Plussing is a technique which allows people to improve ideas without using a harsh or judgemental language.[13]

Unlike brainstorming where members of the small brainstorming group vote on the best idea, in plussing, no one idea is better than another. Each idea is used to create a better overall idea. So the goal of plussing is that when an idea is criticized, the criticism should contain a plus—a new idea which builds on the flaws of the original idea in a productive manner.[13]

The addition of 'and' opens up possibilities, while usage of 'but' can give a sense of a negative feeling. It can close the person. The focus is to not turn down any idea but see how it can be made better.

Hence, 'Yes, but...' becomes 'Yes, and...' and 'That won't work...' becomes 'What if...'.

Here are a few examples.

Let's talk about a situation wherein an operational excellence leader is reviewing the work of a lean change agent involved in streamlining the factory operations. He does not like much of what has been done. However, he still identifies one aspect of the deployment and uses it to build on his good work instead of confronting what he disliked. In this case, he finds that the lean change agent had done a good job in balancing the load of employees, though he had missed on the critical point of behaviour change which is imperative for sustaining the benefits of technical changes which had been brought about. He then says, 'I like the way you have done the load balancing while streamlining the factory operations and what if we were to see how the mindsets can be used to sustain the change?' The OPEX leader delivers a feedback to build on. The use of 'and' does not imply judgement as the word 'but' would have. This approach opens up the possibilities of discussing this matter further. This is an example of how criticism can be used to make work stronger.

Another example is that while doing an analytics transformation, an individual comes with an idea for data analysis which is incomplete. Your response could be the following: 'I like the way you have done the data analysis and what if we were to do a regression analysis to establish causation?'

In plussing, negative feedback becomes palatable. It's precise, timely and natural so that it does not appear harsh.

While working on a problem, teams can individually come up with ideas and then meet to critique and debate on each other's ideas using the plussing technique.

The principle here is that you criticize only if you have something constructive to say.

The Rule of Yes, But, And

This is another technique which can be there in your toolbox. Proposed by Roberto Verganti and Don Norman, here, one sees the confluence of criticism and ideation. This is how it works. Let's say Deb proposes Idea X and Tim perceives a flaw in it. Tim provides a constructive feedback by saying 'this is good prototype of a dashboard but can we strengthen by .....'. He then follows a way to overcome or avoid the flaw, resulting in Idea Y and this is the 'and'. Deb then does the same. He acknowledges the Idea Y and provides a feedback in the same manner. Deb critiques it and develops it further to get an outcome. Others can jump in the process to share their inputs.

As Roberto Verganti and Don Norman say in their *Harvard Business Review* article, the 'but' anticipating the 'and' is essential.[14] The first step of critique is an opportunity to review inputs on the weakness of the idea which could be half-baked, which Deb could not spot himself in the above example. This forces Deb to delve deeper into the next iteration. The beauty of this approach is that with each iteration, one goes into a deeper analysis.

Office Design

In today's connected world, we don't get time for solitude.

This is further accentuated by the way office spaces are being designed today. Many companies are going in for open-plan offices. There are organizations where hot-desking is quite common. This emanates for companies focus on cost savings. It is also being done because leaders still believe that teamwork is important for creative thoughts and coming to work with innovative solutions.

Somehow this kills the creativity of the workplace. The noises in an open office can be a major source of distraction. In an open office, when so many people are sitting around you, how can you be creative? This is despite this fact that the World Economic Forum has been putting creativity as a key skill for the 2020s.

Tom DeMarco and Timothy Lister in their book *Peopleware: Productive Projects and Teams* talk about how the quality of workplace has an impact on the performance of teams. In their study, they found that more than education and experience, workplace has by far a greater impact on worker's performance. They studied this during their 'Coding War Games', which was used to measure the productivity of different companies. The best performing teams had workspaces which were free of interruption and quiet and had more space for their work.[15]

Essentially, effective workplaces are bigger and quieter and have fewer interruptions.

I have seen shared service centres wherein employees are packed like sardines in an open-pan office. The leaders then expect their teams to be creative. This is a paradox.

So what is the solution? The answer lies in the 'cave and commons' workplace designs, which has both common areas which can pull together for critical face-to-face time and private spaces (caves) where one can work without being interrupted by colleagues walking by or cube chatter. These designs enmesh quiet informality with intense commitment. The design is such that it provides not only opportunities for interactions and cross-pollination of ideas but also plenty of private spaces for the employees.

This approach to workplace design was pioneered in the 1960s by American cognitive and computer scientist Marvin Minsky when setting up a research laboratory at Massachusetts Institute of Technology. He changed the existing office structure to create an open space in a hallway intersection.

This was later popularized by Apple when John Sculley was its chairman (1983–1993).

The company then was facing the problem that computer designers wouldn't come to work. They were not able to concentrate in typical modern offices which had small cubicles in large, wide-open rooms. Hence, they stayed at home to do technical work. What the Apple executives realized was that best ideas are nurtured when there is a feeling of community and the engineers can toss suggestions around at the water cooler. Such suggestions become products. John Sculley was an architect by training. He decided to do something radical. In the 1990s, he decided to open a research and development complex which provided private spaces for each researcher and designer plus common areas for informal meetings. The designs of such offices were such that there were workspaces for tasks requiring high levels of concentration and common areas for team meetings, conversations and discussions.[16]

The advantage of such a workplace design is that people have a common space to meet when there is need and they can also retreat into the caves for generating ideas. As Leigh Thompson, professor at the Kellogg School of Management at Northwestern University, mentions in a *Harvard Business Review* article,

> Every organization needs the right balance of caves and commons—and what that precise balance depends on what the organization's particular goals and challenges are, and more

granularly, what the immediate situation of a work team is. The overarching truth is this: there is no question that physical distance creates barriers to communication. However, constant co-habitation can decrease performance, particularly when people are working on creative tasks.[17]

As Leigh Thompson says in the book *Creative Conspiracy: The New Rules of Breakthrough Collaboration*, 'True collaboration often calls for periods of focused, independent work interspersed with periods of intense, structured team interaction.'[18]

Ambient Noise

Research work of Ravi Mehta et al. has shown that moderate levels of ambient noise enhance the performance in creative tasks.[19] A noise level of 70 dB was found to be suitable versus a low noise level of 50 dB or high noise level of 85 dB. Both low and high noise levels hurt creativity. What the researchers found was that moderate noise levels induce a higher construal level which promotes abstract processing, and this leads to higher creativity. When noise levels are high, it reduces information processing and thus impacts creativity.

Begin Ideation Session with an Embarrassing Story

Next time you are ideating in a group, this strategy can come handy. Before beginning the session, let the members share a recent embarrassing story. Research done by Elizabeth Wilson, Leigh Thompson and Brian Lucas of Kellogg School of Management have found that teams which shared embarrassing stories generated 26 per cent more ideas and wider variety of ideas than groups which shared stories of pride and achievement.[20]

Embarrassing stories let creative juices flow.

Sharing embarrassing stories reduces concerns about the future embarrassment of ideas not being up to the mark. What also happens when people share their embarrassment is that they are liked by others. This leads to more trust among team members. This improves the quality of ideation. Contrary to that, when participants begin the session with their success or brag stories, it boosts their confidence. But this has a negative effect. They tend to self-censor, as they don't want to look bad after their story of great accomplishment.

After reading about the above research, I have tried this technique for ideation sessions with senior management and the other with a research and development team. Compared to similar sessions which I had done earlier, I found this technique also to deliver great results.

Next time you come across some leader who tells a team to be themselves in a room and brainstorm* all possible ideas for solution, you know he is getting it wrong. Always remember that the way we have brainstormed is not the best way to ideate.[21]

REFERENCES

1. Osborne FA. *Applied imagination: Principles and procedures of creative problem-solving.* New York, NY: Charles Scribner's Sons, 1953.

2. Furnham A. The brainstorming myth. *Bus Strat Rev* 2000; 11(4): 21–28.

3. Mullen B, Johnson C and Salas E. Productivity loss in brainstorming groups: A meta-analytic integration. *Basic Appl Soc Psychol* 1991; 12(1): 3–23, https://www.tandfonline.com/doi/abs/10.1207/s15324834basp 1201_1?journalCode=hbas20 (accessed 8 May 2021).

4. Greenfield R. Brainstorming doesn't work; try this technique instead. Fast Company, 29 July 2014, https://www.fastcompany.com/3033567/brainstorming-doesnt-work-try-this-technique-instead (accessed 8 February 2021).

---

* Research show that groups brainstorming electronically, when properly managed, do better than individuals; the larger the group, the better it performs. The same is true of academic research—professors who work together electronically, from different physical locations, tend to produce research which is more influential than those either working alone or collaborating face to face.

5. Diehl M and Stroebe W. Productivity loss in brainstorming groups: Toward the solution of a riddle. *J Person Soc Psychol* 1987; 53(3, September): 497–509.

6. Berns GS, Chappelow J, Zink CF, et al. Neurobiological correlates of social conformity and independence during mental rotation. *Bio Psych* 2005; 58(3, August): 245–253, https://www.sciencedirect.com/science/article/abs/pii/S0006322305004634 (accessed 8 February 2021).

7. Charlan JN, Personnaz M, Personnaz B, et al. The liberating role of conflict in group creativity: A cross cultural study. IRLE Working Paper No. 90-03, 2003, http://irle.berkeley.edu/workingpapers/90-03.pdf (accessed 8 February 2021).

8. Kohn NW and Smith SM. Collaborative fixation: Effects of others' ideas on brainstorming. *Appl Cog Psychol* 2011, https://onlinelibrary.wiley.com/doi/full/10.1002/acp.1699 (accessed 8 May 2021).

9. Galton F. Regression towards mediocrity in hereditary stature. *J Anthropol Inst* 1886; 15: 246–263.

10. Taylor DW, Berry PC and Block CH. Does group participation when using brainstorming facilitate or inhibit creative thinking? *Adm Sci Q* 1958; 3(1, June): 23–47.

11. David B. How criticism creates innovative teams. *Harv Bus Rev*, 22 July 2013, https://hbr.org/2013/07/how-criticism-creates-innovati (accessed 8 February 2021).

12. Slims P. *Little bets: How breakthrough ideas emerge from small discoveries* New York, NY: Free Press, 2011.

13. Lehrer J. *Imagine: How creativity works*. New York, NY: Houghton Mifflin Harcourt Publishing Company, 2012.

14. Verganti R and Norman D. Why criticism is good for creativity. *Harv Bus Rev*, 16 July 2019, https://hbr.org/2019/07/why-criticism-is-good-for-creativity (accessed 8 February 2021).

15. DeMarco T and Lister T. *Peopleware: Productive projects and teams*. 3rd ed. Upper Saddle River, NJ: Pearson, 2013.

16. Markoff J. Where the cubicle is dead. *The New York Times*, 25 April 1993.

17. Thompson L. Give workers the power to choose: Cave or commons. *Harv Bus Rev*, 27 March 2013, https://hbr.org/2013/03/give-workers-the-power-to-choose-cave (accessed 8 February 2021).

18. Thompson L. *Creative conspiracy: The new rules of breakthrough collaboration*. Boston, MA: Harvard Business Review Press, 2013.

19. Mehta R, Zhu R and Cheema A. Is noise always bad? Exploring the effects of ambient noise on creative cognition. *J Consum Res* 2012; 39(4, December): 784–799, https://doi.org/10.1086/665048 (accessed 8 May 2021).

20. Wilson, ER, Thompson L and Lucas B. Pride and pratfalls: Recounting embarrassing stories increases creativity. *Int J Des Creat Innov* 2020; 8(1), https://www.tandfonline.com/doi/abs/10.1080/21650349.2019.1662735 (accessed 8 May 2021).

21. Business Insider. What's the optimal size of a creative brainstorming group? n.d., https://www.google.com/amp/s/www.businessinsider.com/whats-the-optimal-size-of-a-creative-brainstorming-group-2012-8%3famp (accessed 8 February 2021).

Chapter 32

Strategies for Behaviour Change

Many OPEX transformations fail not because of deficiency of tools and methods but because they fail to change human behaviour. Changing human behaviour is required whether it's an internal customer (employee) or external customers and consumers who finally consume your product. As a matter of fact, behaviours are the unseen forces which decide the success and failure of a transformation. For example, while catalysing an OPEX transformation in insurance operations, one of the underlying foundations was how effectively the new ways of working were embedded in the company. Or let's talk about a transformation which focuses on increasing revenue from high-net-worth customers of a bank. While you work on processes, automation solution and capability building, there is one more thing which you need to do. You need to work on influencing customer behaviour. This is where the solutions need to be designed for behaviour change.

Hence, it helps to understand the basics of human change.

What I talk about here is based on the work of Daniel Kahneman, Robert Cialdini, Stephen Wendel, B. J. Fogg, Daniel Pink, Nir Eyal, Charles Duhigg, Richard Thaler, Dan Ariely and many others whose names have been included at the end of the book.

What are behaviours?

Behaviours are actions from a person in response to the external stimuli or the immediate environment.

Probably, the biggest issue before OPEX leaders is how to make behaviour stick.

To understand behaviour, we need to appreciate how our mind decides what to do next and what actions to take. We need to refer to the work done by Daniel Kahneman.[1] We have two ways in which we do our thinking. They are called System 1 and System 2 thinking. These are the two ways in which we process information. Our everyday decisions are carried out by one of them. They are elaborated as follows:

- **System 1:** It is the intuitive or emotional mode of thinking. It is fast and automatic. These are unconscious actions and generally not aware of how it happens. System 1 uses rules of thumb and past experiences to instantly give an assessment of a situation. It is executed without much effort. This is also done when there is a constraint of time. It typically occurs under HALT (hungry, angry, tired and late) or when someone is under the condition of illness and emotional distress.[2]

  It works well when the situation is familiar but prone to errors in unfamiliar situations. Here, we use our emotions and sensations, which often is called are 'gut feeling'. So when one says that they decided something through 'gut feeling', it means it's a System 1 thinking.

- **System 2:** This is a deliberate, analytical and rational approach to thinking. We take time to execute this and are conscious about what we are doing. It requires effort and is used for a complex situation. The outcomes are reliable. It is typically used when we want to decide on something big and something which may not be familiar.

System 2 is mobilized when System 1 does not provide an answer. They can work independent of each other and can even disagree with each other. They can also happen in parallel.

The bulk of our everyday decisions are done through System 1 thinking.

So what are the mechanism that the mind uses to make the decisions which are a part of System 1 and System 2 thinking. These are summarized in Figure 32.1.

Any new behaviour starts with System 2 thinking, which is deliberate decision-making which happens in the pre-frontal cortex of the brain. This is the goal-directed system for new and infrequent behaviours. They are guided by attitude, goals and value. Once the behaviour is learnt, the action is pushed to the basal ganglia, which is the more primitive part of the brain. These don't require thought and are guided by cues, triggers, heuristics and experience.

What needs to be remembered is that most of our behaviours and 'what to do next' happen without ours being conscious about it. They happen intuitively, though there are occasions when they are an outcome of conscious thinking. In such cases, our mind takes control of our behaviour and forces us to do things which could be habitual.

System 1	System 2
• Habits • Intuitive response • Self-concept • Heuristics	• Conscious focus / Deliberate Thinking

Figure 32.1. Mechanisms to Make Decisions

TOOLS MIND USES FOR ACTIONS

The following are the tools which our mind uses to drive our actions:

1. Our habits
2. Intuitive responses
3. Self-concept
4. Heuristics
5. Conscious Focus/Deliberate thinking

1. Habits

Habits are repeated learned patterns of behaviours which are trigged by the context. They are automatic, unconscious and responses to specific cues or triggers. They happen subconsciously and the person may even not be aware that he has got it within himself.

Habits are a huge part of our lives. As per the research done by Wood, Quinn and Kashy, around 45 per cent of human behaviour can be considered habitual in the sense that actions are repeated daily or almost daily in the same physical setting and with little or no conscious thought.[3]

Habits are built in one of the two ways. The first approach is when there is a cue and you do a certain routine. When you repeat this, the habit gets formed. For example, when you come home from the office (cue), you keep your laptop at a specific place (routine). And this you do without thinking every day.

Cue ————> Routine

The second approach to habit formation is when a third dimension of 'reward' gets added up. The reward at the end of the routine makes us repeat the behaviour. For example, you are walking in a shopping mall and get the smell of coffee (cue), you get into a Starbucks for a cup of cappuccino (routine) and then enjoy the outcome of the flavour of a coffee (reward).

Cue ————> Routine ————> Reward

Many OPEX efforts fail because of failure to adopt new habits or change the ones which are there. It's important to remember that behaviours may find difficult to stick if they are not translated to habits.

There are a few things which we need to remember as far as habits are concerned. These are discussed further.

Changing Habits Is Not Easy

Once a habit is formed, it rewires the brain to a certain stimulus and response. It happens automatically without the person even realizing it. Research work done by Webb and Sheeran has found that intention to change behaviour has little relationship to actual behaviour change.[4] The other reason is that habits never go away. Once they are formed, they don't really get undone. What really happens is that it lies hidden within a person. However, if exposed to the right context, the habit reappears.

Habits Make Behaviour-building Easy

When behaviours are changed by building habits, it becomes easy to adopt. When behaviours are converted to habits, it is easy to execute as the conscious mind does not need to bother on how it's to be done. This is because when our conscious mind is required for taking an action, it may not take hold. When behaviours are changed by building habits, the mind does not need to think about them. It becomes automatic. The mind makes it habitual.

Habits Need a Trigger

The habits would need a cue or a trigger. We have already discussed it earlier. The cue could be of various types. Some of its examples are as follows:

1. **Time:** Our cues can get triggered by a certain time of the day, for example, automatically reaching out for the kettle every morning for making a cup of tea.

2. **Context:** The cue can be triggered by a context. For example, placing a sanitizer at the entrance of a workplace can nudge people to use it when entering the office.

3. **Object:** The cue can get triggered by an object. For example, seeing sneakers may make you think about running.

4. **Sound:** The cue can be a certain sound which brings back memories of a certain habit.

5. **Person:** Habits can be triggered by a person. For example, when an OPEX team started being led by a leader who had a reputation of no-nonsense approach, the team members started closing actions on time.

6. **Intrinsic reasons:** These include things which happen internally within us such as hunger and thirst.

Habits Need To Be Repeated

For a behaviour to become a habit, it needs to be done repeatedly. A 2009 research by Phillippa Lally et al. at Behaviour Research Centre found that it took anywhere between 18 and 254 days to develop a new habit.[5] The average time was 66 days.

Habits Begin with Deliberation

Any habit begins with conscious deliberation, and this happens in the pre-frontal cortex area of the brain. This is where System 2 thinking happens. But as we practise and repeat a behaviour, the habit system of the brain which is the basal ganglia becomes engaged and takes increasing control of the behaviour.[6] The habit system of the brain is not responsive to motivation, goals and long-term rewards. Instead, it's cue-driven, which learns through repetition or a certain sequence. Once it forms a part of memory, we don't need to engage with the pre-frontal cortex. All this happens without any one even being aware that a behaviour has become a habit.

2. Intuitive Responses

There are behaviours which get triggered by our past experiences and associations. So when we are in a familiar and semi-familiar state, our reactions can get triggered based on a previous experience. For example, a friend of mine became gloomy when he heard anything about Irish explorer Ernest Shackleton. This is because he would hear about him from his previous boss with whom he had a terrible experience and who bullied him. This is also true when you see a customer seeing a new product; he may automatically judge it based on his past associations and experiences which he may not even be conscious about. Hence, for product designers, it's important to understand the past experiences and associations of users so that there are no surprises later.

3. Self-concept

Self-concepts are facets of ourselves, which are built in different situations and contexts. We have different self-concepts and mindsets for home, office, club, when among friends, etc. Each of the contexts triggers different behaviours. Self-concepts can also be looked as self-narratives about who we are and what we stand for. There could be situations when we may respond to the world by asking a simple question: 'Is this something that aligns with whom I am?' Everyone has multiple self-concepts which get triggered based on cues in our environm:nt. The takeaway for behaviour change is understanding the mindset which people are in and can help us to approbate how they will respond to a situation. Hence, if you are able to activate the right self-concept, it can trigger the right behaviour. Behaviour change experts sometimes need to work on changing how a person sees himself.

4. Heuristics

As we saw earlier, our mind does not do conscious work on most of the occasions. Habits and intuitive responses are ways that prevent our mind to do conscious work. There is another way which prevents the mind to do conscious work and that is through shortcuts called 'heuristics'. A heuristic is a mental shortcut which allows an individual to make a decision, pass a judgement or even solve a problem without much mental work. They work well in certain situations, while in others they can let you go on a wrong path. These heuristics trigger our actions in myriad ways, for example, a simple message from a retailer that a certain product is available for only one day and in a limited quantity. We take the help of 'scarcity heuristic' and make ourselves value the product more and we run after it. So when there are difficult problems, our mind looks for ways to solve those easily and one way is these heuristics.

5. Conscious Effort/Deliberate Thinking

This is about consciously deliberating before taking a decision and actions. This typically happens when situations are unfamiliar and an important decision is to be taken. We humans have a limited capacity for conscious attention. We only bring our conscious attention into focus when we are working on something which is important or there is something unusual. While doing so, we do the required cost–benefit calculation.

STRATEGIES FOR BEHAVIOUR CHANGE

Various experts have suggested various approaches to behaviour change. What I share here has been learnt from the works of David Neal, Stephen Wendel and B. J. Fogg. The first six strategies are from Dr David Neal's work.[7]

Ensure Stable, Supportive Environment

Having a stable and supportive environment is a must for habit formation. If the environment is not created for the desired habit, even with the best of intention the person will struggle. The environment comprises (a) physical setting, (b) product environment and (c) action sequence. The physical setting should be stable and not change. The product environment refers to whether the product or supplies are present at the same location every time. On the action sequence, whether there are predefined steps into which the behaviour can be embedded.

For example, when a food company was undergoing a quality transformation, one of the focus areas was ensuring lower microbiology levels in the food product. Towards this, one step was inculcating the habit among shop-floor workers to wash their hands properly before getting into the plant. This was achieved by placing hand wash basins which were created at the entry of the shop floor (this is a stable physical setting which does not change). At each of the basins, soap dispensers were placed so that employees don't struggle with soap (adequate product supply). There was also a dryer for people to dry their hands. Then the workers were taught the sequence which they needed to follow which comprised the following:

Wet your hands —> Lather your hands with liquid soap from the dispenser —> Scrub for 20 seconds —> Rinse your hands —> Dry your hands under the dryer. (This is an example of an action sequence.)

Leverage the Context!

This is about leveraging the existing context and comprises the following: (a) leveraging disruption in context and (b) piggybacking on existing behaviour.

Disruption

When there is a disruption in the context, the existing routines get impacted. They are not as automatic as earlier. This could be due to a change of home or a life event such as the birth of a child, marriage and a new job. For example, a banking operations team had a process adherence issue with an existing team. When the leader of the team replaced part of the team with a new set of people, the process adherence levels increased. Research done by W. Wood, L. Tam and M. G. Witt in 2005 found that when people have recently moved from one home to another, they are more successful at implementing desired health behaviours.[8] Or it could be a pandemic like COVID-19 when people were locked at home and their habits had to change on how they buy things or how they do banking, both of which had to be digital options. Those who were uninitiated to online options had to adopt them for survival.

Piggybacking

This is about bolting new habits into existing behaviour and routine. Here, it helps to mentally connect the new behaviour to the performance with that of another behaviour. For example, embedding the practice of having multi-vitamin tablets after breakfast works, as it ensures you don't forget it.

Make It Simple

If you want people to adopt a certain habit, make it easy for them. To make this happen, the focus should be on removing all the frictions and impediments. It's important that people should perceive that the new behaviour is easy to perform. So the typical frictions which should be eliminated are as follows:

- Reduce the number of decision points before they can start with their new behaviour.
- Bring down the number of steps to execute the new behaviour.
- Reduce the perceived effort to do the routine. For example, in Shanghai, to encourage citizens to avoid taking the car, there are cycles kept all across the city which citizens can pick and use for going from one place to another.

Have you ever wondered why buying on Amazon has become a habit? It's because of their easy process and one-click ordering. Customers can at once enter their billing, shipping and payment information and buy anything going forward. Once the patent around 'one-click' button for ordering ended in 2017, it has is being other e-commerce companies.

Cues and Rewards

We have discussed this earlier. We need to remember two things here. Setting a rule such as 'if X, they do Y' helps. For example, if flossing is something you forget at times, you can set a routine which could be 'if brushing, they do floss'. The other thing to be kept in mind as mentioned earlier is that rewards also play a role. For example, during the pandemic, one rewards for children to wash their hands at regular frequency was a pleasant smell on the skin after the wash.

Practise and Repeat

Habits get solidified through practice and repetition. We don't learn things by observing them. They get ingrained through practice. Learning a problem can happen through verbal instruction but if you have to form a habit, it can only form by actually doing it repeatedly. We need to remember that we can understand things by reason (just like maths) that does not engage with the habit system of the brain which is the basal ganglia.

Companies have to provide opportunities to employees and customers to practise the new behaviour. It's not surprising that companies are coming up with experiential stores for trying new products.

Build Meaning and Motivation

Sometimes it may help going beyond cue–routine–reward and give meaning to the efforts. What may help if we give a deeper meaning to the proposed habit change? This gives clear purpose, and the person can identify it. This is especially suitable where a person's newly formed habit is turning weak. For example, if a person wants to go out for a jog every morning to reduce weight, he does it for some time and starts losing interest. Here, carving it around a deeper meaning can help. For example, anchoring it around physical health and happiness can be very helpful. These additional reasons help to not only keep the motivation level but also embed the habit further.

Ability

Ability is an important enabler in behaviour change. It has been defined differently by different thought leaders, and we shall see some of them later in this chapter. Ability refers to whether one is able to take the desired action. I am summarizing here the four dimensions of 'ability' as recommended by Stephen Wendel[9]:

- **Action plan:** This refers to the steps which are required to take the action.

- **Resources:** The person must have the resources required to act. These include money, material and other resources.

- **Skills:** The person must have the necessary skills to act.

- **Belief in success:** This is about self-efficacy. The person should feel that he shall be successful at the action.

What's important for behaviour change for OPEX is to have a clear 'how to do', possess the required capability and also provide the required resources.

Timing

This is about creating the required sense of urgency so that people work on the desired behaviour change. As recommended by Stephen Wendel, there are four ways how the sense of urgency can be created for behaviour change:

- **External pressure:** Here, an external agency pushes an entity or an individual to adopt a creation behaviour. For example, businesses in India need to file GST (goods and services tax) returns on a regular basis or else they can be penalized.

- **Internal pressure:** This could be because of biological and personal reasons which force us to act and include things such as hunger, thirst, boredom and stress. For example, the stress emanating from staying at home during the current pandemic has forced people to exercise at home.

- **Specific objective:** This is driven by putting time-based objective on oneself to act on something. For example, a person may say, 'I need to complete the presentation' versus 'I need to complete the presentation by 8 pm on 25th June'. The latter drives sharper actions.

- **Consistency:** This happens when we want to stay true to what we have committed in the past. This is especially true if our commitment has been to others. In that case, we would like to be consistent with our prior proclamations. Hence, when we publicly commit to something, we go out of the way to adhere to it.

Behaviour change is an integral part of all OPEX transformation. Often, transformations fail not because of gaps in the structure or methodology but because the desired behaviour change has not taken place. The above strategies can come in handy.

MODELS FOR BEHAVIOUR CHANGE

The following models can be adopted for behaviour change.

B-MAT Model

This model was proposed by D. J. Fogg of Stanford University. It says that for behaviour change to happen, we need motivation, ability and trigger. All the three need to converge at the same moment to make this possible. If behaviour change is not happening, one of the three elements is missing.

$$\text{Behaviour} = \text{Motivation} \times \text{Ability} \times \text{Trigger (B = MAT)}$$

Motivation includes pleasure/pain, hope/fear, acceptance/rejection, etc. Ability is how to execute the do. Triggers are prompts to act. We will look at them in detail later.

In this model, ability and motivation can be traded off. What this means is that if the ability is high, people may overcome low motivation to do a task. Similarly, if motivation is high, people are willing to overcome the shortcomings in the ability. Just motivating a person will not make him act on something. Similarly, just having an ability will not make a person act on a behaviour. What the model does is that it tells you why people are not performing the behaviour which you want them to perform.

As you can see from Figure 32.2, if someone does not want to carry out the desired behaviour change, he has low motivation. And if it is very hard to do, the person has low ability. If you are on lower left hand side of the model, nothing will happen. So our focus should be

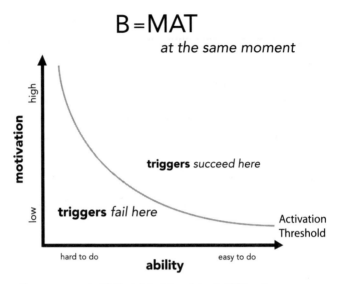

B=MAT

at the same moment

triggers *succeed here*

triggers *fail here*

Activation Threshold

motivation — high / low

ability — hard to do / easy to do

Source: Groenewegen A. BJ Fogg Model explained. SUE, n.d.,
https://suebehaviouraldesign.com/bj-fogg-model (accessed 9 February 2021).

Figure 32.2. Fogg's Behaviour Model

on making it easy for the person which means increasing his ability.
Any triggers placed on the right hand side of the threshold will lead
to behaviour change; triggers on the left hand side will probably show
no behaviour change. When a combination of motivation and ability
places a person above the activation threshold, then a trigger will
cause that person to perform the target behaviour. If the person is
placed below the activation threshold, then a trigger will not lead to
target behaviour. Motivation and ability are inversely related. When
things are easy to do (i.e., you have high ability), you need less
motivation. On the other hand, when things are hard (i.e., you have
low ability), you need more motivation.[10]

Let's understand each of the elements in detail.

Motivation

According to Fogg, motivation is a key element in behaviour change.
When motivation levels are high, you can make people do difficult

things.[11] As motivation plummets, people can only do easy things. There are three broad areas of motivation.

- **Sensation**
  This motivation pertains to pleasure and pain.

- **Anticipation**
  This involves the feeling of fear and hope. Fear is related to some sort of loss which could be health, wealth, looks, etc. Hope is related to something good happening in future. According to B. J. Fogg, hope is the most ethical and empowering motivator.

- **Social Cohesion**
  This pertains to social acceptance and rejection. We are motivated to do things which gain us social acceptance such as acceptance by peers, friends and society at large. Something which gives us a sense of belongingness can be a great motivator. People are also motivated to avoid any negative consequences which will lead to them being socially rejected.

Ability

If you look at Figure 32.2, 'ability' is on the X-axis. It moves from 'hard to do' (difficult) to 'easy to do' (simple). One way to make people do a certain behaviour is to make them enhance their ability through training. But Fogg believes that people are lazy; hence, it's more about making the behaviour easier to do. In other words, make things easier. So instead of focusing on trying, focus your efforts on making things easier.

The model talks about six different factors which contribute to ability. They are as follows.

- **Time**
  If the target behaviour requires time and there is scarcity of time (as we are busy or in rush), we are less likely to do that behaviour.

- **Money**
  When people have limited financial resources and the target behaviour costs money, they are not likely to carry out the behaviour.

- **Physical Effort**

  If a behaviour takes a lot of physical energy such as walking a long journey to buy a product or service, people are not going to take actions.

- **Mental Effort**

  If a behaviour needs a lot of cognitive effort, we are less likely to take actions. We are less likely to engage with the behaviour also when our minds are consumed in something else. This also includes whether we believe we can do it. As we have learnt from Daniel Kahneman, we are as it is trying to cut our cognitive load.

- **Social Deviance**

  If the target behaviour is against the norms of the society, it will not be adopted.

- **Habit/Routine**

  If the behaviour is a part of the existing routine, we are more likely to do it. If the new behaviour is not a part of the routine, we may not do it. For example, a person may stick to the existing routine of going to the bank and not adopt a digital solution provided by them.

Trigger

This is the cue or the call to action for someone to act on a behaviour. There are three types of triggers which nudge someone to act on a behaviour.

- **Spark**

  This trigger is applied when there is high ability and low motivation for the target behaviour. Here, the target has to be designed using motivational elements. The type of things which can be looked at are the benefits of doing the behaviour, drawing on emotions such as fear, approval from colleagues, etc. For example, the deadly impact of COVID-19 has been sufficient to make people wash their hands on a regular frequency.

- **Facilitator**

  This trigger is used when there is high motivation and low ability to do the target behaviour. The focus here is on simplifying the task, making it easy to do or making something free and even making it cognitively easy. For example, if you are trying to eat healthy food but are struggling, a weekly newsletter which has easy-to-make recipes for a healthy meal can be of help. We can go through it and plan our weekly meals. Another example is Amazon's 'one-click' option. The other example could be contactless payment options in retail stores which make it easy for customers to check out.

- **Signal**

  This is applied when both motivation and ability are high. For example, the micro-nudges we get on social media and WhatsApp.

The B = MAT model provides an elegant approach for behaviour change. It is more applicable for persuasion using moment triggers. However, if you are looking at a strategic application the COM-B model is better. Let's understand this model.

COM-B Model

This is another model which can help in behaviour change as a part of OPEX transformations. This model was proposed by Susan Michie, Maartje M. van Stralen and Robert West of Centre for Behaviour Change, University College London, in 2011.[12] The model proposes that 'behaviour' is a result of 'capability', 'opportunity' and 'motivation'.

Capability

This refers to whether we have the knowledge, skills and abilities required to engage in a particular behaviour. This comprises the following.

- **Physical Capability**

  This is about physical skills and ability to execute the desired behaviour.

- **Psychological Capability**
  This is about having effective mental processes to carry out the desired behaviour. This includes knowledge, cognitive ability, interpersonal skills and someone's ability to self-regulate or control one's behaviour.

Motivation

This refers to what might energize us to do the targeted behaviour. This has two sub-elements.

- **Reflective Thought**
  This is about consciously thinking whether to do the behaviour or not. This includes how it is linked to one's identity and beliefs.

- **Automatic Response**
  This pertains to how our habits, impulses, inhibitions and emotional responses impact the targeted behaviour.

Opportunity

This refers to the physical and social environment which supports the behaviour or makes it possible. This includes prompts from the environment.

- **Physical Opportunity**
  This includes availability of desired facilities and services, triggers, layout and design which can influence the behaviour. For example, to make customers do more digital transactions, it's imperative that there is easy availability of Wi-Fi.

- **Social Opportunity**
  This includes how the people around look at the desired behaviour. Who are people modelling the behaviour and is there a social approval for the behaviour of those around? Is there any cultural ethos which can drive or inhibit the behaviours?

Susan Michie et al. recommend full range of intervention types which include education, persuasion, incentivization, coercion, training, restriction, environment restructuring, modelling and enablement.[13]

Table 32.1. Intervention Types

Education	Increasing knowledge and understanding by informing, explaining, showing and providing feedback
Persuasion	Using words and images to change the way people feel about a behaviour to make it more or less attractive
Coercion	Changing the attractiveness of a behaviour by creating the expectation of an undesired outcome or denial of a desired one
Training	Increasing the skills needed for a behaviour by repeated practice and feedback
Restriction	Constraining performance of a behaviour by setting rules
Environment Restructure	Constraining or promoting behaviour by shaping the physical or social environment
Modelling	Showing examples of the behaviour for people to imitate
Incentivization	Changing the attractiveness of a behaviour by creating the expectation of a desired outcome or avoidance of an undesired one
Enablement	Providing support to improve ability to change in a variety of ways not covered by other intervention types

Source: Michie S, Atkins L and West R. *The behaviour change wheel: A guide to designing interventions.* 1st ed. London: Silverback Publishing, 2014.

We shall see how it can be used in our OPEX effort (Table 32.1).

Road Map

So how does one go about changing behaviours. Here's a road map which can be followed, which has been adapted from Michie's work (Table 32.2).

To ascertain the relevance and applicability of an intervention use the APEASE criteria. It can also be used to structure the intervention so that the deployment is done in a flawless manner.

Table 32.2. A Road Map to adopt the COM B Model

Steps	Activity	Details
Step 1	Target behaviour	Identify the targeted behaviour which you want to change or embed in the enterprise.
Step 2	Do a COM assessment	Do an assessment on capability, opportunity and motivation. Identify which of the three to target to get desired change
Step 3	Intervention matrix	Select the intervention type from the list which has been proposed by Susan Michie et al. as mentioned in Table 32.1.
Step 4	Prepare the hows	Specify the intervention on how it can be delivered. When deciding on the type of intervention use the APEASE framework.
Step 5	Action plan	Come up with a detailed action plan on who will do it, when will it happen and resources required.
Step 6	Implementation	Implement the actions in the plan.

A Acceptability = How far is it acceptable to the stakeholders

P Predictability = Can it be implemented at scale within the intended context, material and human resources?

E Effectiveness = How effective is the intervention in achieving the objectives?

A Affordability = How far it be afforded in the intended scale?

S Side-Effects = What are chances that it will result in unintended negative or positive side-effects?

E Equity = How far can it be equitably applied across the various hierarchies of the company?

Usage of the COM-B and B-MAT Models

Having gone through the two models, you must be wondering where they are applicable.

The B-MAT model should be used for a specific point of solution in a context. The examples are as follows:

- Enhancing adoption of self-service in a bank
- Improving adoption of an app by customers
- Improving usage of a new payment solution by employees
- Increasing use of gymnasium by employees.
- Enabling mortgage customers to pay on time

The COM-B model should be used when behaviour change is being looked at as a strategic agenda. The applications could be as follows:

- Embedding the culture of 'accountability' in a business
- Designing a wellness programme for employees
- Building a workplace where employees collaborate
- Building a customer-centric company

REFERENCES

1. Daniel Kahneman. *Thinking, fast and slow.* New York, NY: Farrar, Straus and Giroux, 2011.

2. Croskerry P. The importance of cognitive errors in diagnosis and strategies to minimize them. *Acad Med* 2003; 78(8): 775–780.

3. Wood W, Quinn JM and Kashy DA. Habits in everyday life: thought, emotion, and action. *J Person Soc Psychol* 2002; 83(6): 1281.

4. Webb TL and Sheeran P. Does changing behavioural intentions engender behavior change? *Psychol Bull* 2006; 132(2, March), https://www.researchgate.net/publication/33038447_Does_changing_behavioural_intentions_engender_behavior_change (accessed 9 February 2021).

5. Lally P, van Jaarsveld CHM, Potts HWW, et al. How are habits formed: Modelling habit formation in the real world. *Euro J Soc Psychol* 2010; 40: 998–1009.

6. Hollingworth C and Barker L. How to use behavioural science to build new habits. WARC Best Practice, June 2017, https://www.

thebearchitects.com/assets/uploads/TBA_Warc_How_to_use_behavioural_science_to_build_habits.pdf (accessed 9 February 2021).

7. Neal D, Vujcic J, Hernandez O, et al. *The science of habit: Creating disruptive and sticky behavior change in handwashing behavior.* Washington, DC: USAID/WASHplus Project, 2015.

8. Wood W, Tam L and Witt MG. Changing circumstances, disrupting habits. *J Person Soc Psychol* 2005; 88(6): 918.

9. Wendel S. *Designing for behavior change: Applying psychology and behavioral economics.* Newton, MA: O'Reilly Media, 2013.

10. Fogg BJ. A behaviour model for persuasive design. In: Chatterjee S (ed.) *Proceedings of the 4th International Conference on Persuasive Technology.* New York, NY: ACM, 2009.

11. Fogg BJ. The behavior grid: 35 ways behavior can change. In: Chatterjee S (ed.) *Proceedings of the 4th International Conference on Persuasive Technology.* New York, NY: ACM, 2009.

12. Michie S, West R, Campbell R, et al. *ABC of behaviour change theories.* 1st ed. London: Silverback Publishing, 2014.

13. Michie S., van Stralen MM and West R. The behaviour change wheel: A new method for characterising and designing behaviour change interventions. *Implement Sci* 2011; 6, https://implementationscience.biomedcentral.com/articles/10.1186/1748-5908-6-42 (accessed 9 May 2021).

Chapter 33

The Privacy Paradox

Humans as customers want control; they want to be convinced and also want personalization. They want products and services to be delivered when they want, where they want and in the form they want.

All these are possible only through customer data. Search engines such as Google and Bing ask us to allow to access our information, and we don't mind sharing our details with them, not realizing that they can be retrieved for any other use by them. When you purchase or search something on Amazon or Flipkart, your purchase and search history is stored so that they can provide products which match your search/purchase.

Customers don't shy away from sharing their personal information for receiving these benefits. Yet when you ask them about their privacy, they show concern about someone else owning it and their likelihood of getting misused for things they are not aware of or have given consent to. This dichotomy between what people think about data and what their actual behaviour is called the privacy paradox. While they show concern about privacy, they undertake actions which do little to protect that.

The term 'privacy paradox' was first used by Barry Brown, an HP employee, in 2001. In a study on online shopping behaviours, Brown found that though customers expressed concern about their privacy, they continued to use their loyalty cards which tracked their behaviour.[1]

Today, we see consumers proclaiming that they want privacy but will not make any effort to be conscious about it, share information only when required and even delete the data.

I know a CEO friend who is very concerned about privacy and very often he will talk about how technology is taking away our privacy. Yet when it comes to sharing his personal information on various online sites, he does not hesitate to do so.

The issue of privacy paradox came to the fore after the 2016 US presidential elections in which Cambridge Analytica used data of people without their knowledge to target advertisements and social media posts for influencing voters in the elections.[2]

Research done by Susan Athey of Stanford Institute for Economic Policy Research and Christian Catalini and Catherine Tucker of MIT found that when you offer incentives to people, it influences their privacy decisions. They examined 3,018 students and found that majority of them were willing to provide emails of friends for a free pizza. As the study concluded, 'people are willing to relinquish private data quite easily when incentivized to do so.'[3]

Clearly, if we talk to customers, they would proclaim that they want 'privacy'. But they would also say that they want to be convinced and want personalization.

But why do customers behave this way? The following are the main reasons:

- They are not aware of the impact of their sharing of data.

- They are poor at judging the risk associated with this action of theirs.

- They see the benefits of the technology more than the associated risk.

- They look at it as a cost of getting free access. This is especially true with respect to Facebook, Twitter and Google. Just because these are free, they are ready to pay the price.

- They have got used to it. Can you think of life without Google today?

- They are not aware of the alternatives.

- They don't know how to protect their privacy. There could be many Facebook users who may not know what they need to do to make sure their data are safe.

However, in a post-COVID-19 world, companies would increasingly use technology for safety and contactless delivery. Hence, we should clearly tell them how, where and what would be done with personal data.

So how does a company address the privacy concerns of the customers? Here are a few antidotes.

MAKE PRIVACY AN ELEMENT OF YOUR VALUE PROPOSITION

Let privacy be an element of your core value proposition. One company which has done this very well and even communicated to the customers is Apple. As the company says, privacy is a fundamental human right. It has also made privacy one of its four core values.[4] Not only that, privacy has been at the centre of its product design efforts. So when you use an iPhone, privacy is embedded in the entire experience such as six-digit passcodes, Touch ID, Face ID, two-factor authentication and Find My features. Privacy is clearly a differentiator for Apple from its competitors.

MAKE PRIVACY POLICY DIGESTIBLE TO CUSTOMERS

Customers often don't know their rights. They also have little idea of the regulations around their privacy and the data they share with companies. Hence, it would make immense sense for companies to share the regulations and privacy policies in a way that it's easy for the customers to understand. Quite often customers just accept the privacy conditions without reading them, as it is difficult to read and understand. Hence, it's suggested to share with the customers the distilled elements of the privacy policy so that they can understand what they are getting into. This can go a long way in building trust with customers. One company which does it very well is Keepsafe—a cloud-based digital platform which allows users to control the privacy of their digital content. They have distilled their privacy policy into four sentences (see Figure 33.1).[5]

CLEARLY COMMUNICATE WITH CUSTOMER

It's important to explicitly communicate to customers the purpose of the data which is being collected. Tell them when, where, how and who will connect the data. Give them the option to decide which data they should allow you to use and which data should be deleted. They should also be told what the benefits and downside of data sharing

---

Privacy Policy: Keepsafe

1. We don't look in your Keepsafe.
2. We look at data to improve ourselves.
3. We safeguard your identity.
4. We only reveal your data for legal or safety reasons.

Source: Keepsafe. Keepsafe's privacy policy in four sentences. 3 May 2017, https://www.getkeepsafe.com/policies/ (accessed 9 February 2021).

Figure 33.1. Keepsafe's Privacy Policy

would be. The benefits should be so powerful that the customers would not mind sharing a bit of their privacy to get the outcome.

GIVE POWER TO CUSTOMERS

The data that you collect from customers should result in an experience which gives customers control, convinces them and results in something meaningful. The customer clearly realizes that what you can do for them through data, they cannot achieve it themselves. Think about search engines such as Google which give the power to customers to search for anything which they need, or a GPS device in cars which allows a driver to navigate a city without having to know the way. When your data provides such power, customers will be willing to share their data.

USE LEGISLATIONS FOR EMBEDDING CUSTOMER CENTRICITY

Many companies see legislations such as General Data Protection Regulation (GDPR), California Consumer Privacy Act (CCPA) and Nevada's Online Privacy Law (Nevada's Senate Bill 220)[6] to be an irritant. Actually, it's quite the opposite. These provide a framework to manage the privacy of customers and build trust. They not only give control to customers but also demonstrate that the company is following good data practices which are fair, compliant and transparent. This can be very reassuring. Customers get the opportunity to decide how their data should be used and they know that they can get access of their data when they want or their data can be deleted. Regulations force customer centricity and help to address a key concern of customers which has long been overlooked.

AVOID USING THIRD-PARTY DATA

This is because they could be from sources which are unreliable and can quickly become outdated; as a result, they may not have a direct link with the customer. As it is in a post-GDPR world, companies which use third-party data will be forced to take customer's consent if they plan to sell their information. This may not be agreeable to customers. What it also means is that companies which buy third-party data would have to make efforts to ensure compliance. This is indeed something which companies would like to avoid.

While designing customer value proposition, bring privacy issues to the fore. Even if you have a great product, but if you don't address privacy issues, you will fail. Don't bring privacy discussions for a later stage of your product design and experience discussions. Let it bubble up at the very step of the design. In a post-COVID-19 world, safety may win for some time but once there is a vaccine and things settle, there will be noise around privacy. So it's better to be upfront with customers.

REFERENCES

1. Brown B. *Studying the internet experience.* Publishing Systems and Solutions Laboratory, 26 March 2001, https://www.hpl.hp.com/ techreports/2001/HPL-2001-49.pdf (accessed 9 February 2001).

2. *The New York Times.* Cambridge Analytica and Facebook: The scandal and fallout so far. 4 April 2018, https://www.nytimes.com/2018/04/04/ us/politics/cambridge-analytica-scandal-fallout.html (accessed 9 February 2021).

3. Wong M. Pizza over privacy? Stanford economist examines a paradox of the digital age. *Stanford News*, 3 August 2017, https://news.stanford. edu/2017/08/03/pizza-privacy-stanford-economist-examines-paradox-digital-age/ (accessed 9 February 2021).

4. Apple. Privacy. n.d., https://www.apple.com/privacy/ (accessed 9 February 2021).

5. Taylor J. The privacy paradox and the marketer's dilemma. *Forbes Council Post*, 19 November 2018, https://www.forbes.com/sites/ forbescommunicationscouncil/2018/11/19/the-privacy-paradox-and-the-marketers-dilemma/?sh=16bd3d8e20c4 (accessed 9 February 2021).

6. InfoLawGroup. Nevada enacts new online law privacy law requiring opt-out rights for data sales. 4 June 2019, https://www.infolawgroup. com/insights/2019/6/4/nevada-enacts-new-online-privacy-law-requiring-opt-out-rights-for-data-sales (accessed 9 February 2021).

Chapter 34

Nine Laws of Customers

Customer-centricity is the true north of a company. Customers are not only the most valuable asset of the company but also the life blood for business survival. Not surprisingly they are an integral part of OPEX efforts. Often improvement efforts fail not because of intention or effort but because we don't seem to understand the world of customers. This comprises customer expectations, their behaviours and the unique nuances around them. As I navigated the terrain of improvements over the last three decades, I realized that there are some key lessons which I have distilled as the 'nine laws of customers'. Anyone embarking on an OPEX needs to keep them on the radar. While designing and working on the transformation, these laws need to be kept in mind.

FIRST LAW: CUSTOMERS DON'T KNOW WHAT THEY WANT

When I began my journey of OPEX in 1990s, knowing the customer was about gathering a voice of the customer by conducting a focus group. In it, sets of volunteers were brought together to discuss a particular product or service. However, the problem with this approach was that the participants did not share their view with candour due to politeness, peer pressure and lack of participation by few.

Henry Ford was right when he said that customers often don't know what they want because they just don't know. If he had asked the customers what they want, they would have said that they want a faster horse. This view was also echoed by Steve Jobs, who did not believe in techniques of market research. Even if they have a sense of what they want, they may not find it easy to express it.

Hence, the antidote to this is observing customers in their context. Here, the researchers don't just listen and watch, they immerse themselves in the experiences of the people they are studying. This means moving into people's home. They stay with them, eat meals with them, follow people in the gym, observe what they do in the kitchen, accompany them to the supermarket and shadow them as they do their daily chores. While they do this, they look for physical, cognitive, social, cultural and emotional elements present, which impact the overall experience. There are various tools which can used which include ethnography, cultural artefacts, POEMS (people, objects, environment, messages and services) etc.

SECOND LAW: CUSTOMERS DECIDE EMOTIONALLY AND JUSTIFY RATIONALLY

Humans are irrational creatures. We have looked at System 1 and System 2 in Chapter 32. A lot of our decisions are made using the intuitive thinking process.[1] Many of the things that we decide are based on our emotions. It's not that logic does not play a role. It does, but it may not be an overriding role in the way a customer decides.

When you ask them later on why they decided what they decided, they may not be able to tell it accurately. Hence, evoking the right emotions is critical in driving customer decisions. Customers buy a Ferrari not for transportation but for prestige. If transportation was just the objective, they could have gone for a Maruti 800. They buy an expensive product to meet their aspirations. Businesses need to make sure that the right emotions are evoked to drive the maximum value. They also need to know which emotions need to be avoided which can drive the customers away. What is important to remember is that customers have emotional expectations which need to be addressed. Companies have a great opportunity to influence the customer through emotions. Let me give you an example of how context plays a role in customers' decision-making. A wine store tested how music impacts sales. On the days, when they played classic music from French composers, 80 per cent of the customers bought French wine, while on the days German music was played, the sale of German wines was more than French wine.[2] Here, the customer behaviour was influenced without even their knowing it. Companies can influence their customers by encouraging their System 1 in mind to respond in a way they desire.

THIRD LAW: CUSTOMERS SEEK THINGS WHICH REQUIRE LEAST EFFORT

Have you ever wondered why customers want things to be effortless and easy? Many of us would say that this is because we are lazy. Actually, the reason is different. Our ancestors used their energies for things which were essential for survival such as fleeing wild animals and predators, making fire and hunting food. Hence, our ancestors were focused on easy things to evade energy-consuming efforts. Those who did not do so did not survive for long.

Our brain has System 1 and System 2 thinking, about which we have read earlier. When we use System 2 thinking, our cognitive resources are used, and this depletes our energy. As Dr Marcus Raichle of Washington University School of Medicine found, the brain weighs

2 per cent of the body weight but accounts for 20 per cent of body's total energy use.[3] Humans focus on saving their energies for important activities in their lives such as working, parenting and negotiating. Hence, if people are forced to do something, it must be worthwhile for them. As a result, we use heuristics (shortcuts) for executing things, solving problems, learning and discovering new things. The outcome of these shortcuts may not be perfect, but it helps in achieving the immediate goals. For example, when we are buying a product online, our decisions are often based on thinking that what's popular and selling more must be a good product. Hence, we also purchase it. Or when we are at a luxury store, our decision to buy something could be based on the appeal of the salesman than the quality of the product. Both of them are examples of how customers use heuristics in decision-making.

While working on a transformation which involves customer experience, you need to first ascertain whether the activity is important for the customers and do they have the required cognitive resources to do it. Establish whether an 'easy experience' is important to customers or they would like to engage in an 'effortful experience'. If the customer needs to do something in a noisy, distracting environment, an effortless experience will be valued. For example, iPhones are designed in such a way that one can use them without much thinking and cognitive requirement. But when customers are locked down at home as during the COVID-19 pandemic, they may want to try do-it-yourself products. Hence, in such cases, what the customer values is effortful experience which requires their full involvement.

FOURTH LAW: CUSTOMERS EXPECT A COHERENT EXPERIENCE

In today's always connected digital world, customers can start engaging with a company on a website, then move to the mobile phone and then visit the store. What they want is that in each of these channels and touch points, they should feel the same. Customers move from one channel to another and the information does not travel with them. They want to navigate from one channel to another without having to start over again or repeat themselves. They expect consistency across all interactions, and hence companies need to present a single face to them. They want to be remembered. When customers have to restate and re-enter information, it wastes their time and make them feel that the company does not care for them. They expect the same kind of experience from a company, whether they communicate online, in a store or branch, on the phone or anywhere else. Let's see how it will work. If you browse a retailer's website for a trouser and then walks into the store the next day, the staff out there should know that you have spent 40 minutes looking for the trouser on the company's website the day before. The in-store visit should be a continuation of that journey which began online—not a new start. This is called an omnichannel experience. Today, customers spend a lot of time online and their purchase journey can cut across multiple channels, offline and online. You may get an email about a deal on a refrigerator while at office which you see on your smartphone. You browse about the product features and reviews while coming back home. The next morning you ask questions about the product on chat bots. Finally, you place an order from your desktop during the weekend. This is an example of a customer's purchase journey. The customer expects seamless experience across channels, and companies need to have an omnichannel strategy to make this happen.

FIFTH LAW: CUSTOMERS WANT TO BE IN CONTROL

We humans want to be in control of things. We want to control our destiny, and we hate outside forces getting involved in what we do. For example, if we have taken a taxi and are travelling from one place to another, we expect that there will be freedom to decide the route, especially when there is a paucity of time. Or if you are travelling business class in a plane, you expect the air hostess to offer you drinks when you like it and as many times as you like it. When we have a sense of control, we feel free and relaxed. Research done by R. T. Mills and D. S. Krantz found that the blood donors who were allowed to choose the arm from which blood was to be collected reported less pain.[4] Clearly, loss of control seems to have resulted in stress, anxiety and even anger.

Sriram Dasu and Richard Chase recommend that through clever application of process design and psychology, we can give customers a sense of control.[5] They talk about two types of control which include 'behaviour control' and 'cognitive control'. Behaviour control is about giving a sense of control in customer actions that before, during and after the counter. Cognitive control is a perception that events are predictable and derived from our past experience with the system. While the customer may not control the service process, the past experience in the system makes us believe that things are 'in control'. For example, if a customer is buying a phone, the company should make sure that he has sufficient access to product information. This gives him a sense of control and he feels comfortable to buy it. Businesses can provide sense of control in myriad ways such as self-service, giving visibility to the service as it gets delivered, offering a product or service when and where they want it, and providing plenty of information on product features and service issues. Thanks to technology and the internet that there are many opportunities for companies to cede control to customers with the service delivery process. Companies should dissect the customer journey and see activities where they can cede control. Where providing control is not possible, create an illusion of control. For example, while standing in an orderly queue at an immigration counter, we feel a sense of control as we see people moving, and we know that we shall reach the end shortly. And most importantly, reduce the number of choices so it's easy for the customer to buy a product and not waste time in evaluating which one to buy if the options are large. Choice overload can frustrate people. Apple seems to have got this right. When you have to buy an Apple phone, the customer has to navigate between few choices. Old versions are killed on time.

SIXTH LAW: GET SENSE OF CUSTOMER VALUE BY USING THE PIRATE METRICS

The Pirate Metrics were proposed by Dave McClure. He is an entrepreneur, angel investor and founder of 500 start-ups. He first talked about it in a 2007 Ignite Seattle talk, and it has been popularized by his video and his presentation on SlideShare. His view was that any start-up should focus on five key metrics which he called AARRR. Although they were meant for start-ups, they could be used for any business. The reason they are called Pirate Metrics is that an entrepreneur is a bit like a pirate who has to navigate the hidden currents and having the right metrics will help to navigate better.

The five metrics are aligned with the customer lifecycle stages and help businesses to know where they should focus their marketing and sales effort. The metrics are designed in such a way that they represent the key behaviours of the customers. The metrics are as follows[6]:

- **Acquisition:** This refers to the lead generation strategies which are done through various channels, whether inbound or outbound. This is when the customer finds you. Examples of metrics are customer acquisition cost per channel, number of leads and website visit.

- **Activation:** This is when customers try your product or service and see value in what you offer. This is when the customer uses your product.

- **Retention:** This is about the number of customers who come back after initially trying the product or service. This is when the customer continues to use the product.

- **Referral:** This is about current customers referring other customers.

- **Revenue:** This refers to the money which you make from customer activity. This is when the customer pays you.

The reason why I am sharing this here is that I believe that OPEX teams should know about these metrics. They will get a big picture view of the business. Before they get into any project, they should look into the AARRR metrics. In fact, these metrics will provide insights on where they can focus on.

SEVENTH LAW: CUSTOMERS SHOULD BE VISIBLE TO ALL EMPLOYEES AND ALL THOSE INVOLVED IN PRODUCTION, DELIVERY AND SERVICE

Whether an employee is doing a customer-facing job or is part of a back office or doing a role of a janitor, each one should know their customers. For some of them, there could be more than one customer. For those in customer-facing roles, their customer is the person who buys the product or service from the company. In case of roles which are not customer facing (as in a back-office role or the role of janitor), they could have more than one customer. Their immediate customers are the users of their work (also called internal customer), and they also have the end consumer who finally purchases the products and services. What's important here is to make sure that each one of them not only knows the profile of their immediate customers but also the end consumer or the customer who pays for the product or service. They need to have an understanding of both types of customers' needs, wants, pains, aspirations and context. I have come across companies where back office people don't know who the end consumer is, and they just come, do their job and pass it on to the next person or department in the process. When employees get to know about the end consumer, they know whether their work is adding value to their lives or not. It is a critical element in building a customer-focused organization. Businesses need to regularly conduct awareness sessions for their employees to let them know what the customer is seeking and how they can serve better. In B2B businesses, the companies just can't stop with the external customer who buys their product; they have to also understand the world of end users of their products. In platform business models, companies may have more than one customer, as they facilitate interaction among large numbers of participants. For example, an Uber has three customers: users of cars, drivers and corporates. Employees serving each of them directly or indirectly need to know the broad profile of each of the customer sets.

EIGHTH LAW: CUSTOMER RELATIONSHIPS ARE BUILT ON TRUST

All businesses have customers. The only way to make sure that the customers keep coming back is by building trust. It is a fundamental thing to building stickiness in the relationship. Company reputations are dictated by the trust customers have in the firm. We all love Amazon because it has been able to build trust with customers. Trust helps to build loyalty and increase customer's lifetime value. When customers trust a product or a service, businesses don't need to spend time and effort to explain the value which gets delivered to the customer. As customers trust more, they don't mind ceding control. For example, if you are working for a manufacturing company which has been consistently receiving good-quality raw materials, it may slowly reduce the amount of quality check which it does on receipt of the materials or just go by the quality certificate given by the supplying company. A key element in building trust is reducing the risk for the customer. When risk reduces, it elevates the trust between the customer and the company. Businesses need to consciously undertake trust-building actions so that it solidifies their relationships with customers. Actually, trust can be an amorphous concept if we do not know the components.[7] The following are the building blocks of trust:

- **Reliability:** This is about constantly meeting what has been promised to customers. This includes dimensions such as quality, timeliness and safety.

- **Convenience:** This is about making it easy for the customers to do business with the company. This includes things such as easy invoicing for customers and one-click ordering.

- **Responsiveness:** This is about making sure that the company is there to respond and help the customer when there is a problem.

- **Applicability:** This is about making sure that the product or service meets the unique needs of the customer. It includes offering personalization of product and service.

- **Emotions:** This is about evoking the right emotions during the customer journey so that the customer feels comfortable dealing with the company.

OPEX professionals need to consciously design in the trust components into the value proposition and also the customer journey. What should also be remembered is that trust should also have to be infused as a key element of organizational culture so that it becomes a part of the way of working in the company. Employees must be told about it, they have to be trained and it needs to be demonstrated in their day-to-day interactions even within the company. It also must be embedded into job designs especially for those who are interacting with the customers. For example, a frontline staff should know how to demonstrate trust by demonstrating behaviours, such as eye contact, smiling, respect, listening and showing empathy.

So building trust requires looking at the 'hard' and 'soft' elements of the enterprise. The former includes things such as processes, IT system, infrastructure and policies. The latter includes employee behaviours and organizational culture. The key mantras to remember for building trust are listening to customers, conveying to them about company's risks and problems, never exploiting their vulnerabilities and going out to help them when they need you.

NINTH LAW: CUSTOMERS EXPECT AMAZON-LIKE EXPERIENCE FROM ALL COMPANIES

I was advising a multinational company in the B2B sector to become customer-centric. As a part of that exercise, I had an opportunity to speak to many of its customers. When I asked them what sort of experience they expected from the firm, it was quite interesting to see that many of them said that they would prefer an Amazon-like experience. Remember that this was a B2B player not connected with e-commerce, yet the customers expected businesses to be like Amazon. This has happened because of what I call the Amazon effect. This is a phenomenon where Amazon has created a new benchmark of customer experience with unrivalled product inventory, great prices, effortless buying process, free shipping (for Prime customers), easy returns, robust packaging, high product reliability and time-bound problem resolution. The Amazon effect has impacted customer expectations across industries. Irrespective of what products or service a company makes today, customers compare their experience with that of Amazon. So in a way, Amazon is the competitor of every business.

What should businesses do, especially when doing what Amazon does, may not be possible. My suggestion is that companies should look at the practices of Amazon and other companies (may not be from the sector) which are doing a great job in engaging the customers. They should then pick up practices and implement them over a period of time. For example, if a company is looking at Amazon, it could begin by adopting its mission, which is to be earth's most customer-centric company. Then maybe it could look at their shopping experience, shipping and so on. Achieving what Amazon has achieved may not be possible, but the company has shown direction to all businesses on what a great customer experience looks like. The takeaway for businesses is that the customer's expectations may be influenced by some other player who is not from the same industry. So providing best-in-class customer experience performance in one's industry does not guarantee success.

REFERENCES

1. Shaw C and Hamilton R. *The intuitive customer: 7 imperatives for moving your customer experience to the next level.* London, Palgrave Macmillan, 2016.

2. North AC, Hargreaves DJ and McKendrick J. The influence of in-store music on wine selections. *J Appl Psychol* 1999; 84(2): 271–276.

3. Raichle ME and Gusnard DA. Appraising the brain's energy budget. *Proc Natl Acad Sci U S A* 2002; 99(16): 10237–10239. doi:10.1073/pnas.172399499

4. Mills RT and Krantz DS. Information choice, and reaction to stress: A field experiment in blood banks with laboratory analogue. *J Personal Soc Psychol* 1979; 37(4, April): 608–620.

5. Dasu S and Chase RB. *The customer service solution*. New York, NY: McGraw Hill, 2013.

6. Pedicini A. AAARR Metrics. n.d., https://www.product-frameworks.com/AARRR-Metrics.html (accessed 10 February 2021).

7. Soudagar R, Iyer V and Hildebrand VG. *Customer experience edge*. New Delhi: Tata McGraw Hill, 2012.

8. Heid M. Does thinking burn calories? Here's what science says. *Time*, 19 September 2018.

Chapter 35

Know the Types of Customer Data

As you embed customer centricity in a company and focus on personalization, you will have to make use of customers' data. This could be for designing better products, designing experience and for personalization. In today's world of the internet, we are inundated with data. However, companies need to know which consumer data to use which will help them to achieve the desired objectives. Today, companies collect so much data or have access to so much data, but they need to know its quality and the reach it can give to them. While data are required to provide a better product proposition to customers, they are all not equal.

This also became critical in a post-GDPR (General Data Protection Regulation) world, wherein compliance around data becomes critical. For those not familiar with GDPR, it is the regulation that requires businesses to protect the personal data and privacy of EU citizens for transactions that occur within EU member states. So what are the types of customer data?

ZERO-PARTY DATA

This a term coined by Forrester. This is the data which is willingly shared by the customers to the company. Forrester describes this as a class of data which 'a customer intentionally and proactively shares with a brand. It can include purchase intentions, personal context and how the individual wants the brand to recognize her'.[1] This is collected by getting in touch with customers and them giving permission to use the data. This data is owned by the customer and should never be used or sold without their consent. They are a great asset for personalization, and customers state what they want from the company. It also helps in better targeting of customers. Customers could also give this data for some value in return. They would expect better product recommendations, offers, services and personalization. This is also called content data as both are aware of the benefits and use of data. For the data that the customer shares, he could get a value in exchange which could be discounts, exclusive contents, personalized recommendations, social kudos, loyalty points, VIP treatment, etc.

Advantages

- You get to know exactly what the customer wants
- It provided high accuracy and clarity on zero-party data
- Success of marketing, personalization and promotion efforts is very high
- It helps to build deep relationships with customers
- Given the privacy concerns, it can help to address customers' concerns about data
- Customers own the data during the entire experience and can revoke access when they want
- It addresses the privacy concerns of customers
- It meets the requirements of data regulations

Disadvantage

- Seeking too much data can overwhelm customers

Sources

This is collected by asking directly from the customer on their need, preference and personalization requirements. Companies can also use the following:

- Questionnaires
- Polls
- Quizzes
- Social stories

FIRST-PARTY DATA

This is the data which is collected by the company itself. It is most accurate and relevant. The data is owned by the company, and the company does not need to pay for it. The company here has a direct link with the customers. If you want to know about customers, first-party data is probably the best. It's called first-party data, as it is collected by the party firsthand. They are best data for retargeting a customer. Typically, this data is collected during the purchase process and used for retargeting a customer. For example, if you have searched something online, you would have seen banners around the product to follow you. The recommendations that you see after searching for a product on an e-commerce site are outcomes of first-party data.[2]

Advantages

- You have visibility on how the data was collected
- It provides you greater accuracy about your customers
- You have visibility about the recency

- It can be a source of competitive advantage as only you have access to the data and your competitors can't access it
- Your company has control over the data
- Your customers have better control over the data and its deletion
- It is considered to be the most valuable
- It does not cost anything for use and reuse

Disadvantages

- It may be difficult to scale and may require significant investment in technology.
- It does not allow you to reach new customers about whom you don't have information.
- Data is restricted to the scope of your operations. For example, an app for fitness will have details about your health and demography, but it may not have other details to know your persona.

Sources

- Websites
- Emails
- Point of sale
- Text messages
- Call centre
- Mobile site
- CRM
- Social media profile
- Surveys
- Customer feedback
- Mobile app
- In-store beacons

DIFFERENCE BETWEEN ZERO-PARTY DATA AND FIRST-PARTY DATA

The difference between zero-party data and first-party data is that the former data is given by customers in exchange for a value, while the latter is gathered during customer interaction, specifically during the purchase process. Also, zero-party data is owned by the customer, while first-party data is owned by the company. Also, first-party data is rich in implied interests of customers and provides a peek into their past behaviours. On the other hand, zero-party data provides details on customers' interests, purchase intention and what they prefer. Also, first-party data is collected without customers' explicit knowledge and volition and data is intended to be used more broadly to provide an overall better experience to them.

SECOND-PARTY DATA

Here, the company uses another company's first-party data. The company provides the data to another company on payment or for internal benefit. The other company can be a service provider like a market research agency or there could be a partnership with another company to share the data, for example, a manufacturing company sharing customer data with a sales partner.

This can also happen when the other company providing you the data has a product or service which targets your customers, for example, a hotel chain having a partnership on data sharing with an airline.[3]

Advantages

- It helps to get over scale limitations.
- It allows a company to improve its marketing and promotion activities, as it helps to get data beyond existing customer base.
- It helps in improving sales effectiveness, as it provides details about customers beyond what you already have and provides potential leads.

- It aids in personalization.

- It provides endless possibilities but you have look for partners.

- The data source is reliable because you're leveraging your trusted partners first-party data.

Disadvantages

- You don't have control over the data.

- It only works when there is no conflict of interest or competition between the two parties.

- Although its reach is more than first-party data source, it's confined to the customers of second-party customers. The reach is limited to the partner's data source.

Sources

This would be similar to the first-party data sources. It's only that it's owned by someone else and not your company.

THIRD-PARTY DATA

Here, an entity collects data which may not have a direct link with the customers. The company collects data from various sources and sells it to companies. These companies are into collecting, aggregating and selling data. This is typically bought when companies need a large amount of data. The data could be available to your competitors as well; hence, there could be questions. Typically, the company collects data from various sources and then sells it to customers. There could be some data which it could collect itself, but a majority would be from other sources. When you get an e mail from a company you don't know, it could be because your data has been sold to them and you are not aware of it. The third-party data should be used in conjunction with first-party data. It should be used as a complement to your first-party data. Never use it as a replacement for the first-party data collected by you. Instead, it's recommended that you analyse the first-party data for consumer behaviour and then compare it with the third-party data.

Advantages

- It provides a great opportunity to scale your data sets.
- It can be made available quickly—you can pay and get it off the shelf.

Disadvantages

- There can be issues around accuracy and recency.
- It costs money.
- There can also be issues around data privacy.
- While there can be good data, there can also be a lot of junk data.
- Data could be stale and could be sold for customers who have aged, moved cities and have had changed in life events and preferences.
- You could be breaking the law, as CCPA (California Privacy Rights Act of 2020) and European data laws (GDPR) allow customers to opt out of the data being sold to third parties, and this will impact the entities.
- You do not know who collected the data, when it was collected and where it was collected.
- The data being available to competitors may not be a source of competitive advantage.

Sources

It typically comes from a company which is into buying and selling of data. Here, the company does not have a direct connection to the consumer whose data is collected. Its sources may include websites, social media, surveys subscriptions, etc.

Given the data regulations, it's important to understand the impact of the type of data which you are using. In the current regulatory environment, leaning towards more zero-party data might be a good idea for customer experience and product design professionals.

REFERENCES

1. Richard J. The personalisation and privacy paradox. *AdAge*, 25 March 2019, https://adage.com/article/wayin/personalization-privacy-paradox/317085 (accessed 10 February 2021).

2. Haberman R. Consumer data types, explained: The difference between third-party, second-party, and first-party data. Jebbit, 1 August 2019, https://www.jebbit.com/blog/consumer-data-types-explained-the-difference-between-third-party-second-party-and-first-party-data (accessed 10 February 2021).

3. Simpson J. What are first-, second- and third-party data? 23 March 2016, https://econsultancy.com/what-are-first-second-and-third-party-data/ (accessed 10 February 2021).

Chapter 36

The Power of Open Big Room

While rolling out an OPEX effort, the power of open communication is the key. Employees need to know what's happening and how the progress is. An open communication is required not only for collaboration but also to seek ideas. To effectively do this, I always recommend setting up a large room wherein people come in and see and discuss matters pertaining to OPEX. Go around your office. Look for a room which has large empty walls. Covert it into a war room for aligning and discussing matters pertaining to OPEX. If you don't have an empty room in your office, I would suggest you get one created, as it is one of the most powerful communication and alignment tools in an OPEX journey. You could call it a war room, a bridge, an *obeya* (Japanese for a large room),[1] a problem-solving room, a bootcamp room, a command centre or an adrenalin room. These are dedicated spaces for teams to meet and discuss specific matters/issues for a specified period of time.

This room should have a specific purpose, that is, to solve an organizational problem which helps to take the performance to a new level. This is not to be used for business review meetings but for irregular meetings which are focused on things beyond the ordinary. They are typical issues which challenge the enterprise and need resolution. It could also be used for meetings to discuss issues around a gap.

An open room bereft of pillars and partitions but with empty space in the centre signifies and does the following:

- It is a small representation of a boundaryless enterprise where members collaborate freely.

- Since there are no partitions, it shows that silos have been brought down.

- A room with free empty space helps people to freely move around without any hinderance.

- Since all teams stand and work, it becomes very difficult for anyone to deny being part of the team.

- The setting is such that everybody is on the same plane and standing; hence, there are no hierarchies.

- It allows real-time collaboration instead of banking on emails and rushed meetings.

- It fosters common understanding on issues.

- It helps to get alignment and buy-in on critical issues /matters.

- When issues/problems are visually depicted, it becomes easy for the employees to understand.

- It allows to focus on issues, as all relevant people are present, and their focused effort is on it.

- It helps to pool in collective expertise of the team.

- It makes a problem visible in front of everyone and brings out issues which could have been hidden.

These rooms can be used for myriad things such as problem-solving, root cause analysis, customer journey mapping, project status, new product development and metrics.

Let me share with you all an example. One of my clients who are into packaging products had this major quality issue which was tarnishing their brand name. Despite being a true innovator, this was an issue which they were not able to solve. There were multiple efforts from the teams in technical services and quality but in vain. Despite all the corrective and preventive actions which the teams had come up with, the problem continued. This went on for almost 18 months so much so that 2 of their major accounts decided to stop their business with them. It's around that time when they brought me in to help the company navigate a journey of OPEX. As a part of the roll-out, we set up an open big room near the shop floor. It was going to be used for discussing all issues pertaining to OPEX. I nudged the teams to get all relevant people into the room and do a thorough root cause analysis. For the first time, a cross-functional team comprising sales, technical services, manufacturing, quality, supply chain and finance came together to discuss the issue. For the first team, there were representatives from functions who were not involved in manufacturing process doing a deep-dive on an issue pertaining to product quality. What this exercise did was that functions who had earlier just blamed such as sales, got involved in the process. Representatives of finance were involved, as they were involved in generating the customer claims. It was an exercise of understanding the customer journey and dissecting the root causes. The walls were filled with customer journey maps, empathy maps, charts, fish bones, 3 legged 5 whys, etc. It was interesting to note members walking around watching their work which was being done on the wall. They were writing, debating and participating, irrespective of their hierarchy in the company. The four-day focused exercise saw brilliant outcomes. Not only did the teams challenge each other, but the teams which were earlier blaming were now a part of the solution. All perspectives were on the table. The result was a list of countermeasures, many of which addressed the root causes and the way the customers were so far involved. After the actions were taken, the problem got resolved.

Remember that this room should have the bare minimum stuff. There could be a cupboard in one corner for keeping the necessary items. These include flip charts, Post-it notes, easel boards, markers, sketch pen, A3 sheets, PDCA (plan–do–check–act) templates, mood stickers, etc. There could also be a table. You could also have a computer to retrieve information. There could be a projector in case something needs to be displayed and retrieved from. You could have a few chairs but not too many. The participants could sit around the table to discuss the issues.

Keep in mind that the open big room should not be far away from where the real action is; otherwise, employees may not use it. I know of a company wherein they set up this big room for the shop-floor workers to discuss and solve their problems. The mistake was that, it was set in an office which was almost a couple of kilometres away from the manufacturing plant. As a result, no one used it, and it saw a natural death. Make sure that this room is in a comfortable setting and not uncomfortable that people find it difficult to spend time there. For example, a steel plant put together this room not far away from the furnace. Given the inclement temperature, teams did not want to spend time there.

There are people who ask me that why do you need such a space if everything can be stored and retrieved from a computer. What the big room does is to make things visible. I am a big supporter of doing things with hand and the power it gives to employee involvement. Think about a room wherein people can play around with Post-it notes, pens, etc., and not look at the computer screen which shows a set of data which everyone in the room can't play around. It's okay to have a digital display of metrics but make sure that there is a space for people to use boards/walls for problem-solving. There are companies which are using digital involvement tools which help in not only visual management but also problem-solving.

Those who believe that they don't have a separate room in the company, I suggest them to find a dedicated place in one corner and cordon it off using white boards. These white boards can then be used for writing and visually depicting what is being discussed.

To me, this open room is almost like the brain of the company where ideas around making the company better get analysed, synthesized, digested and prioritized. This is the place where organizational barriers melt and one gets nuggets to take the enterprise on a journey of excellence. Important issues are all there on the walls and not hidden in someone's computer or log book. Use it and get great benefits. If you don't, you are missing a great operation excellence practice.

REFERENCE

1.   Jusko J. Obeya: The brain of the lean enterprise. *IndustryWeek*, 30 September 2016, https://www.industryweek.com/lean-six-sigma/ obeya-brain-lean-enterprise (accessed 10 February 2021).

Chapter 37

Knowing the Mechanics of Teams

When I started working in the early 1990s, one thing that we were told was that it's teams and not individuals which make organizations great. As a matter of fact, the 1990s were the period when companies globally were adopting total quality management (TQM) as a means to achieve organizational excellence. One of the pillars of TQM was teams. My first lesson on the power of teams was from a quality management diploma programme which was run by Professor Amar Kalro of IIM Ahmedabad at Ahmedabad Management Association.

The power of teams in building excellent companies was further solidified during my days at Hindustan Lever (now Hindustan Unilever Limited). Dr P. Bannerjee, who was then the head of Corporate Quality, told me what excellent teams did to the enterprise. My later stints in ICICI Bank and Standard Chartered brought in newer perspective on teams and the magic that they created for businesses.

One thing which became very clear to me was that if you have an embed OPEX in an enterprise, hire people who are smarter than you. Try and have skills which are complementary in nature. What this meant was that don't hire your clones. Instead, hire for diverse skills which will strengthen your journey of OPEX. So what are some of the things which you need to keep in mind as far as teams are concerned?

DIVERSITY GIVES STRENGTH

A team entrusted to embed OPEX should not be a collection of individuals who are clones of the leader. This is a mistake that I have seen OPEX leaders committing while building their teams. The power of an OPEX team comes from diversity. Diversity increases creativity and encourages the search for novel information and perspectives, leading to better decision-making and problem-solving.

This means diversity of professional experience, diversity of industry exposure, diversity of educational background, diversity of skills, diversity of perspective and diversity of age. Let me explain you what I mean by each of them.

- **Diversity of expertise:** This means including team members who have various expertise and professional experience. This could mean having team members who have worked in various functions such as operations, finance, human resources, sales and marketing. They bring different perspectives. Don't worry if they don't have the relevant problem-solving skills. You can always train them up. Let them be with the OPEX team for some time and then send them back to their core functions.

- **Diversity of industry experience:** This means having team members who have worked in another industry. For example, an OPEX team of a manufacturing company should look at hiring talent from the service sector, especially someone who has worked closely with customers. This would not only bring a perspective from a different industry but could also help to embed a customer-centric mindset. Similarly, a bank keen on focusing on efficiency could look at hiring people from manufacturing who can transplant the shop-floor practices to a banking back office.

- **Diversity of age, gender and race:** This means that the OPEX team should try and have members of all generations and all genders. Let there be young members, mid-aged and those who are not far from retirement. We cannot forget the insights which could come from someone who has just graduated from a college or the wisdom which can flow from someone who has years of experience behind them. I find it weird when companies decide that all members of the OPEX team will be of a certain age group. It helps to have a mix of all the genders.

For example, the effect of gender diversity on organizational performance was looked at by Cristian Dezsö of the University of Maryland and David Ross of Columbia University. They looked at Standard & Poor's Composite 1500 Index.[1] They examined these firms to management from 1992 to 2006 and found that on average, 'female representation in top management leads to an increase of $42 million in firm value.'

Another interesting research was done by Richard Freeman and Wei Huang. They examined the ethnic identity of 1.5 million scientific papers written between 1985 and 2008. What they found was that papers written by diverse groups received more citations and had higher impact factors than those written by people of same ethnic groups.[2]

An OPEX leader once told me that they don't hire women because there was a lot of hard work to be done on the shop floor. This is such a flawed thinking in today's world when women are excelling in all spheres of life.

COGNITIVE DIVERSITY: BEYOND WHAT IS SEEN

In a *Harvard Business Review* article, academicians Alison Reynolds and David Lewis talk about cognitive diversity.[3] According to them, cognitive diversity is about cultivating and embracing a team with a difference in perspectives and information-processing styles.

Cognitively diverse teams have a unique advantage while working on problems, approaching a change and performing in complex situations. Cognitive diversity is not predicated by factors such as gender, ethnicity and race. A cognitively diverse team helps a team to interpret information using different perspectives. It also reduces bias in decision-making.

What we also need to remember is that cognitive functions have two broad dimensions which include how we gather information and how we make decisions. This entails whether individuals gather data to make sense of a situation or they make more intuitive sense of what they see. Also, while making decisions, do they use logic and reasons or is it based on what they feel right or aligns with their values?

Unlike race, colour, gender or ethnicity, cognitive diversity is not visible. By seeing from outside, one cannot know how an individual processes information and responds to a change.

The mistake that we often do is to hire people like us. We do this because we tend to gravitate people like us. But the result of this is that we create an organization of like-minded people.

Businesses have to consciously recruit teams which have cognitive diversity. When teams are put together for problem-solving, this has to be kept in mind. What needs to be remembered is that if you have a homogeneous team, people find it difficult to stick their neck out. This is because they want to conform. What's also important to remember is to look beyond race, gender and ethnicity while putting together a diverse team.

DIVERSE TEAMS, PROBLEMS AND HOW THEY OPERATE

Diversity does have its problems. It causes discomfort; it can be painful. The interactions may not be easy. Building trust is arduous, and there are greater chances of conflicts. The teams can also be less cohesive. But it brings in a silent power to the teams.

When there is diversity, team members know that there would be perspective difference. This forces them to change how they behave. When team members are different, participants know that the opinions and perspectives are going to be different. They know that their perspectives will not get easy acceptance. They change their expectations. Unlike a homogenous group where ideas would have got accepted easily, they know that they will need to work hard to come to a consensus. Hence, they work harder both cognitively and socially.[4] This may be a painful process, but the outcome is better.

DIVERSE TEAM AND FACTS-BASED THINKING

Teams which have diverse members influence the behaviour of the group. This enhances critical thinking and makes the group's thinking more accurate. Research done by Samuel Sommers has some interesting facts. The research examined the multiple effects of racial diversity on group decision-making. As a part of the study, 200 people were assigned to a six-person mock jury panel, whose members were either all white or included four white and two black participants. They were shown a video of a trial and had to decide on the guilty. What the research threw up is that the diverse panel of jurors not only raised more questions but also made fewer errors. Even if the errors occurred, they were corrected during deliberation.

As David Rock and Heidi Grant observed in a *Harvard Business Review* article, diverse teams encourage greater scrutiny of each member's actions.[5] They are more likely to constantly re-examine facts and remain objective. They also keep members vigilant in their work and keep their cognitive resources sharp to perform the tasks better. Research done by Katherine W. Phillips, Katie A. Liljenquist and Margaret A. Neale also shows that diverse teams may outperform in the decision-making because they process information more carefully.[6]

MAKING DIVERSE TEAMS WORK

Managing a diverse team brings in its own challenges. It's not only more conflict-prone but also less cohesive. The following are a few things to keep in mind.

Shared Vision, Goals and Objectives

Create a shared vision of the problem that the team is working on. Make sure that the team members explicitly understand the outcomes and how their work will be impacting them. Make sure that the vision, goals and objectives are not only understood but also accepted by all. What's critical to remember is that lack of understanding of their precise roles and responsibilities impacts the performance of diverse teams.

Shared Access to Data and Information

It's important to make sure that all members have access to all relevant information. Be it data around sales or marketing or production or finance, let all team members have access to data. They should be able to use data and information for informed decisions. In case if there is data that is confidential we should make it clear to employees. What companies should avoid at all cost is certain team members have important information while others don't. This could be due to various reasons but should be avoided. Remember, shared information is cornerstone of effective collaboration. It provides single version of truth and transparency around data builds trust among teams. The more open are team members in sharing information, the greater the opportunity for them to interact among themselves. This solidifies the cohesion between team members.

Co-location, Virtual Working and Geographical Integration

There has been this belief that diverse teams should be co-located for better interaction and collaboration. As per Ling et al., co-location is considered an important element of joint working, encouraging informal contact, resulting in increased mutual understanding, quicker and easier communication and expedited problem-solving, and facilitating learning across professional boundaries.

Over the last few years and now in a post-COVID-19 world, teams have been operating virtually. There have been this belief that virtual working is good for transactional work but may not be good if you are innovating. This is what I also believed till I facilitated virtual problem-solving with a multidisciplinary team based in various geographies. It is indeed possible to hold problem-solving sessions and innovation workshops virtually, but what is required in closer geographical integration? The sessions need to be highly managed and facilitated well. What's critical is to keep the enthusiasm of the team up. Having communication platforms such as Slack, Microsoft Teams and Discord helps greatly. We also need platforms such as Microsoft OneDrive and Google Drive, which allow sharing documents with team members.

During the pandemic, we have been seeing virtual hackathons for solving problems. These have been very effective and have delivered results. They start with the problem, sketch a possible solution to that problem, design that solution and then launch a prototype. All this happens within 24–48 hours. These are attended by diverse teams such as developers, designers, marketers, nurses, doctors, students, scientists and teachers. They are tiring but satisfying for the participants. These virtual hackathons have been set by organizations such as The Global Hack, MIT and Australian Computer Society and were participated by individuals from around the world. Clearly, virtual problem-solving by a diverse team is possible.[7]

Creating an Inclusive Environment

A key element in managing a diverse team is creating an inclusive environment. As a matter of fact, without an inclusive team, a team will not be set for operating successfully. Without an inclusive culture, teams will not be set up for success. Actually this can result in their leaving the organization and the benefits of a diverse team will not be realised. For businesses, what this means is to define what is inclusion. For those uninitiated to this topic, inclusion is a workplace culture where employees with diverse background feel comfortable to be themselves , work in ways that suit them and work towards achieving the objectives that make the company successful. As Aleah Warren mentioned in an article in *Fast Company*,

> Less-than-inclusive work cultures also tend to encourage 'covering', or efforts to de-emphasize or 'cover up' something about yourself that's different from the majority group. Covering shows up in many different ways, from changing your appearance (for instance, wardrobe or hair style) to fit in with the majority, or declining to advocate for your own group as a way to prevent yourself from being perceived differently.[8]

Clearly, covering leads to lesser commitment to the company. And when an individual hides the difference for which he was hired, the company loses out as it loses the benefits of those differences.

SUSTAINING THE HETEROGENEITY OF DIVERSE TEAMS

With time, the positive impact of diversity gets lost. The heterogeneity of a team gets homogenous. Members start to think, talk and act alike. With time, groupthink also sets in and team members start aligning to the majority opinion. What's also seen is that diverse teams have higher turnover and that a team breaks into subgroups of similar people.

The solution to this lies in clearly explaining to all members the challenges of diverse teams and how it helps a team to succeed. What seems to work is when team members have a good understanding of each other's competency and how they can complement each other for better team success. For example, Deb knows that he is not very good with numbers and Tim also realizes it. And that's where Tim supports Deb, as he has very good analytical skills. Similarly, since Deb is good at creative problem-solving, he supports Tim when he needs it.

The other solution lies in building redundancy. Researchers Edward Bishop Smith and Yuan Hou have a proposed a structural solution to this problem.[9] They call it redundant heterogeneity. What they suggest is that the heterogenous teams are just not within a hierarchical level but the diversity is matched by similar team members' characteristics at other hierarchical levels.

The other thing to do is to teach members about the difference and cultural sensitivities. After all, members may engage in different ways. It's important to not pre-judge them and engage with an open mind.

The leaders of these teams have a big role to play in making diverse teams work. Here are a few things that they should do.

PACKING A TEAM WITH TOP TALENT

Trying to make a team of top talent can be a recipe for failure. A successful team is one in which the members collaborate effectively and are interdependent on each other. Having too many top talents results in members not coordinating effectively. This happens in sports as well as animal world also. In sports, when a team has too many star players, it affects the performance. Research done by Roderick Swaab et al. has found that there is a limit to the benefit top talents bring to a team. They looked at three sports: basketball, soccer and baseball.[10] They calculated both the percentage of top talent on each team and the teams' success over several years. In the case of basketball and soccer, they found that top talent did in fact predict team success, but only up to a point. In the case of basketball, which has greatest proportion of elite athletes, it performed worse than those with more moderate proportions of top-level players. Why does this happen?

This happens because the top talent wants to focus on becoming top dog and not on achieving superior team performance. Their pursuit to sustain their star status prevents the attainment of team goal.[11] In case of sports, for such individuals, the reason for this could be that their personal records may become greater even if it is at the cost of team goals. What the researchers found was that the percentage of top talent on a team affects intra-team coordination.

This problem is also found in the animal world. When a colony of hens has too many dominant, high-producing chickens, conflict and hen mortality rise while egg production drops.

Let me give you and example of a services company which was setting up an OPEX team. It picked up top talent from the marketplace. These were individuals who had made a name in the space of business improvement. However, what was observed was that the team failed, giving very little result for the company. Each of these individuals felt that they were larger than life and felt little need to collaborate with others. Their focus was also on increasing their profile in the marketplace. They spent a lot of time in speaking at conferences, writing articles, etc. A cold war also erupted, as each one of them thought to be better than the other. And they were eyeing the top job of the OPEX leader. The impact of this was that team failed to deliver much and had to be reconstituted.

Since OPEX is largely a team sport, having a large proportion of top talent in the team is not advisable.

SIZE OF TEAM

As discussed teams are an integral part of all OPEX transformation. Typically, these are cross-functional efforts. To make sure that all relevant stakeholders have their mindshare in the project, we include them in the project team. As a result, the project team becomes large and sometimes unmanageable. Sometimes the team count also increases because there is this belief that adding more people will help in sharing the load. Unfortunately, they do not make things easy but create problems, which impacts the larger OPEX effort.

To understand this better, we shall refer to the work of some of the finest experts in this domain.

Brooks' Law

This law was proposed by Fred Brooks in his 1975 book *The Mythical Man-Month*. His work was on software projects, wherein he found that 'Adding manpower to a late software project makes it later.' This is now known as Brooks' law.[12]

This happens because of the following reasons:

- The increased communication which is required among the new team members reduces the time available for each to do productive work.

- There is a reduction in experienced personnel available for development work, as they are used for training of the new personnel.

However, it should be kept in mind that Brooks' law is applicable to tasks which are not divisible (tasks which cannot be broken into smaller components) and projects which are late. An example of non-visible task is that it takes one woman nine months to produce one child but nine women can't produce a baby in one month.

In case the task is divisible like cleaning rooms in a hotel, adding people does decrease task duration up to a point.

Work of Lawrence Putnam

Lawrence Putnam Sr, is a legend in the field of software estimation and management. In his book *Five Core Metrics: The Intelligence behind Successful Software Management*, he talks about his repeated observation that a large team took five times more the number of hours than a small team.[13] To understand the right team size, he undertook a study which looked at 491 medium-sized projects in various companies. There were projects with between 35,000 and 95,000 'new or modified' source lines of codes. These information system projects were completed between 1995 and 1998. What he found are as follows:

- Smaller team of five to seven people delivered in less time.

- Significant increase in effort occurred when team sizes reached nine or more.

2226305906 | (22) (263) (059) (06)
Before and after chunking

Figure 37.1. A Indian Telephone Number

- Once the teams grew larger than eight, they took dramatically longer to get things done.

- Groups containing three to seven people required about 25 percent of the effort of groups of nine to twenty to get the same amount of work.

Clearly, Putnam and Myers emphasized that teams of five to seven people delivered in less time and also significant increase in effort occurred when the team size reached nine or more. Clearly, the teams which have people less than eight deliver in less time. Also, there was a significant increase in effort when team sizes increased to nine or more.

Miller's Law

George Miller was an American psychologist, who was one of the doyens of cognitive science. He proposed that the number of items an average person can hold or process in their working or short-term memory is 7 (+ or − 2), making the average range of 5–9 items. This is now known as Miller's law.[14] Short term memory refers to the mechanism that allows us to retain small amount of information for a very short time. Gorge Miller concluded that bits, the basic unit of information, don't affect memory span as much as the number of information chunks being memorized. The term 'chunks' in cognitive psychology refers to collections of basic familiar units which have been grouped together and stored in a person's memory. What he taught us is that the size of the chunks did not seem to matter. We could hold in our short-term memory seven individual words as easily as seven individual letters. An example of chunking is the way we remember phone numbers. When it's chunked, it's easy to remember (Figure 37.1).

Channels of Communication

Communication is central to any team. If it is not effective or is impaired, it can impact the outcomes which the teams have to deliver. While setting up teams for OPEX, we need to keep in mind the number of communication channels between the team members. The following formula can be used to figure out the communication path numbers for teams:

No. of communication channels $= \dfrac{n \times (n-1)}{2}$

Where n = number of team members

A team of 4 has 6 channels

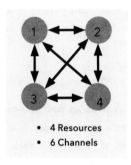

- 4 Resources
- 6 Channels

A team of 5 has 10 channels

A team of 5 has 10 relationships. There are 10 different combinations of how team members can interact and develop a relationship with other team members. Each pair of people represents one relationship. Effective teams need to have strong relationships between each of the team members.

Similarly, a team of 7 will have 21 channels, while a team of 9 will have 36 channels.

Increasing the number of team members from 7 to 9 increases the number of communication channels to manifold.

As team sizes increase, the team members spend a lot of time on communication, and this impacts their productivity. Also, what is seen is that members lose socially as they don't want to lose on productivity. Team size should not become so much that it becomes unwieldy to manage relationships and also impacts productivity.

Work of J. Richard Hackman

Richard Hackman has researched on effective teams. He has studied teams from airplane cockpit crews to musical ensembles. He authored a book called *Leading Teams: Setting the Stage for Great Performances*, wherein he delved into what it takes to foster and establish effective teams.[15] One of the things he proposed in his book was that no team should have a membership in double digits. His preferred size was six. What his study had found was that the number of performance problems increases exponentially as the team size increases.

Learnings from the Second World War

The fire team is the smallest organized unit of a military organization. They can be found in the US Army, British Army, Australian Army, etc.[16] A fire team typically has four soldiers, comprising a fire team leader, an automatic rifleman, a grenadier and a rifleman. Fire teams make up squads; squads make up platoons.[17] Army lieutenants lead platoons as part of an infantry rifle company. A squad comprises 9 people which includes two fire teams and a squad leader. The size of a squad shrank from 12 to 9 during Second World War, as it was difficult to manage this team under stress.

Jeff Bezos's and Brad Smith's Rule

When Jeff Bezos founded Amazon, he instituted a rule which was that every internal team should be small enough to be fed with two pizzas. This was not done with focus on cost or to reduce food bills. This was done with the objective of efficiency and scalability. As was reported in an article in *The Guardian* in April 2018, a smaller team spends less time managing timetables and keeping people up to date, and more time doing what needs to be done.[18] But it's the latter that really matters to the company. Amazon has lots of small teams which work together and access common resources to achieve the larger objectives of the firm.

When Brad Smith was the CEO of Intuit, he also had a similar rule. He was a big supporter of innovation. He advocated small teams of employees to boost innovation. He urged teams to be kept small at four to six people—no more, he noted, than can be fed by two pizzas.

Scott Keller and Mary Meaney Insights

In the book *Leading Organizations: Ten Timeless Truths*, Scott Keller and Mary Meaney recommend an optimal team size between 6 and 10.[19] They have found that as the team size grows beyond 10, the effectiveness of the team diminishes substantially. What happens is that there is a formation of sub-teams and members have less ownership for the group objectives. There are higher chances of groupthink. On the other side, when the team size is less than six, there is a lack of diversity, which impacts the quality of decision-making. There is very little strategic cover for spearheading strategic priorities. There is also a challenge around succession.

What's Our Recommendation

I think we have seen sufficient evidence that large-sized teams don't add value. They become an impediment. We cannot be inclusive and include all functions, job titles, star performers and all relevant stakeholders. We cannot avoid emotionally tough conversation on why someone was excluded. What should be kept in mind is that only members with relevant knowledge, capabilities and diversity are included in the team.

The optimal team size, we believe, should be 7 plus/minus 2.

To keep all the stakeholders engaged, I would suggest to hold regular sessions with them, take their inputs and answer their doubts and queries. Take it also as an opportunity for them to poke holes on the work which the team is doing.

REFERENCES

1. Dezsö CL and Ross DG. Does female representation in top management improve firm performance? A panel data investigation. *Strat Mgmt J* 2012; 33: 1072–1089, https://doi.org/10.1002/smj.1955 (accessed 10 February 2021).

2. Freeman RB and Huang W. Collaborating with people like me: Ethnic co-authorship within the US. *J Labor Econ* 2015; 33(3, S1): S289–S318.

3. Reynolds A and Lewis D. Teams solve problems faster when they're more cognitively diverse. *Harv Bus Rev*, 30 March 2017, https://hbr.org/2017/03/teams-solve-problems-faster-when-theyre-more-cognitively-diverse (accessed 10 February 2021).

4. Phillips KW. How diversity works. *Sci Am* 2014; 311(4, October): 42–47, https://www.scientificamerican.com/index.cfm/_api/render/file/?method=inline&fileID=9F4FCDB9-A5B3-40AB-A9A525 FDC71156AB (accessed 10 February 2021).

5. Rock D and Grant H. Why diverse teams are smarter. *Harv Bus Rev*, 4 November 2016, https://hbr.org/2016/11/why-diverse-teams-are-smarter (accessed 10 February 2021).

6. Phillips KW, Liljenquist KA and Neale MA. Is the pain worth the gain? The advantages and liabilities of agreeing with socially distinct newcomers. *Personal Soc Psychol Bull* 2009; 35(3): 336–350. doi:10.1177/0146167208328062

7. Mann G. Virtual hackathons can help you solve coronavirus problems without leaving your home. *The Conversation*, 30 April 2020, https://theconversation.com/virtual-hackathons-can-help-you-solve-coronavirus-problems-without-leaving-your-home-136956 (accessed 10 February 2021).

8.   Warren A. Why diversity in hiring is only one part of the puzzle. *Fast Company*, 5 February 2020, https://www.fastcompany.com/3056351/why-diversity-in-hiring-is-only-one-part-of-the-puzzle (accessed 10 February 2021).

9.   Smith EB and Hou Y. Redundant heterogeneity and group performance. *Organ Sci* 2014; 26(1, 1 September), https://doi.org/10.1287/orsc.2014.0932

10. Roderick IS, Schaerer M, Anicich EM, et al. The too-much-talent effect: Team interdependence determines when more talent is too much or not enough. *Psychol Sci* 2014; 25(8, 1 August): 1581–1591.

11. May C. The surprising problem of too much talent. *Sci Am*, 14 October 2014, https://www.scientificamerican.com/article/the-surprising-problem-of-too-much-talent/ (accessed 10 February 2021).

12. Brooks FP, Jr. *The mythical man-month: Essays on software engineering.* Boston, MA: Addison-Wesley, (1975) 1995.

13. Putnam L and Myers W. *Five core metrics: The intelligence behind successful software management.* New York, NY: Dorset House, 2003.

14. Miller GA. The magical number seven, plus or minus two: Some limits on our capacity for processing information. *Psychol Rev* 1956; 101(2): 343–352.

15. Hackman RJ. *Leading teams: Setting the stage for great performances.* Boston, MA: Harvard Business School Press, 2002.

16. Tobin J, ed. *Ernie Pyle's war: America's eyewitness to World War II.* New York, NY: Simon and Schuster, 1987.

17. Department of the Army. *The Infantry Rifle Platoon and Squad.* Field Manual No. 3-21.8, 28 March 2007, https://arotc.uncc.edu/sites/arotc.uncc.edu/files/media/FM%203-21-8%20%20The%20Infantry%20Rifle%20Platoon%20and%20Squad.pdf (accessed 10 February 2021).

18. Hern A. The two-pizza rule and the secret of Amazon's success. *The Guardian*, 24 April 2018, https://www.theguardian.com/technology/2018/apr/24/the-two-pizza-rule-and-the-secret-of-amazons-success (accessed 10 February 2021).

19. Keller S and Meaney M. *Leading organisations: Ten timeless truths.* London: Bloomsbury, 2017.

About the Author

Debashis Sarkar is one of Asia's leading organizational improvement experts. He is recognized globally for his thought leadership in customer-centricity and operational excellence. Over the last three decades, he has enabled myriad businesses and helped them to perform better and become profitable. He is the Managing Partner at Proliferator Advisory & Consulting, which has clients in Asia, Africa, Europe and the Middle East.

Author of multiple books and papers, his ideas have been adopted by companies worldwide. A much sought-after speaker, he is invited from the world over for keynotes and workshops.

He has been a business improvement pioneer. In the early 2000s, he introduced 'lean thinking' to service businesses in Asia and played a significant role in developing it into a management practice. He is also credited to have created new tools for change and continuous improvement. Over the last decade, he has also been working on building an improvement practice which leverages principles of behavioural economics and psychology.

He is a Fellow of the American Society for Quality and recipient of multiple recognitions. Notable among them are Phil Crosby Medal and Simon Collier Award. He is also the recipient of the first Quality Champion Platinum Award from Quality Council of India, which is the highest award for quality from the Indian government.

To know more about him, please visit https://debashissarkar.com/

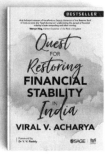

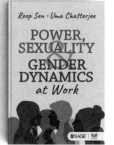